CW00403276

"Exciting, authentic account from the man who has filmed & survived in almost every single one of the world's extremes – and still come out smiling!"

Bear Grylls
Adventurer and TV Presenter

"Whether I found myself perched on the diving cliffs of Acapulco, Mexico, ready to jump, or being strapped to a bull in a pen waiting to be thrown off, much to the amusement of 5,000 baying Texans, Mungo has an uncanny knack of making it all seem fine. I don't want to sway your opinion, but he's a great lad and much loved by me and my family, but I'll leave that for you to decide! With tutoring from Mungo, the Flintoffs are prepared for 'End Days' scenarios – I have learnt to pitch a tent in less than an hour, can get a good fire going on the third attempt and I carry a head torch and karabiners pretty much everywhere I go."

Freddie Flintoff
Ex-England Cricket Captain and TV Presenter

"Mungo is, in my opinion, one of the best cameramen I've worked with. He is always in the middle of the action and tells the story perfectly."

Simon Cowell
X Factor and Britain's Got Talent

"I've worked with Mungo on many TV shows. He is just a great guy to work with. Amazing at his job, professional and hard-working. He never complains, always has a smile on his face and the team he works with adore him (and he's jolly handsome too!)."

Davina McCall
TV Presenter

"In television, it boils down to what's on the screen. What makes Mungo a legend is what he does to make it happen. It's all about style, grace, authenticity – and guts."

Richard Wiese
Host of ABC's Born to Explore and former president of The Explorers Club

"I think travelling should be fun and making documentaries as you go gives it even more meaning and creativity and so the people you go with have to add to that mix... and Mungo certainly does."

Russ Malkin

Producer – Long Way Round & Long Way Down

"When I first met Mungo, I immediately warmed to him. He followed me across the wilds of New Zealand for an entire week – and no matter how hard it was to shoot, he'd always get that shot. And thanks to his chilled demeanour and collection of hilarious stories from across the globe, it's a pleasure not only to work with him, but then to go to the pub and chat about life. Because if anyone is living the dream, it's definitely Mungo!"

Tobias Mews

Adventure Sports Journalist (Telegraph Men columnist),
Filmmaker & Endurance Athlete

"What can I say about Mungo the exceptional cameraman. From the minute I met him we never stopped laughing and we soon became great friends. We have travelled the world together and made some great TV shows – he is one of the most talented cameramen I've ever come across. I thoroughly recommend this book, which is a fantastic read and insight into what a cameraman goes through."

Charley Boorman (TV Adventurer)

LIVING THE DREAM

More Extreme Adventures of a TV Cameraman

PAUL 'MUNGO' MUNGEAM

FILMING WITH...

BEAR GRYLLS
CHARLEY BOORMAN
KATE HUMBLE
FREDDIE FLINTOFF

Published by Zaccmedia
www.zaccmedia.com
info@zaccmedia.com

Published October 2014

ISBN: 978-1-909824-52-2

British Library Cataloguing-in-Publication Data
A catalogue record for this book is available from the British Library.

Other books by Paul "Mungo" Mungeam:
Mungo the Cameraman - ISBN 978-0-955565-00-7

Printed and bound by CPI Group (UK) Ltd, Croydon, CR0 4YY

This book is dedicated to my father, Chris Mungeam

Without your wisdom, belief, total support, constant encouragement and unconditional love I would never have achieved any of this (let alone writing two books!). You are a hard act to follow, Pa, but I'll try my best.

Son x

Most of the TV shows mentioned in the book can be viewed on **YouTube**. Watch before you read and you'll get a far greater insight into the story.

CONTENTS

ACKNOWLEDGEMENTS

There are far too many people to mention fully by name here, but my thanks goes to:

All the camera op's and sound op's I have worked alongside and now have the privilege of calling my mates.

The directors who have worked with me and chosen me as their 'shooter', and the producers who have trusted their precious TV series with the likes of me.

The presenters and contributors who have allowed me to point my camera at them and trust me to portray them in the best light possible.

The outstanding safety teams who have enabled us to push the boundaries, while keeping us in one piece – I've trusted my life with you.

Special thanks to Fred, for writing the Foreword (you're a good man!). And also to all those who are mentioned in the stories that are told in these chapters – what amazing adventures we have experienced together – let's hope there are plenty more to come in the future.

Thanks to Paul Stanier – Zaccmedia, who had faith in this

book when the 'big fish' publishers deemed it too small time for their portfolios – let's hope they live to regret that decision!

A huge thank you to my family, who have put up with me being absent and often keeping quiet about what I was really up to, to save them the worry. I love you all.

Finally, thanks to YOU for reading this book – I genuinely hope that you not only find it interesting and amusing, but that you also take something away from it that may enrich your life and the lives of others around you.

Mungo

AUTHOR

Paul Mungeam (known in the TV industry as 'Mungo') was born in Royal Tunbridge Wells, Kent, United Kingdom in April 1971. From his earliest days he had creativity, sport and adventure in his blood. Following school he spent three years studying Fine Art in Sydney, Australia, after which he worked as a Youth Worker, before 'falling' into TV through new contacts.

Over the last twenty years Mungo has travelled to over eighty countries, filming for all the major broadcasters (BBC, National Geographic, NBC, Discovery, ITV, Channel 4, etc.) and working with some of the biggest names on TV – some of whom have become friends for life.

During these extensive travels he has experienced firsthand the sublime to the ridiculous – stories which he shares in his two self-written books: *MUNGO – The Cameraman* (ISBN 978-0-9555650-0-7. Hardback) and now *MUNGO: "Living the Dream"*.

Some of the stories featured are sad and some are shocking, but guaranteed some of the tears shed will also be in sheer amusement.

FOREWORD

I still find it the most unsettling, most uncomfortable and bizarre feeling having a camera shoved in my face. Especially when they expect me to be mildly entertaining. So, it's probably a good thing that the person behind the lens is someone you trust, respect and most importantly, like.

Entering my first major television series *Freddie vs the World* (or at least a few retired sportsmen), I first met the crew at Heathrow Airport. I put on my usual confident front, but in truth I was feeling like a child on his first day at school.

As I met everyone and shook hands, I met Mungo – a Cameraman I'd heard had worked with Bear Grylls, Charley Boorman and Simon Cowell. I couldn't help but think, what will he make of having to shoot an ex-cricketer with little experience in TV? I doubt Simon Cowell constantly asks, "Was that alright? You will tell me if it's shit?" Or, Charley Boorman asking, "How do you start this bike?" Or, Bear Grylls asking, "How do I tie this knot?"

Luckily he realized, and was happy to accept, that on this assignment he was going to be far more than just a Cameraman. It would also entail being a director, drinking partner, human alarm clock, bedtime monitor, travel buddy, agony aunt, mentor and ultimately a great friend.

Whether I found myself perched on the diving cliffs of Acapulco, Mexico, ready to jump (!) or being strapped to a bull in a pen, waiting to be thrown off, much to the amusement of 5,000 baying Texans, Mungo has an uncanny knack of making it all seem fine.

Since that first series, I've been lucky enough to go on some amazing adventures in Africa, Australia, Borneo, Canada and Brazil. I've slept on deserted islands, in caves and rainforests and done them all with a mate.

At first, I never dreamed I could live or sleep in such places, having been a spoilt cricketer who never even had to carry his own bags. But now with tutoring from Mungo, the Flintoffs are prepared for 'End Days' scenarios. Also, I have learnt to pitch a tent in less than an hour, can get a good fire going on the third attempt and I carry a head torch and karabiners pretty much everywhere I go.

Not only has he taught me these survival skills, but I could never have become a professional boxer without him being there every step of the way. Obviously his keen eye and artistic shooting angles were great, but just having someone in my corner who I could talk to openly and honestly was invaluable.

It's little wonder that now, when I get offered TV work, one of my conditions is that Mungo has to be on it! Though, these days, I seem to be at the back of a queue which depends on Bear's or Simon's diaries.

That's my experience of Mungo. I could almost write a book on him myself!

I don't want to sway your opinion, but he's a great lad and much loved by me and my family – but I'll leave that for you to decide!

Andrew 'Freddie' Flintoff MBE
Former England Cricket Captain and now TV Presenter.
May 2014

1

MAN VS ARCTIC

FEATURING: BEAR GRYLLS AND WILL FERRELL

Driving my Land Rover through the back roads of Chiswick in London, my mobile phone rang. I pulled the car over to the side of the road and answered....

"Hello?"

"Hi Mungo, my name's Anne and I'm calling from a Production Company in Bristol, and we were wondering if by any chance you are free at the moment and may be able to help us out?"

"Hi Anne... I may well be free – what's going on?"

"We are shooting a *Man vs Wild* special with Bear Grylls and Will Ferrell in north Sweden, about 500 kilometres inside the Arctic Circle. Our Cameraman has just broken his ankle whilst ice climbing on the recce and we are due to start shooting tomorrow and are in desperate need to replace him. You've come highly recommended by Bear, so is there any chance you might be available?"

"Poor guy, but yeah, sure. How soon would you need me there?"

"Well, as soon as possible. How soon can you leave?"

"When's the next plane?"

"There's one that leaves Heathrow for Stockholm in two hours."

"OK, if you can get me a ticket, I'll be on it!"

She said she would do her best, so I ended the call, threw my phone on the passenger seat, wrenched the steering wheel around and swung the car back in the direction of my apartment in Wandsworth.

Arriving home I locked my car, and rang for a taxi that could take me to the airport. I was asked when I would need it. "In fifteen minutes," I replied. The Production Company staff were desperately pulling strings to get me on the next flight. I ran upstairs to my bedroom, grabbed a big black North Face kit bag and went to my clothes drawers.

Over the years I have accumulated a vast amount of 'kit' (clothing and equipment) for all different environments and conditions. I am constantly challenged to find places to store it all where I can get my hands on it quickly remembering where everything is.

One of my lower drawers is allocated to 'Colder/Ski Weather'. Throwing the empty kit bag onto the wooden floor, I pulled open the drawer and looked at the mass of hats, gloves and thermal underwear. Right, I thought... What does one wear in the Arctic? I had never been to the Arctic before and I had no time to make calls to pick the brains of friends who have been in those extreme icy conditions. I'll just have to take pretty much everything, I thought.

So, I took the drawer out and practically tipped the entire contents into the bag, which swallowed the items leaving little room to spare. I then slid the bag to the other side of the room, shuffling around the bottom of my bed and began to search through my more unusual 'specialist kit' horde, with the likes of compasses, handheld GPS devices, international plug adapters, snap fluorescent emergency lights and a pre-packed survival kit, or 'Grab Bag' as we often call them.

Again I said to myself, "Right… what will I need in the Arctic?" It wasn't only a case of having never been to the Arctic environment before, but more to do with the fact that as everything was so last minute I didn't really know where we would be staying – hotel or camping? Also, apart from filming I had no clue of, generally, what I would be expected to do when there.

I decided that I would take the basics, two European plug adapters, my trusty surge protected four way power extension lead and the 'Grab Bag' – survival kit… just in case.

I looked at my watch. I had little time to spare before the taxi arrived, so zipping up my bag threw it over my shoulder and ran downstairs to the bathroom. Scurrying around I threw the bare necessities into my travel wash bag; toothbrush, toothpaste, deodorant, contact lens solution and spare lenses – just in case. Next was the all-important medicine tin; a pre-packed tin with all sorts of general medication in their foil strips: Benadryl for hay fever or any other allergies, Ibuprofen for muscle pains or strains, Paracetamol for headaches/hangovers (!), Sturgeon for any strange travel conditions and Strepsils for a sore throat – from experience, there's nothing worse than being in the middle of nowhere with a throat feeling like you are gargling cut glass. This can also be very detrimental to one's work, when not being able to swallow without pain so breaking up a good night's sleep. Wash bag complete – zip.

The final items I grabbed were my big green Parker/down jacket and my new, leather walking boots. Almost to the second when finishing doing up my laces, the front door bell rang, the taxi had arrived so I took my keys off the hook and made sure all the house lights and central heating were off. As I picked up my now swollen kit bag and hopped down the stairs to the front door, I patted my jeans back pocket, making sure that I had my wallet and passport. I greeted the taxi driver and as we headed off towards the airport, I sat on the back seat and in my head silently went through a mental checklist, making sure that I had everything that I could possibly need. Having said that, the fact that my flight was scheduled to leave in just over an hour and a half meant that realistically I had no time to turn around even if I had forgotten something – I'd just have to buy any essential items at the airport.

One of the factors of filming in remote locations is that you need to be well prepped and self-sufficient. It's not like working in a foreign city or town where you can just pop to the shops because you may well find yourself hundreds of kilometres from civilization.

Part of my usual routine, as I'm sat in a taxi heading out to a shoot, is to call people – I told my neighbour and good friend Jules, who lived in the apartment below me, that I would be away for a week, so he would know my flat upstairs was (or was meant to be) empty. I phoned my father, which is now part of my routine, just in case something happened while on a trip. He would know where I would be and he was always armed with my 'Emergency File', informing him of all the details of my health insurance, passport details and emergency numbers etc. I would also take the time to call my mum and three older sisters, to let them know that I was going away and where I would be should anything happen to me or them while I was away.

This may seem over the top, but I've always thought that in an emergency situation you can always help yourself and others by pre-planning... just a habit I have got into over the years.

Still in the taxi, in between calls, Anne rang again to confirm that I was booked on the flight and gave me the flight number and details etc. It was all going according to plan.

Within an hour of arriving at the airport, I was on the plane on my way to Stockholm. It was less than three hours since I had taken the initial phone call while on my way to Chiswick to see some friends.

It was late evening by the time our flight arrived in Stockholm, and as I was about to step through the door to exit the aircraft, a lady in a yellow/green fluorescent jacket stepped out in front of me...

"Are you Paul Mungeam?" she asked.

"Yes," I replied.

"Please follow me." She made her way down the stairs onto the tarmac and opened the rear passenger door of a white estate car.

"Please get in and wait for me here... do you have your luggage tags and can you describe your bag to me?"

I peeled off the luggage tag that was attached to the back of my passport, gave it to her and added "My bag is a big, black North Face holdall, it shouldn't be too hard to recognize. Would you like a hand with it?"

"No, please remain in the car," she said as she closed the door and disappeared, walking under the belly of the aircraft.

I sat there wondering what on earth was going on... Was I in trouble? This must all be above board, as she was an official airline employee – having said that, I didn't check her name tag, I simply gathered this by the fact that she was wearing a luminous jacket. Should I have given her my luggage tag? Either way, it was too late now. So I did as I was told and just sat there.

A few minutes later she opened the trunk of the car. Cold night air hit me. I heard a groan as she lifted my heavy bag into the back. After slamming the car door she walked round to the front and got into the driver's seat. We drove off.

To my surprise, rather than heading towards the arrivals terminal, we seemed to be driving towards the perimeter fence. If this was VIP treatment, we were going a very strange route... where was she taking me?

At the fence we passed through a security gate and on to what looked like a private road. Realizing that we had now left the airport I piped up, "Shouldn't I have gone through customs etc. before leaving the airport?" She replied, "We haven't got time for that." Somewhat naively I decided to not ask any more questions.

Within a matter of minutes we turned into another gate, through security and drove onto a very dark and seemingly desolate airfield. In front of us, way in the distance I could see the occasional flashing green and red light of what must have been another aircraft.

As we approached the flashing lights I could just make out the feint silhouette of what looked like a Lear Jet. I jokingly said to the lady driving, "I guess that's my jet?" To my astonishment she replied, "Yes." I slumped back in my seat and smiled from ear to ear.

Pulling up to the small executive jet aircraft, the door opened and the stairs came down. A man in a pilot's shirt poked his head out and then descended the steps. Shaking my hand he introduced himself and welcomed me onto the flight. With that he ushered me up the stairs and then retrieved my bag from the car and stowed it somewhere in the fuselage.

The inside of the plane was relatively small but absolutely luxurious. There were only six seats facing each other. Each seat was more like a La-Z-Boy armchair; big, wide and made of a grey/beige leather, the kind of chair that when you sat in it, it would envelope itself around you like a big hug. As I am tall, my usual problem of finding enough leg room on flights was not going to be an issue tonight.

I sat in the furthest chair from the front door, mainly so that I could look back down the plane and see what was going on... I was still unaware that this jet was solely for me. That was until the pilot climbed aboard, pulled up the steps and shut the door. He turned to me, gave a welcoming smile and said, "Good evening, Mr Mungeam, welcome on board. We will shortly be taking off and heading to Kiruna."

I must confess, at this point, inside I was exploding with excitement. However, I thought it only right to act as if this happened the whole time. So, I sat in my chair and flicked through the pile of magazines at my side. I really wanted to browse through *Heat* magazine and see who had been snapped in an embarrassing pose this week, but instead I chose the *Financial Times,* as somehow this seemed more fitting. I really fancied a beer, but I asked for a gin and tonic. This act continued until the pilot and his second-in-command shut the door and told me they would check up on me during the flight. Like a typical man, I then started to lounge around and check out all the drawers and cupboards etc. around the cabin! I chuckled to myself, this was seriously cool.

However, I then had to draw upon some sobriety as in a few hours I would be landing in a strange land, with dangerously low temperatures. I would then have to work out just what was going on and what was going to be professionally required of me.

A couple of hours later, we descended from altitude and the Lear Jet landed in the winter wonderland of Kiruna. I looked out of the window and it looked very bleak. It was around 2 a.m. and it was snowing heavily. There was a thick layer of snow surrounding the runway and as we pulled up to a halt, a big car pulled up to the base of the steps.

I said my thank yous to the aircrew and then jumped into the car. The taxi driver sorted out transferring my bag and then hopped in and we drove off.

"Welcome to Kiruna," the man said in a strong Swedish accent.

"Thank you very much... I've never been this far north before. Where are we off to?" I replied.

"I shall drop you off at your hotel... the journey will take about thirty minutes."

As it was so late (or should I say early!) I didn't press the poor guy with more questions about Kiruna etc. He had obviously scored the graveyard shift, working all through the night, and so I just sat back in my seat and looked out of the window.

Kiruna is the most northern city in Sweden. Set 145 kilometres within the Arctic Circle it is, in relative terms, a very small bastion of civilization surrounded by a very wild environment. Predominantly forest and wilderness make up this area, but the city survives by supporting and servicing the local mines. The summers in Kiruna are short and the winters are long – very long!

It was March and as I sleepily gazed out of the taxi window, I could see the snow falling steadily, lit by the orange glow of the street lights. It was beautiful, silent and quite a different scene to that which I had started my day in.

Minutes later, tiredness really started to set in. I arrived at my hotel just after 2:30 a.m. The night porter let me in and gave me my room key and a note.

Thanking him, I shouldered my bag and headed for the lift to my room. I read the note written by my old mate Duncan (1st Assistant Director) It read:

Hi Mungo. Welcome. Hope the flight was OK? Get some rest as your call is downstairs at 05:30 for breakfast to leave hotel at 06:00. Sleep well. Duncs x

Closing my hotel room door behind me I threw my bag on the floor and looked at my watch... it was 02:45. This night was going to be as short as one of Kiruna's summers. With that I got my head down.

05:15 – I woke to the most despised sound in my world, the alarm clock. I jumped in the shower to force my reluctant body to wake up. Having only had a few hours of sleep, it was going to have to be busyness and adrenalin that would keep me going today.

As I dried off I wondered what I should wear for the day ahead. I still had no idea of what exactly we would be doing, where we would be going or what the weather conditions would be like. It was a tough call. I opted for the universal 'ski' dress of layers: thermal underwear, liner socks then ski socks, waterproof salopettes (waterproof trousers), T-shirt over my thermal top, a light fleece, a heavier fleece and then my waterproof jacket. Sturdy walking boots, gaiters, hat, gloves and finally my down jacket stuffed into my day sack. "That should do for breakfast," I chuckled to myself deliriously, as I left the warm sanctuary of my hotel room.

Downstairs, stripped down to my thermal underwear top and salopettes, I entered the breakfast room and immediately started looking for familiar faces. Not surprisingly our team were the only guests tucking into breakfast at 05:30. I was pretty sure even the birds outside were still fast asleep, huddled up together in the warmth of their nests.

I headed straight towards the tea making facilities. Being a true Brit, I struggle to operate in the mornings without a large mug of tea. Shortly after grabbing some bread and cheese I felt a huge pat on my back and it was Duncan, "Hello Mungo!" he said as he gave me a big hug. "Well done for getting out here so quickly. Take a seat while I grab myself a coffee and then I'll take you through what we've got planned for today."

I first met Duncan on *Lads' Army*, a reality style series for ITV where a reconstruction of 1950s National Service had been set up. From day one we got on famously. Following that, we stayed in touch and then worked together on various other shoots all around the world – such as *The Search* (Channel 4) where we filmed in France, Italy, Peru, Guatemala and India. Also *Escape to the Legion* set in the Sahara Desert (where Bear had made his break into mainstream television). Up until this point the last series we had worked on together was *The Hottest Place on Earth* for the BBC (which I will write about in a later chapter). His job as '1st Assistant Director – A.D.' basically entails being the cement that holds the bricks together on a shoot. He runs the filming schedule and ushers people to the right place at the right time etc. Duncan is exceptional at his job and always deals with people while wearing a smile on his face (even if sometimes through gritted teeth!).

As Duncan explained the plan for the day, which was to recce the locations for the start of the main shoot tomorrow, he also introduced me to various members of the team.

Dave – Rope and Safety Co-ordinator and Woody – Survival Consultant were both ex-military. Their role was to advise Bear, but they also looked after the health and safety of the crew (critical roles when the crew have to be concentrating on looking through the camera, while at the same time being careful as to where their feet may be). Dan was the other Cameraman on this two-camera shoot. Fortunately, he was still in good shape following Rob's accident the previous day. There was also Buster

– Camera Assistant, David – Director (whom I'd also worked with before on *The Search*) and then Steve – Executive Producer. Last, but by no means least, were the soundmen, Pete – whom I had previously worked with on multiple shoots and Sean whom I had never met until now.

They were all very nice chaps and immediately made me feel very welcome.

The backbone of filming such a series as *Man vs Wild* (*Born Survivor* as it's known in the UK) is having a team who work very well together. They each need to respect and trust each other, as well as executing their individual roles professionally, while hopefully having fun and enjoying the shoot. It is also critical that they look out for each other's safety, as support.

The majority of this crew were regular members of the team that film the *Man vs Wild* series, where Bear goes on his solo adventures. This special episode was quite a bit different in practical terms of the filming and safety issues, due to there being a guest joining him, that of course meant that there were two people doing everything, and one of those people will not be the 'superman' that is Bear Grylls! This adventure would have to be meticulously planned out prior to setting off with the A-list comedy actor Will Ferrell.

Just a few minutes before we left the hotel, Bear bounded into the breakfast room. He came straight over and gave me a big hug. It was a while since I'd seen him, so it was good to catch up again – albeit through unfortunate circumstances for injured Rob. As we caught up chatting he made himself a bread roll, wrapped it up and stuck it in his day sack.

I first met Bear while filming *Escape to the Legion* for Channel 4 in the Sahara Desert. We had always got on well and had stayed in touch following that shoot. I had followed Bear's astronomic rise of career with keen interest. He had certainly done very well for himself. While catching up with him over breakfast, I noticed how he had visibly changed since I'd last seen him. He was looking leaner, fitter and more groomed. Granted the last time I had spent any significant amount of time with him was in the desert when he had a French Foreign Legion crew cut (skinhead).

Some people in the UK find Bear's extravert and sensationalist style of presenting terribly un-British, but to his credit there are now over a billion people in the world who have watched his shows. America particularly love him and his eccentricity. He's ex-Eton, ex-SAS, good-looking, posh and as hard as nails – the closest thing to a real life James Bond.

The task for our day ahead was to go on a technical recce, to plan and map out where we would film the following day. So, today there would only be a handful of the crew required to go. It was decided that Bear, Dave, Woody, Steve, David, Dan and I should make up the recce team. The others stayed back in the hotel and took some time off, a welcome break for recovery from the previous shoot that week. Once we were all fed, watered and in good shape, we left the cosy, warm hotel and stepped out into the brutally cold air and snow. Outside it was still dark as we left the hotel and we piled into two 4x4 vehicles and headed off.

By the time we reached our destination, the low winter sun was starting to reluctantly peak its head over the distant, blue horizon. Our first stop was the local helipad. As we disembarked our vehicles saw two seriously cool-looking, bright red helicopters. These were going to be our primary form of transport for the next three days.

I have worked with helicopters for many years now, but no matter how many flights you tally up in these remarkable machines, you never get bored of them.

Leaving our day sacks in the office of the hangar, we were introduced to our lead pilot, a young guy called Tommy. After pleasantries, Tommy led Bear, Dave and I out to the six-seater Eurocopter. As we stood beside the impressive aircraft, Bear explained to me that his and Will's first stunt would be rappelling (abseiling) out of the door as the helicopter hovered at around 50 metres. Dave's job was to work out how to safely rig the rappel ropes to the anchor points inside the helicopter. He set to work with Tommy to work out the best way of doing this. Yet, Dave not only had to think about Bear's and Will's rope safety, he also had to work out a safety rig that would allow me to be anchored to the chopper, with a full body harness, in a way that allowed me to lean out of the aircraft with a big camera on my shoulder, to follow all the action.

Having only met Dave about an hour ago over a croissant, I watched him at work and was impressed by his knowledge and expertise in rope work. He knew instantly what to do, fixing the most critical of rigs in the simplest fashion.

I was to find out later that Dave had spent many years in the Royal Marine Commandos. He was an expert in mountain and Arctic warfare, plus on top of this, like Bear he had summited Mount Everest. There was no doubt in my mind that we were in the very best hands.

After thirty minutes or so, discussing what I needed to do to film the sequence and how Dave would rig the chopper, it was time to head out into the wilderness to carry out the recce.

At this point the other boys joined us and one by one we climbed into the chopper. Taking our seats we fastened our belts and put on the headsets.

Looking ice cool, wearing a baseball cap and a pair of stylish Oakley sunglasses, our pilot Tommy breezed through the pre-flight checks and started the rotors.

When you ride in a helicopter for the first time it is a strange sensation. I guess we're normally so conditioned to travelling in planes that we half expect the aircraft to need a good run at speed, in a forward motion, before eventually leaving the ground. Yet, when you're in a helicopter you can feel the rotors winding up above you, as you sit stationary with everything around you gently vibrating. As they pick up speed, the noise and vibration becomes louder and stronger, until the pilot releases the brake. Then, not unlike a spinning top, the helicopter is seemingly sucked up off the ground and into the air.

Once the shallow hover is deemed stable, the pilot dips the nose of the chopper and that's when the forward motion begins.

The beauty of the helicopter is the incredible visibility of your surroundings and, of course, the overall manoeuvrability of the aircraft. You can fly a lot slower than an aeroplane, a great deal closer to the ground and you can turn on a sixpence (dime) or totally stop in mid-air.

As we all sat hovering at about 10 metres above the helipad, Tommy casually yet expertly dipped the nose and with a deep thundering sound, we zoomed off towards the wintery wilderness and snowy mountains.

It took us a good forty minutes to reach the huge valley that was carved out between the two mighty mountain ranges. The ground far below us was covered in deep white snow, only punctured by the speckled black markings of trees and other seasonal plant life.

Snaking its way down through the centre of this remote valley floor was a frozen river only really visible by the indent of the snowy 'S' shape and the occasional frozen lake-like clearing. The temperature on the ground was close to -20°C.

The main objective of this recce was for Bear to scour the terrain and work out where he would lead Will the following day. At the same time this served as a chance for us to work out how we would technically follow and film their journey.

The ultimate aim of the programme was to drop Bear and Will from the helicopter into the top of a hostile, snowy gully. Once on the ground, we would join them and together we would start making our way down the deep gorge, overcoming whatever obstacles stood in our way, eventually arriving in the open valley below. After finding food and shelter for the night, the following day we would continue on foot over to the other side of the valley and up the mountainside that stood opposite. Eventually, when on the summit of the distant mountain, Bear and Will would light a fire to create smoke as a signal to the helicopter that they were ready to be extracted. Sounds easy, doesn't it? It certainly wouldn't be.

Having been brilliantly flown by Tommy into one or two potentially suitable gullies, Bear and Dave agreed that the last one seemed like our best option. We hovered with the vast sheer rock walls of the gully perilously close to our rotor blades, as the boys spotted an area deep in the gorge that they believed Bear and Will could safely rappel into. When this had been briefly discussed and agreed, it was time for us to try to land in that exact spot.

On the day, when Bear and Will had safely rappelled to the ground and the rope had been cleared away, we would have to perform a 'hot' landing – briefly touching the skids on the snow while maintaining spinning rotors and power on the chopper engine for a quick getaway.

Manoeuvring the aircraft to get us onto the ground was very dangerous, but Tommy was exceptionally cool and precise as he gently lowered the front of the skids onto the icy ground. In haste we flung the doors open and, grabbing our day sacks, all climbed out of the chopper and knelt down in the snow directly where we had disembarked.

This previously undisturbed gully can't have known what hit

it. The chopper was making its deafening thudding noise, which reverberated around the natural stony cavern, as the spinning rotors kicked up a frenzied blizzard of bitterly cold previously virgin snow.

As we knelt, we were violently buffeted around by the extremely powerful wind machine. We stowed our packs under our legs and then bowed our heads down, clamping our waterproof jacket hoods to our faces with our gloved fists. When the last person was out, the doors were methodically fastened closed. Dave, who had positioned himself out towards the front of the chopper so Tommy could clearly see him, then signalled thumbs up. With a nod, Tommy skilfully rose and cleared the chopper away. He would disappear back to base until we called him in, via satellite phone, later in the day.

The plan while filming this sequence the following day was to have an additional helicopter, which would fly in sync with ours to allow Dan (2nd Camera) to film air-to-air footage. This extra helicopter would deliver Dan onto the gully floor prior to the epic rappel and would then clear away. We would have to allow enough time for the snowstorm to settle (created by the downdraft of the chopper) and also give Dan a chance to get into a good position from which to film the rope descent from the ground.

Throughout the whole recce led by Bear, Steve and David took notes of the logistical plan which would later be drawn up into a shooting schedule.

As Tommy's helicopter rose higher and higher, the deafening sound slowly began to fade. As it reached safe turning height out of the gully, the nose bowed away to the right and within seconds it had disappeared over the mountain and out of sight. At that moment it was as if a blanket of silence had been thrown over us all. The snowy conditions always created a muted, dull sound, yet compared to the thunderous din of the chopper, it felt as if the silence could have knocked us over.

One by one we all stood up and brushed the snow off our jackets and loaded the packs onto our backs. We spent a few minutes standing in a group and discussing what would happen the following day, when we "do this for real". We would have the additional chopper, more people and a serious amount of camera, sound and climbing kit to add to the equation. Right now, we had the luxury of taking our time to think about it... but the following day, every minute and movement would count. Time would be of the essence.

Methodically each member of the team went about looking at different facets of this wild landscape and considered how they would best execute the action on filming day. Bear, Dave and Woody went looking for the best route down the narrow gully, as Dan and I spied out the most suitable positions from where we could capture the best angles when filming the unfolding drama.

Moving on foot, from our landing zone we followed Bear's lead and started to track down the steep, imposing gully. We moved carefully, because underfoot the going was treacherous. Beneath the layer of snow and ice under our feet, we discovered a frozen riverbed, which we could faintly hear gushing below. This buried Arctic river was covered with a layer of ice. It would most likely differ in thickness the further we followed it. We needed to be very careful as the last thing any of us wanted at this early stage of a long day in such freezing conditions was to get wet feet. To aid our footing, each of us carried a pair of crampons. When we hit particularly steep slopes of ice we would strap the spiked accessories onto our walking boots. These gave us traction where before we would have been certain to slip and fall.

Thirty metres or so down the steep gully, the first obstacle we came across was a frozen waterfall with a lethal 10 metre steep slope. It pointed straight down. We decided that to be safe we should rig a casual belay rope system down to the bottom. Bear helped a few of us and Dave and Woody helped the rest. Two by two we slid down like penguins and in no time we gathered again at the base of the drop. On the recce this was all relatively easy but we were only too aware that the next day, with all our film equipment and almost double the amount of people, even this relatively small obstacle would prove to be quite an effort and pretty time-consuming.

Further down the gorge, still following the frozen river that churned beneath the ice under our feet, we came across a second obstacle. This one was major. There before us was a huge horseshoe-shaped vertical drop-off. Still flanked by the two sheer rock faces that created the jagged gorge, the sight before us was truly spectacular.

Peering over the top we saw that the drop was sheer and fell vertically for at least 30 metres. Not only that, but on the lip of the overhang was an enormous snow cornice (a lip of ice and snow that perilously pushes out over the drop). This must have been at least 2 metres in depth and width, and it gave the impression of a large wave that had been frozen whilst still in motion. If you walked on this cornice, your weight would almost certainly burst through the ice and consequently break the entire lip off. This would be incredibly dangerous as it crashed down the cliff, taking you and anyone else with it.

However, filming wise, this huge drop-off and cornice would be a fantastic obstacle for Bear and Will to have to tackle. So, for now, we were careful to leave the awesome cornice fully intact. We skirted around the far left-hand side of the rim and as carefully as possible rappelled all the way down without disturbing the perilous snowy lip. This proved to be a slow process as, in order to leave no trace, all seven of us had to descend one by one.

In order to safely and confidently rappel, you must embrace the correct technique. The more upright you stand the harder and more dangerous it will be. This is due to the more likelihood of your feet slipping down and hitting your head or face on the rock. The correct and safest method is to sit back into your climbing harness so that you are standing 90° to the rock face. To do this you have to learn the golden rule of climbing: Trust your rope!

In this particular instance, staying right out at 90° was critical, as the rock face was covered in snow and ice. Crampons can only work if your spikes are digging into the surface.

By now we had been in the formidable gully for almost three hours and the temperature in the shadows of the mighty walls was rapidly dropping.

We needed to press on.

From the bottom of the final drop you could see in the distance the way out of the gully, which would lead us down onto the edge of the vast valley. As we headed down further, the going got heavy underfoot with very deep snow drifts, so we had to stop and exchange our crampons for snowshoes.

Traditionally snowshoes looked like tennis rackets strapped to the feet. These days technology has somewhat advanced the design and now they look more like plastic skateboard-shaped decks with curled up front ends. The toes of your walking boots slide into a cup and, like cross-country ski bindings, your heel is free, allowing your whole foot to move in a scissor-like action. The base of the snowshoe swings with your step and not only creates a greater surface area upon which you can walk over deep snow without sinking, but jagged metal teeth below the binding also dig into the snow and give you extra traction.

All the time we were travelling we were chatting about the shoot and making notes. Bear and Woody were seeking out points of interest regarding survival skills and tips. For example, what plant life was available for edible foraging and what other 'tools' could be made from natural sources that were to hand.

Eventually we reached the base of the valley and there we decided to stop for lunch. We had all made our own sandwiches for the recce at breakfast and had also stowed in our packs some thermos flasks full of hot, sweet tea and coffee. Out in the expanse of the valley, the weak winter sunlight made the temperature noticeably warmer. Yet despite these slightly higher temperatures we still had to be mindful not to let ourselves get too relaxed – which would lead to us getting cold in seconds. If we became too cold it would be very hard to get warm again.

The basic rule of working in extreme cold conditions is not only to dress, but also to 'work' on the principle of layers. If you are about to take on some physical activity which is likely to make you sweat, then you should strip off some of your layers – depending on the extent of the physical demand of the exercise. Sometimes you need to literally strip down to just your thermal top and your waterproof jacket. This way you will start cold, but then as you exert some energy, you will not overly sweat.

The key to the success of this method is that when you stop you must immediately reapply extra layers to retain your heat. Sweating is the body's way of expelling heat, but in super-cold environments, the minute you stop working you will keep sweating – if that sweat should turn cold, your whole body will rapidly chill. Adding more layers will keep you consistently warm and your core body temperature will not lose its heat. In these extreme conditions if this is not controlled it can very easily be fatal!

After a quick bite to eat we were back to it. Next, we had to trek across the valley, cross the snaking frozen river and head towards the mountain on the other side. As we set off it was clear that the terrain underfoot was still tough. The following day Bear would lead Will and us all through this, so for now to save time and our energy (which we would definitely need to reserve for the following day) we decided to call in Tommy with the helicopter. The final part of the recce would be done from the air while returning to the helipad. On route we skimmed over the terrain where Bear estimated that he and Will would be likely to end up and get extracted from. The plan was set.

By the time we arrived back at the hotel, it was mid-late afternoon and rapidly growing dark. We were met by those of the team who had been left behind and, being the good lads that they are, found out that they had spent the last few hours prepping all the kit in our absence. This was a great team effort, but to be fair, there wasn't a whole lot to do in Kiruna on a day off.

Due to my lack of sleep the night before, by now I was absolutely shattered. So, to make the most of my last ounces of energy, I decided to sort the finer details of my camera kit out before an early supper and then crashing into my bed.

I went straight into the 'kit room', which was a hotel conference room which had been allocated for our use. The boardroom table and chairs had been moved back to the mustard-yellow walls and the room now brimmed over with camera and sound equipment. Battery chargers hummed away and the contents of the tough plastic 'Peli' cases spilled out in organized chaos.

Asking Buster (Camera Assistant) where my allocated camera was, he guided me to a corner of the room on the right. There I found my Sony F800 camera, wide angle lens, battery charging station which was fully loaded with batteries and a pile of Stock (XDCAM discs that we record our footage onto, which long ago replaced video tapes).

Buster had done a great job, so all I really needed to do was run my eye over all the various bits and pieces making sure it was all there. Then most importantly, I need to adjust and personalize the camera settings, and finally set my viewfinder.

Each Cameraman will have his own preferences for how he is used to operating his camera. Some use 'Zebras' (stripy signal that indicates your level of exposure on the viewfinder picture) but some don't. Some crank up their 'Peaking' (highlighted contrast lines that help your accuracy when focusing – if the subject is 100 per cent in focus, the brighter the peaking lines will appear) – yet others don't. Then the most basic of adjustments is of that to your own eye. You can slide the viewfinder's magnifying glass towards or away from your eye, thus enabling you to adjust the picture to suit your vision.

There are also many in-camera and viewfinder display settings that we will adjust, but I'll save you the details. If you're really interested, go and buy yourself a Sony camera manual!

As I sat in the kit room relaying the basics of the plan to Pete (Soundman paired up with me), Duncan popped his head round the door and asked that, after a clean-up, we could make our way to the ballroom where we would be have a brief production meeting before supper, to discuss in detail the plan for the shoot the following day.

Returning to my room tiredness hit me like a truck, yet I knew that despite the next days being 'full on', it was only two days. Compared with the duration of most other shoots, this would be a breeze. I took a long, hot shower, dressed in my 'civvies' and headed back downstairs to the hotel ballroom.

As I helped myself to a drink and found a seat in the circle of chairs, one by one everyone started to arrive.

The last people to walk in and join the circle were Will (Ferrell) and Gretchen (representative from the Discovery Channel US).

They had just flown in from LA and so were operating on a different time zone and were somewhat fazed out.

Will Ferrell is an American comedian, actor and writer who is hailed as one of the funniest men in Hollywood. In his mid-forties, he is surprisingly tall in the flesh and has a mop of light brown curly hair, which in itself presents quite an amusing image. He first came to the spotlight during his cameo performances on *Saturday Night Live*, but since then has a very impressive list of film credits under his belt, such as: *Old School, Elf, Anchor Man, Blades of Glory* and *The Other Guys* to name but a few. He is particularly well known for his dry, sarcastic, off-the-wall humour. Often the kind of humour where you don't know whether he's being serious or cracking a joke. Seeing how Bear would cope with this larger-than-life character would be fascinating.

Will took his seat in the circle. He seemed pretty quiet and a little overwhelmed by stepping straight into such a gathering. Like so many things in the entertainment and TV world, projects such as this for the 'Talent' (celebrities) are so 'flash in a pan'. They will literally turn up at the last minute, throw themselves into whatever is required and then, before you can blink, they'll be ushered off onto the next engagement. Having just arrived from the US, Will would have one night to try to get some sleep (fighting jet lag) and would then be thrown into the wilderness with Bear and on the adventure of a lifetime. Truly a baptism of fire!

Duncan warmly welcomed and thanked everyone for being there and roughly spelt out what the purpose of the meeting was, before handing over to Bear.

Bear made a special welcome to Will, and then extremely eloquently introduced the whole team to his guest. I was impressed by Bear doing this, because most 'Presenters' that

I work with rarely know everybody's name or what part they actually played in the team. Bear systematically worked his way around the circle and named each individual and explained what he had worked on with them previously, what they did as a job and then he would praise each individual in some way. I thought, if ever there was an example of great leadership it was this, making each member of the team feel included, important and valued.

Will then replied to Bear's welcome, saying how excited he was by being there and was not entirely sure just what he was about to let himself in for. No matter what Will said, even if he was trying to be serious, he just came across as funny – this must be one of the curses of being a well-known 'funny man'. The only context that people are used to seeing you in is cracking lines that are aimed to be humorous. There were one or two snorts of laughter breaking out around the circle, but Will, being a seasoned pro just reacted by pulling a face that magnified the amusement of the team.

When the pleasantries were over, it was down to business. Duncan, David and Steve took the lead and intricately led the team step by step through the plan for the next two days of filming. We only had a window of forty-eight hours in which to film the complete hour-long episode, so no matter what the elements threw at us, we had no choice but to knuckle down and nail it. Every member of the crew listened intently, and a few questions were asked in order to achieve absolute clarity over the schedule.

About an hour later, the meeting drew to a close and the group were adjourned. Dinner was served and then we all split off and retired to our rooms for a final night of rest before launching into the main shoot.

Shoot day:
5:15 a.m. I woke, again to the dreaded alarm. This time, after a full night's sleep, I sprung out of bed and hopped into the shower. I already felt the adrenalin kicking in of the challenge that lay before us. Getting dressed this time was a matter of routine and within a few minutes I was closing my hotel door and heading down to breakfast.

Having learned from the previous day's recce just how physical this shoot would be, I followed the example of Bear and made myself an extra sandwich to eat as a snack mid-morning. This would act as a good boost to my energy levels and would see me through until lunch.

After breakfast, the crew were all fed and watered. So, we gathered in the kit room and each person collected his respective kit and spares for the day.

It was an impressive sight as we made our way out to the convoy of 4x4s. This time we were fully tooled up, laden with heavy kit bags, cameras and sound kits.

Soon we arrived at the helipad. I dropped my kit in the office and joined Dave out at the six-seater helicopter. There I helped him secure the ropes and straps to the preordained anchor points and then climbed into my full body harness. Dave attached a karabiner to the ring on the back of my harness, positioned in-between my shoulder blades. He would use this to attach me, using a large karabiner, to a secured rope just before Bear and Will were about to exit the helicopter. We measured it up so that I would be able to lean right out on the skids over their heads as they rappelled out of the helicopter. We also rigged a safety line, to which I would attach the camera. This was a precaution in case I slipped or dropped the camera – this safety line would prevent the heavy camera falling down on top of Bear and Will, which could easily kill one of them.

As soon as Dave was happy and all the rigging was squared away, we went back into the office to gather the troops. Duncan allocated people seats in the two helicopters which were being pre-checked and warmed up. And so, we all climbed into our 'birds' and loaded up.

With the two helicopters flying out in formation, it looked like a scene from the film *Apocalypse Now*. From the ground it must have looked impressive and it certainly felt very cool to be a part of – I remember thinking, "There must be harder ways of earning your living!"

On the way out I rode with Bear, Dave and Pete. As we flew over the wilderness and came in line with our particular valley, we started to film the opening piece to camera – Bear speaking/presenting to the camera – setting the scene by introducing the show.

While we were flying in and filming the piece to camera, Dan was in the other helicopter shooting air-to-air (one chopper filming the other chopper while airborne). They then ran ahead and dropped Will off at an old wooden hunter/fisherman's hut in the middle of the valley, not too far from our gorge.

As we approached the small hut, you could see Will standing outside so we reduced altitude and made our approach.

David (Director) Pete (Sound) and I jumped out and shot a quick sequence of Will waiting for Bear to pick him up.

As I filmed, Will stood outside the hut and spoke to camera as Bear's chopper took off again. Tommy made a very wide circle, which was necessary to make the sequence work, before actually coming to pick Will up.

Being the ultimate professional, Will didn't disappoint and said to the camera: "I don't know how I got myself into this... I don't even like camping!"

Then as the chopper returned he added, "Maybe the chopper's

taking me back to Acapulco?" It was definitely the way he delivered it, that made it so amusing.

Bear's helicopter touched down on the snow, with the engines still roaring. Sitting with the door slid right back, Bear beckoned for Will to run over. Will responded and, dipping his head, ran low toward the helicopter as I chased behind, all the while filming. As Bear welcomed Will and hauled him into the aircraft you can see my reflection in the helicopter window (not something I would normally be bragging about, as the crew are meant to remain unseen).

David, Pete and I then also climbed on board and we were off. Typically with reality-style filming, you have to shoot pretty much everything in one take, as you haven't really got the time to do things twice – you have to be, as we say in the industry, a 'one-take wonder'.

The minute I sat opposite Bear and Will, with my back facing the pilot, Tommy, Pete gave me the nod that he was ready with the sound and I kept the camera rolling. Bear now properly welcomed Will on camera and loosely explained about what they were about to do. When Bear mentioned that they were going to rappel out of the helicopter, Will gave a comedy double take – whether he was clowning around or was genuinely gobsmacked, we'll probably never know. I think it was probably a bit of both.

The pace was blistering and that was how it was going to continue for the next two days, but so far so good.

In what seemed like seconds we had reached the gorge, and Tommy started to carefully edge his way in. At the same time, ahead of us we could see that the second chopper had just dropped off Dan and the other boys, and was now lifting itself out of the tight landing zone. As they cleared and held a distant position, Buster filmed air-to-air with one of the smaller cameras. Tommy then took the lead and hovered perfectly over the pre-allocated position for the rappel.

Bear explained clearly to Will exactly what his actions were to be during the rappel, and that he just had to trust the rope and Bear, of course. The two of them were going to descend together off the one rope. Bear slid the door open and the cabin was immediately washed with a huge gust of ice-cold swirling wind and snowy dust. Bear then threw out the long black rope which hit the ground over 50 metres below. Dan got great shots of this while looking up and shooting from the ground.

Bear, checking his karabiner and harness, then stepped out backwards off the hovering helicopter and stood on the left skid, facing in towards us. Very tentatively Will then shuffled out and followed him.

At this stage, no matter who or where you are, it doesn't matter that the camera is on you. All your focus will be zeroed in to what you and your body are doing. This was not a natural thing to do and the stakes were extremely high. Will was very quiet and there was certainly no joking about now.

I continuously filmed all the action as it happened. I kept checking my exposure, checking my focus and most of all checking that I was recording!

It may sound silly or unprofessional, but it's all too easy to be caught in the moment and be distracted by all that's going on around you that you can actually forget to press RECORD. Any Cameraman worth their salt, when being honest, will admit to doing this at some point during their career.

I was recording (!) as Bear and Will both carefully lowered themselves from a standing position on the helicopter's skid, to now hanging by their climbing harnesses, with their heads at about the skid level. I then stood up and swung around to face them straight on. As rehearsed, at this point Dave, who was overseeing everything regarding all our safety, clipped the large karabiner onto the back of my body harness which meant that I was now safe to hang right out of the chopper. With a tap on the shoulder I turned around to see Dave, who was giving me a 'thumbs up' – I was secure.

I have said on numerous occasions since this shoot, that surely it's the biggest testament to whether you trust and would recommend someone like Dave – when having only known him for less than twenty-four hours, you trust him to clip you on, behind your back in a completely blind position, and then you lean out of a hovering helicopter at 50 metres above a treacherous snowy gorge. I chose to put my trust in him and, being the consummate professional that he is, of course he didn't let me down.

I edged closer to the door as the two guys were carefully positioning themselves to swing under the skid in order to be free to rappel down to the ground. Suddenly there was a problem. The combined weight of Bear and Will on the same line meant that their main descender (figure of eight-shaped rappelling device) got stuck on the lip of the door. Seeing that they were struggling I looked down and saw the jammed descender, so still filming I gave it a kick with the toe of my boot. It came loose, but then got jammed again on the skid. This time Bear had to jiggle their weight around in order to free the descender. Eventually it came unstuck but Will's hand was under the rope which took the full pressure of both their body weight. This could have meant quite a nasty injury for Will's arm, but fortunately, as Bear bounced their weight around, Will managed to squeeze his arm out safely. Seconds later the boys were dangling a few metres under the helicopter and free to commence their rappel.

Dan was stoically filming from the ground all the action happening in the air above. All the while he fought to keep his lens clean from the snowstorm that was being kicked up by the chopper's downdraft. This was a real challenge, but he did a great job.

As the two began to rappel down the rope, the motion forced them into a slow spin. Bear was rigged with a special mini-cam on his wrist which brilliantly captured Will's face as he spun around in mid-air shouting, "Mommy! Mooooommy!" It was a priceless addition to the action sequence.

By this stage I was leaning right out over their heads, having to stretch a little further than originally thought due to the skid blocking my shot as they spun. I remember being caught up in the powerful wash of the rotors and I desperately struggled to keep the camera steady. On top of that I will never forget just how cold that wind was. It felt as if it was burning a hole in the side of my head, like an extreme 'ice cream headache'.

When Bear had skilfully lowered them down so their feet were touching the snowy ground, he gave enough slack in the rope to set them on their knees. Now stable, he unclipped the rope from the descender and his karabiner and then set it free, signalling to Dave, who was kneeling next to me up in the chopper, that it was clear to be pulled up to safety. As Dave heaved the rope up back into the helicopter I kept filming for as long as I could, until Dan and Sean took the chance to run up and meet Bear and Will on the ground and cover their reaction and initial conversation following the stunt.

The first challenge had gone brilliantly. All credit to the whole team who worked in unison to safely achieve a potentially very dangerous sequence.

Will and Bear stood aside as Tommy dropped Dave, Pete and me down and then took off back to base. All being well, we wouldn't see him until late afternoon the following day.

On the ground there was no hanging around, so Pete and I

literally had time to put our packs on our backs and then carry on filming.

I had previously agreed with Dan that I would shoot the wide (safety) 'two shot' of Bear and Will as he would concentrate on the more side on, arty, close-up shots of their faces and points of interest – for example, if one of them was tying a knot, I would shoot both people and Dan would crash in and focus on a tight shot of the hands and rope. This way, we should be well covered not to miss any of the action and in the edit they would also have plenty to 'cut away' to (a generic shot of something without any lip sync, so that they can use it to edit around a scene and patch over an unnatural change of picture).

I took up a general position, pretty much straight in front of Bear and Will, as Dan kept just off to one side – more of a profile shot.

Bear started by giving Will a few accessories that he would need for the adventure ahead: a water bottle, cup, knife, a fire-starting flint and then a Twinkie (an American golden sponge cake with a creamy filling). Never one to miss a trick, of course, the water bottle, cup and knife were from the 'Bear Grylls' branded accessories – a clever bit of product placement advertising.

When Will was fully tooled up, Bear then left him for a few minutes in order to go and gather some branches, just up the hill, that would be used to help them descend any drops coming up.

As Bear scuttled off I remained focused on Will, expecting to get a reaction to what he had just been given. In the mid shot (head to waist) of Will as he knelt down packing his gifts into his day sack, you could see Bear in the distant background foraging around. Will, realizing that Bear was out of earshot, decided to start tucking into his Twinkie bar straight away. He ate the whole thing in about two mouthfuls.

For me, it wasn't so much that he ate the Twinkie bar now

(which was supposed to be a survival/energy ration for later in the day) that was funny. But it was just the way in which he did it... he just has funny bones.

Often when filming funny things, it is a real challenge to keep the camera steady. With the camera resting on your shoulder, the slightest giggle or snort of amusement will of course shake the picture. Not to mention your guffaw being picked up on the microphone held close by. I have to admit that I have been caught out like this on many occasions – sometimes it adds to the scene, sometimes it's totally inappropriate... yet nearly always unavoidable. In this scenario, as Will was acting this out for comic effect, he appreciated that if the Cameraman and Soundman laughed, then he was obviously being funny and so fortunately this time, we were in the clear.

The banter between Bear and Will had started well. Bear berated Will as he carried on acting the clown, but of course the whole episode was always intended to be a bit of fun, with some pretty serious adventuring to add into the mix.

As we walked down to the first obstacle, the 10 metre tall frozen waterfall, due to the experience following the recce, all the crews donned their crampons. Bear and Will weren't allowed this luxury. They would have to improvise or fall over – which they did.

Just before tackling the descent, Bear decided that this river under the ice would be the perfect opportunity for him and Will to fill up their water bottles. So, using a rock, they punched through the four to five-inch ice and managed to reach the water below with their water bottles. This water would be some of the freshest and cleanest in the world, with no source of pollution for literally hundreds of kilometres. Will commented that he was "used to more chlorine in his water". Just one of the joys of being out in the wilderness.

Bear then rigged up a short belay upon which to shimmy down the 10 metre drop. Will was clearly enjoying himself.

Whenever Bear and Will were manoeuvring around an obstacle, Dan and Sean would have to scurry ahead in order to film them arriving at the bottom of the drop – leapfrogging Pete and I. Usually we would try to keep the momentum up, but it was inevitable that sometimes we had to pause proceedings so that everyone could catch up. After all, we weren't going very far without Dave and his climbing ropes.

The frozen waterfall was tackled by all, relatively easily and quickly.

Next up was the 30 metre drop with the 2 metre cornice attached.

The idea at this next challenge was for Will to act as a human anchor for Bear as he walked out to see what the drop was like. Will would be sat down in the snow, digging his heels in firmly and then belaying Bear using the rope that would be passing through a karabiner attached to Will's climbing harness. Sounds easy enough?

This was another potentially very dangerous stunt, so all the crew assembled to recap on how we had planned to cover it on film, as well as working around the big drop safely.

Dan had offered to be roped up and walk beside Bear as he tackled the cornice, the idea being that if Bear fell, then Dan would fall beside him catching all the action and drama on his camera.

I would stay covering Will and see his reaction as Bear inevitably broke through the cornice.

When everyone was set and ready to go, we went for it. Will was sat in the snow, heels dug in, and slowly paid out the rope as Bear walked backwards ever closer to the lip of the drop. Dan walked sideways beside Bear. The atmosphere was actually quite tense. Will was genuinely nervous about being responsible for paying out the rope, and the rest of the team, who knew what was coming... were waiting for the moment.

Suddenly the cornice gave way under Bear's weight, and he and Dan just disappeared in a cloud of snow! Will's body violently jerked as he took the strain, saving Bear and breaking his fall. "Bear!" Will shouted. "Bear, are you OK?" There was silence... "Bear?"

The problem was the remaining cornice was so thick with snow that Bear dangling below couldn't hear Will. There were concerned looks darting around the crew. "BEAR!" Will shouted once more with a lot more volume.

Everybody stood still to listen, and then we heard a faint voice, "I'm OK, Will, just hold the rope tight and I'll try to get out of here." Will muttered under his breath, "This is crazy."

It's not to be underestimated that Will, having just flown in from LA, had never done anything like this. It was completely new to him and, on top of that, his body clock was still on LA time, so he was all over the place.

Dangling beside Bear was Dan who was covered in snow, but still heroically filming Bear attaching his ascender device to the rope, in order to climb out.

It took close to ten minutes for Bear to climb out and as Will had been sitting in the snow for some time now, he had grown very cold. Eventually Bear appeared over the lip of the drop, covered in snow and slightly out of breath. This had been quite an effort. Dave, who had been belaying Dan throughout, then lowered Dan down to the bottom of the drop. He would stay down there ready for when the two guys rappelled down for the lower angled shot.

Despite being cold, Will held fast and waited for Bear to crawl well clear of the drop before loosening his grip on the rope. His hands had 'gone'. Once back on his feet, he then came over to me and Pete, well clear of any danger. He was not one to complain, but I could see that he was really uncomfortable and was properly chilled through. As someone else opened up a thermos flask to give him a hot drink, I gave him my thick ski gloves to put over his lighter gloves.

Make no mistake, this was not a Hollywood actor being precious or being pampered. We were working in dangerously low temperatures and once your body starts to get cold, it's imperative that you take seriously the need to warm back up. If the cold really gets a grip of you, that can rapidly turn into hyperthermia.

After the exertion of his super-physical climb out of the drop, Bear was perfectly warm, so he cracked on with Dave prepping the next manoeuvre.

After a few minutes of warming back up, Will gave the nod that he was up for carrying on. So, returning my gloves, he and Bear headed back out to the area just a few metres away from the drop.

Here, Bear demonstrated the 'Dead Man's Anchor'. This was where he would take two small branches and dig them into the snow, so they literally acted as an anchor. The branches set deep in the snow were very strong, and so with the rope passed around them, this was easily able to hold the weight of the two guys. A clever survival trick. Bear said, "A friend of mine once lowered a body down, using a Dead Man's Anchor with a frozen Hershey bar", opposed to branches. Will replied, "I wonder if a frozen Twinkie would have worked? We'll never know", referring to the one he scoffed earlier. Bear laughed.

Once the Anchor was securely in place, Bear passed the rope around the secured branches and through his belay device and then tied it through the karabiner attached to the hoop on Will's climbing harness. He then described how they were going to tackle this obstacle. They would slowly walk backwards, side by side. As they were both on the same line, they would lower themselves down at the same time.

When they reached the lip of the drop, at the space Bear had cleared by falling through it, they crouched down and onto their knees. Slowly and steadily Bear paid out the rope as they began to descend, and over the lip they went.

At this point, during the short break, Dave had attached a safety line to the back of my climbing harness. This allowed me to walk facing the guys all the way out to the lip. As they went over the lip, I stood on the edge and filmed looking down at them. This shot was good as not only could I film on the long end of the lens their faces and reactions, but I could also crash out the zoom and film a very wide shot, which showed the scale of just how large this drop was.

I kept filming the whole event as Dan, who was positioned a quarter of the way up from the base, also picked up the action from more of a profile angle.

When they reached the bottom, I held one more ten-second wide/scale shot and then left it all to Dan below. Now it was a race to get down to join them. The problem with this particular drop, as we learned on the recce, was that it was slow to get everyone down. However, now the cornice was broken up, it was decided that Pete and I should race down first to carry on filming before Will got too cold again.

Dave moved the rope to the front of my climbing harness and a sling to the handle of my camera. I slung the camera over my shoulder onto my back and then turned and began rappelling down as Dave belayed me.

To save time getting the whole team down these obstacles, we had another climbing expert with us, who was Swedish. He was a lovely guy, but his English wasn't quite fluent.

As I was rappelling, the Swedish guy had roped up Pete. As Pete's sound kit was so much more cumbersome than a camera, Dave decided that he should use the larger gap that Bear and Will had made in the middle of the cornice. By this stage I had reached the bottom and was untying my rope. I looked up to see Pete stepping out onto the lip of the drop. He was saying "No, no, no", trying to communicate to the Swedish climber that he wasn't ready to go over the edge and so wanted the rope to be pulled taut to take his weight. Unfortunately the Swedish guy thought Pete was saying "Go, go, go" so paid out more and more rope, the consequence being that Pete's foot got caught on the edge of the cornice and due to the weight of his sound equipment he swung forward over the drop and then completely upside down! As he twisted upside down his foot knocked a huge chunk of the cornice, which broke off and fell directly onto my head!

It could have actually been quite nasty, but in fact it was one of the funniest things that I'd seen in years, that was before I got a face full of hard-packed snow. Seeing poor Pete dangling upside down from the top of the drop was spectacularly funny and I could barely breathe for laughter. Not only that but he shouted out an expletive (which I can't repeat), which then echoed around the mountain gully.

As I cleared myself from the pile of snow and wiped away the tears from my eyes before they froze, Pete managed to right himself and then complete his descent. Bear, Will and I kept on chuckling about the whole event. Fortunately, Pete was a great sport about it.

For some reason, over the years I have developed an ability, which is not often helpful, to constantly replay events over and over in my head. Seeing them repeated just gets funnier and funnier. This situation was ripe for that and as we carried on walking down the last few hundred metres of the gorge, even though I was filming, I kept on bursting out laughing and then giggling like a little girl. At first Pete joined me in this, but then after the second or third hour of guffawing, I think he grew a little weary of my childlike humour.

Overall, it had taken us five hours to get to the bottom of the gorge and at the start of the huge open valley. As it was close to midday, similar to the recce day, we decided that this would be as good a time as any to stop and have some lunch. To our delight, lunch today was being brought in by skimobile. We stood around the vehicles and made ourselves reindeer sandwiches and sipped hot soup, which were fantastic.

Those who have worked with me a lot say that I am famous for loving my food. In fact, they pull my leg over the fact that at almost every meal we're sat at, I tend to state, "I think this is the best meal I've EVER had!" In defence I think this is mostly due to the fact of having worked so physically hard, I am just incredibly hungry. Having said that, I probably do still say it even on a rest day. There is no doubt... I love my food.

This simple lunch, washed down with some sweet coffee, was enough to completely recharge all our batteries, and within thirty minutes or so we were all raring to crack on.

The first scene we shot after lunch was Bear and Will having a pee! This wasn't planned and wasn't just for comedy effect, but Bear also added that even with peeing there is an important survival tip. You should always check the colour of your urine, and should aim for it to be the colour of champagne. If it's more like PG Tips (tea) colour, then you need to drink more. Sounds funny, but this is critical to one's health in such an environment.

For comic genius Will, this was an opportunity far too good to miss. As he stood side by side with Bear who was already peeing like a racehorse, Will stated, "I think I've lost my penis!" Well, it was -20°C.

We were one-third of the way through our forty-eight hour adventure and we still had a fair bit of ground to cover before sundown.

Shortly after heading off across the valley we ran into some very deep snow. It was literally up to our nuts. So, in order to be physically able to walk while filming, Pete and I attached our snowshoes. We struggled even with our snowshoes on, so you can imagine how hard this was for Bear and Will. Will was as ever in good humour about it, but this took an extreme amount of effort and quickly sapped you of energy. Bear wanted to show Will how to make snowshoes out of live branches. So, they struggled their way to a small group of birch trees and started to pick branches off.

The improvised snowshoes were rudimentary, but would definitely help the guys stand on the snow. Even though they still sank fairly deeply with each step it was far easier than being buried up to your waist.

Having successfully made some ground, heading over the valley floor toward the river, we hit another area of deep snow which had a parallel track to it. At this stage I thought it would be a great opportunity to attempt some kind of tracking shot. So, Woody rode one of the snowmobiles over and as Bear and Will trudged their way through the snowfield, I sat on the back of the snowmobile and rode beside them. Like so many things on location it was a nice idea, but it turned out that the terrain was simply too bumpy to get a clean, smooth shot. So, I quickly scrapped that idea, hopped off the skimobile and joined them again on foot.

The day was getting on now and the low Arctic sun was beginning to fade. On route, the boys had come across a reindeer carcass, left by hunters, which was now (in true Bear Grylls fashion) top of the menu for their supper in camp that evening.

A few hours later we all arrived on the other side of the valley, exhausted. Will had made a sterling effort in his makeshift snowshoes (which had collapsed a number of times) though he was now physically at the point of collapsing through tiredness. Having walked a good number of kilometres with them on, he finally piped up and said, "Bear, don't take this the wrong way, but f@*$k these snowshoes!" Bear laughed, as they did look a bit like they had stamped on a witch's broomstick which had then stuck to the bottom of their boots. Bear then acknowledged that it had been a long day, and that they would make camp for the night in this spot. This was visibly music to Will's ears.

Dan and I were also glad that we had stopped to make camp, as the light was growing almost too low to film in.

Buster had by this point primed the LED 'top lights' which we could use, but I chose to shoot under natural light until we really had to add extra light. The great benefit of being out in the mountains is that snow acts as a fantastic natural reflector, keeping the light levels higher than they would normally be.

It was in this blue-pink twilight that Bear and Will set about building their shelter in which to camp. They used bigger sticks to create the frame of a 'lean-to' shelter and gathered green leafed branches to lay on the floor and stand beside the frame to create walls and a roof. Finally, they had a reasonable covering that pushed snow up against the bottom of the walls to create some kind of insulation. It was very basic, yet was quick and effective.

The finishing touch to their overnight home was to cut the head off the reindeer carcass and then lay the skin and fur on the ground. This was almost a luxury.

Bear was impressive with how quickly he made a fire with some sticks, using a handful of 'Old Man's Beard' (a type of moss that hangs off tree branches and is generally dry and brittle, making a great natural fire starter) which they had found earlier as they were walking out of the gorge. This lifted Will's spirits as not only was he now resting after a full-on day's adventuring, but this fire also meant that he could also properly warm up again.

We were also grateful for the fire, because not only did it give me and Dan more natural light to play with, but the heat also reached out and warmed us up too.

With everyone happy, Bear played 'Mom' and threw the entire reindeer head on the fire. Will kept on referring to the eyeball and made a few comments like "If I had a dollar for every time I've come to Sweden and eaten reindeer's eyeball... I'd be a rich man" and "I call the eyeball!" Needless to say he was joking.

Deeply tired, with glazed-over eyes and a more thoughtful sentiment, he added. "A reindeer head on the fire, that's a crazy image for a crazy day for me. Basically, a whole day of activity that I've never done in my life, nor did I ever think I would. So, thank you for that." He continued, "It's fun to get out there and test yourself in ways that you're not used to doing. It was pretty fun, actually... I have to say."

It's always nice to hear people saying such things when you've spent all day chasing them around, working your ass off. It kind of makes it all worthwhile, as there's nothing worse than working really hard for people who just don't enjoy or appreciate the experience.

Around thirty minutes later the reindeer head was still frozen, but the eyeballs had melted enough to pluck them from the eye sockets to eat. Bear went first. Using his knife he dropped the eye into his mouth and chewed on it. Will just chuckled beside him, in disbelief. Will then asked, "Bad, is it?" Bear replied, "Mmm... Yeah, it's terrible!" However, with all the eating challenges that Bear has faced over the many series of his TV shows, none of them are included for enjoyment, but rather to prove that if you are in a real-life survival scenario, this stuff (although revolting) can help to keep you alive.

Now it was Will's turn to eat an eyeball. Bear passed it to him and without hesitation he popped it straight into his mouth. As he began to chew it his face was priceless. This time it was Bear's turn to do the chuckling.

Bear asked him how it was. Will replied with a grimace on his face and through pursed lips, "Yep... that's terrible." "Well, good on you for trying it," Bear added and then they tucked into some of the more appetizing cheek.

After an extremely frugal supper, the boys got their heads down for the night. Will admitted that he'd never experienced adrenaline rushes like he had done earlier in the day and subsequently that he had never felt so exhausted in his life.

With the close of the sequence, David called "that's a wrap" marking the end of the filming day. However, even though we had finished filming, we were still in the middle of nowhere so our day was by no means over yet. We left the boys at their camp and rendezvoused a little further back down the track. The original idea was that we were going to also camp out near Bear and Will, so the support team had erected a tepee for the crew with a fire pit in the centre of it. Yet, it was decided that there wasn't going to be enough room for us all, so the main crews, me, Pete, Dan and Sean should be taken by snowmobile to a group of log cabins, where Buster could charge our camera batteries and we could get a better night's sleep. It had been a long, tough day, so we weren't going to argue with the decision. I hopped on the back of Woody's snowmobile, rested the camera on my lap and held on to the seat side bars and we took off. The journey out took us just short of an hour, which is a very long time, holding on with one hand to the back of snowmobile, through the Arctic wilderness in the darkness of night. By the time we arrived at the cabins, my right foot was completely numb with the biting cold.

I thanked Woody for his skilful driving and then stomped off to find a hut for Pete and me to share. Pete arrived shortly after me along with the others in a convoy of snowmobiles. We were well and truly shattered, so without hanging around, we quickly dispersed to our shared cabins, dropped our kit and crashed into bed. It was mid-evening, but felt very late when considering our extremely early start, plus we had hardly stopped all day long.

Pete was fast asleep by the time that I got into bed. He was gently snoring away. I soon followed and drifted off.

After just one or two hours of deep sleep I was rudely woken in the dark, by Pete shouting out, "Come on then, let's see it"; "Come on, think you're hard, do you?" I lay in bed and chuckled to myself as Pete, still fast asleep, was obviously fronting up to someone in his dream. He then carried on mumbling and murmuring. By this stage I was sniggering under my blanket like a schoolboy. Pete is normally such a quiet guy who usually keeps himself fully together. Just as my giggling began to cease and despite the entertainment from the bed next door, my heavy eyelids started to win the fight and I began to drift off to sleep again.

But then, to my shock, Pete sat bolt upright and shouted, "Wooooooooooha... BOFF!!!" He then immediately lay back down, rolled over and carried on sleeping quietly. That was it, I was howling out loud with laughter I couldn't control myself. Like when someone farts in a church service, the more I tried to stifle my giggles the more I kept bursting out in hysterics, while again, playing it out again over and over in my head. This continued for an embarrassing length of time and severely reduced my night's sleep. In the morning I was delighted to share the night's entertainment with Pete... then Dan and Sean... then Buster... then Woody... you get the idea. Although Pete did laugh along with us, I can't help but think that he ended up feeling a little embarrassed by the sleep talking/shouting. Loving it, I still call him 'BOFF' to this very day.

The next morning was another brutally early start. We left the cabins in a convoy of snowmobiles way before sunrise, aiming to make it to Bear and Will's camp to film them having breakfast... more reindeer head.

The second day was probably not going to be so 'obstacle challenge' based, but instead we had a lot of terrain to cover, so it was likely to be way more physical in the way of endurance. One thing was set in stone, the two helicopters had to pick us up at least an hour before sunset, in order to make it safely back to the helipad in daylight. So, once again, time was of the essence.

We left camp on foot. Following a previous long, physical day you always start with sore legs. It takes way more than a mug of tea to wake your reluctant muscles up and it's not until you have started some kind of exercise, which increases your heart rate, that you truly feel back in the swing of things.

As we trudged through the knee-deep snow, Bear headed straight for the tallest tree that he could find. He needed to climb the tree in order to look out over the land and get his bearings. Once he'd established where they were, he could then navigate them out of the valley and up to the extraction point on the next mountainside. At the base of the tall tree, Bear made a makeshift rope ladder by tying a series of hoops into a length of rope. Will, still waking up, stood and watched.

We attached the mini-cam back on Bear's wrist and then in just a couple of swift movements he had hauled himself up onto the first big branch which must have been at least 2.5 metres off the ground. Will was suitably impressed. He then attempted to follow. Let's just say that Will's not a natural climber, but he did make it up to the first few branches, where he decided to stay while Bear continued on up to the top of the tree.

We remained filming from the ground, which was agony on our necks due to the angle of shooting up into the tree. I was huffing and puffing due to the effort.

While both of the boys were up the tree, we decided to do some 'pieces to camera' or 'teasers' that would be used as a separate snippet with which to promote the special episode. I wasn't best pleased about this, because my neck and right shoulder was contorted into the most painful of positions. Yet, the shot did look good; relatively extreme and somewhat bizarre. I agreed that we could do the pieces to camera "as long as we were quick". Mercifully, then Bear and Will delivered their lines like two old TV pros, and a few minutes later they were on the ground and we were off again.

We walked quite some distance before coming to the start of the ascent of the other mountain. By the time we had got there the weather was starting to close in and we only had about four hours of daylight left.

A little further on, we saw in front of us an enormous, magnificent-looking frozen waterfall. It appeared almost as if someone had touched it with a magic wand and it had just stopped in frozen animation. At the same moment, we saw a huge eagle fly high above us. This place was somewhat magical. We decided to stop for a quick rest, and as Bear and Will sat down, it started to snow. It was probably the snow and the scenery which prompted the heart-to-heart chat between the boys.

Without stopping, I knelt in the snow just in to the right of Will and framed up a two shot. Will was in the foreground and Bear over his left shoulder, slightly out of focus in the background. This was good. I was comfortable on my knees in the soft snow and knew that as the conversation took place I could pull focus to and from each guy.

Will shared that he was quite blown away by the beauty and the solitude of the wilderness and compared it to working on films in Hollywood. He definitely enjoyed both, but it was the solitude and the peacefulness of this snowy location that impressed most upon him. Bear agreed that this was the biggest draw of the remote locations for him too.

Prompted by Bear's question, "When did you first realize that you were funny?" Will then continued to share how his humour was originally born out of him being somewhat different to his school mates. He was always tall and gangly and so stood out from the crowd. Due to this he always felt a little awkward within his own skin, but the one thing that seemed to warm others to him was that they laughed at what he said. It wasn't a calculated decision to be the 'funny man', but his humour and take on life seemed to charm others. And so, the famous Hollywood comedian was born.

Filming this intimate and revealing chat felt a privilege. It's funny how, no matter who the person is, or how famous they are, when you are out in the elements of a remote location, everybody is equal, just another human being. I have always counted it an honour to meet such big names and be in a position to witness them letting their guard down and at least, for a while, forget their 'fame'. After all, in reality, they are just normal people, doing pretty much the same job, the only difference being that they are positioned in front of my camera and I am behind it. This openness made my respect for Will grow even more.

Once the chat was over, it was time to move on towards the massive frozen waterfall. Our route there was to traverse a very steep snow field. Bear and Will got up, shouldered their packs and took off. Dan and Sean were covering the wider landscape shot from the valley below, while Pete, Dave and I followed Bear and Will in closer quarters. For a while we created a path parallel to them through deep virgin snow, a few metres lower than where they were walking.

With the camera slung under my shoulder, holding it with my hands at hip level, we tracked them as they walked. Underfoot the snow became increasingly deep and so became a real effort to push through. Within minutes the snow was up to my mid-thigh level and in order to carve a path through it, I had to lift my feet and knees as high as I could to make ground. All the while I was still trying to steadily balance the camera while filming. It worked, but was exhausting.

After a good ten minutes or so, my work rate was maxing out, my heart was pumping and my legs were burning with the extreme effort of carving out the fresh path. Bear and Will were still moving along, so I had no other option than to dig deep and just keep pushing on. Occasionally, while concentrating on holding the shot, my foot would get stalled by the snow and I would fall over onto my elbows, desperately keeping the camera body out of the snow. Every now and then Pete, who was following me, would do the same. For Pete the view of his feet was totally obscured by the sound mixer hanging around his waist – this meant that each step was pretty much blind. We found that the coping mechanism was to laugh about it and every time we fell, you could hear a chuckle or a wheeze from behind.

As we continued on through the difficult snow, to add to the effort, the gradient of the slope started to become really steep. At this point, Bear stopped Will and decided that as the snow was fairly icy on top, the chances were that it was layered in a similar fashion below and so would be liable to break and slip as their boots cut through. If any of us slipped, we would tumble down the steep slope and end up on the jagged rocks below. It was deemed necessary to 'short rope' each other, so Bear tied a piece of rope to Will and then hitched it around his shoulder. If Will took a fall, Bear would be able to act as an anchor for him. Likewise if Bear slipped, Will would do the same.

As they set off, roped up, we decided that we didn't have the time to do the same, so Dave moved forward and kept within an arm's length of Pete and I. Having absolute faith in Dave, I concentrated on the filming and carried on, huffing and puffing.

We eventually made it over the steepest section of the slope and I found a spot to stop, kneel down and film Bear and Will as they carried on towards the frozen waterfall. I filmed them walking away on a wide shot, allowing Dan, who was now at the base of the huge ice waterfall, to pick them up approaching him.

The plan worked perfectly.

Dan and Sean, who were slightly more rested, took over the coverage as the boys arrived at the great ice structure, which gave Pete, Dave and I time to catch our breath and then catch up with them again.

The monstrous size of the frozen waterfall was only to be truly realized when stood at the foot of it. It towered over us at about 15 metres and was at least 10 metres in diameter... in short, it was like three double-decker buses standing on their ends in a pyramid fashion.

The idea was to look behind the structure to see if there was an easy way leading up to the summit of the mountain. We only had a couple of hours left before we needed to be calling in the helicopters, so again we had to crack on.

Dan and Sean offered to go in behind the waterfall, so they donned their crampons – a luxury that of course Bear and Will didn't have.

Around the back of the frozen water, the ice was like sheet glass. It was literally like walking over giant ice cubes.

When fully around the back, Bear realized that there was no quicker route out, so using the short rope (still attached from before) he belayed Will down a steep slide of pure, see-through ice. Shortly afterwards he hooked the rope around a solid block of ice and skilfully belayed himself down unaided. At this point Pete and I had leapfrogged ahead, repositioning ourselves to the side of the waterfall where they would be exiting. Within a matter of minutes we could see them flaying around, while trying to walk out on the ice – occasionally slipping over and spinning on their backs like turtles upside down on their shells. As you can imagine, the sight of this was highly amusing, but what made it even funnier was the fact that all the exertion and excitement had 'moved' Will.

Leaving the ice and finding better footing as they came out, Bear was encouraging Will that they only had one more steep climb and then they would be at the top. Yet, Will was quick to interject that he needed a little break... for his bowels! Bear laughed and said, "Is it number ones or number twos?" With a definite air of resignation, Will replied, "Unfortunately, it's the worse of the two that you have to deal with when in the wilderness." With that he turned and staggered off to disappear behind a huge rock close by. As he walked he said, "It's not Man versus Wild... it's Man versus Bowels!" With that he lost his footing and fell flat on his back. We all roared with laughter as the poor guy regained his posture and went off to do what a man's gotta do.

Minutes later, with an obvious weight off his mind, Will rejoined Bear and we all began the final ascent before reaching the summit and their extraction point.

Without doubt we were all physically tired, but due to the

addition of jet lag, Will was finished. This started to really show on this last climb. I think the fact that you know that you are so close to the end causes one to switch off a bit and the adrenaline to calm down, all of which allows tiredness to really take hold.

Dan and I kept leapfrogging up to the top, so we had the climb well covered.

Eventually we all arrived on the summit and almost as a reward for all our efforts, despite it being bitterly cold, the clouds cleared for a spell and there before us was a magnificent view over the surrounding mountains. Literally as far as the eye could see there was nothing man-made. This truly was a wilderness and it was stunning.

After a quick breather, taking in the view, Bear and Will quickly got to making a small fire. Will had stowed some 'Old Man's Beard' in his jacket pocket and Bear had carried some kindling wood in his day sack from earlier that day.

Within minutes they had a basic fire going, which was burning strongly as they foraged around nearby ground for any moss, which when thrown on the fire would increase the smoke as a signal to Tommy in the chopper.

Bear said, "You'll hear the chopper before you can see it up here," and then, sure enough, you could hear that familiar faint thudding of the distant aircraft.

By now the second, smaller chopper had already joined us on the flat summit, so Pete and I ran over to it and made ourselves ready, sitting securely harnessed in the open door ready to shoot the air-to-air extraction. Our chopper then took off again and settled into a low hover from where I had a great view of the others below.

The plan was for Tommy to hover overhead and drop a steel and rope ladder down to Bear and Will. They would then climb a few runs up the ladder and clip in, while Tommy flew off for the final shot, with both of them remaining dangling below the chopper. A 'hero shot', as we've come to call it.

Yet, all didn't quite go according to plan...

As the steel/rope ladder was unfurled from the helicopter, Will was to go first and climb up about four or five rungs to leave enough room for Bear at the bottom. He climbed up the first two or three rungs perfectly, but then literally ran out of steam. The powerful downdraft of the helicopter and his exhausted body proved too much for him. Suddenly he let go of the ladder! Thankfully, he had already clipped himself onto the ladder with a karabiner. But what happened next, no one could have guessed...

As Will let go of the ladder, with his climbing harness attached at waist level, he suddenly spun around, like a Catherine Wheel, and ended up completely upside down! My heart leapt as I filmed all this from the other helicopter, as I thought Will may be in serious trouble. Yet, very quickly Bear jumped up a few rungs and helped him regain his balance and composure. Again, not for the first time on this trip, we all burst into hysterics.

With Will firmly back in position and Bear hooked on below him, Tommy steered the chopper away with the boys hanging on the ladder under it, about 100 metres off the ground. I remember having tears from the laughter flooding down my face as we chased and filmed this stunt... fighting to see what I was filming.

The final stunt was magnificent, as was the closing shot. All very fitting for the end of a truly epic adventure!

Postscript:
Following this first ***Man vs Wild*** *special, Bear went on to film a number of special shows with a select group of celebrities – under the title of* ***Wild Weekends*** *with Bear Grylls.*

Mungo also filmed with Bear:
Escape To The Legion
Escape From Hell
Get Out Alive

Running Wild with Bear Grylls
(The US version of Wild Weekends featuring: Ben Stiller, Zac Efron, Channing Tatum and more)

2

BEHIND THE SCENES

In recent years the BBC Natural History Unit (NHU) have uncovered some of the truths behind how they make their wonderful, glossy, high-budget Nature series. Who makes them and how? They cleverly chose to tag onto the end of each episode of *Planet Earth* and *Blue Planet* etc. short films showing behind the scenes.

I'm sure it was a pleasant surprise for the producers to see the reaction from the viewers, many of who actually say that the *Planet Earth Diaries* are just as interesting (if not more) than the main programme itself. Controversial, but I can understand why.

The people who work on these big NHU projects tend be the best in their field (the BBC can afford them). Yet, they are also totally passionate and completely committed to their area of expertise. They will spend weeks, months, if not years in some incredibly inhospitable environments, just to get the one shot of a rare frog (for sake of example). This is not for everyone.

Over the years I've shot a few wildlife programmes and you need the patience of a saint and an enthusiasm for the subject that will get you out of a warm sleeping bag, early in the morning. Personally, I love the extreme environments, but I don't possess an advanced interest in animals... I like animals, but I am far more interested in people.

On a totally different level, we used to involve the crew on past shows that I've worked on like *Streetmate* (with Davina McCall) or *The Big Breakfast* (with Chris Evans etc.). It is not a new idea, but an interesting shift for the elite film-makers. This new angle of openness in film-making seems to be born out of a response to the savviness of the modern viewer.

Audiences these days are fully aware that there is a film crew with whoever they happen to be watching on their screens. They totally understand that in order for them to see this TV programme, there has to be a camera, operated by a Cameraman. They acknowledge that they can only hear what is happening, being said or sung, because there are microphones recording the audio, all operated by a Sound Recordist. So, on the right occasion, why not show these people and what they do? In doing so they have seemed to satisfy the viewers' appetite for more information and authenticity. Interestingly, some of the NHU cameramen have now made decent careers by moving in front of the camera, such is the demand and interest.

So, what has caused this shift in the audience's interest in the 'Techies', who for years were kept strictly behind the scenes?

In this modern age of computer technology, pretty much anyone can now make a film. You can use your digital camera or even your mobile phone or tablet to film a subject. Then by downloading the images to your computer, you can edit them with simple, user-friendly editing software and then upload them onto the web for the whole world to see. We are no longer tied to complicated film cameras or expensive film processing costs – now for a tiny amount of money we can shoot high-quality video on our everyday handheld devices and edit them with revolutionary simplicity. Every day people can duplicate (to a degree) what was previously only ever accessible to the experts.

The world has changed and so must the TV and Film industry.

Due to this massive shift in technology and viewer awareness, those of us who work in the film and TV business need to move and adapt, in order to keep up with all the changes and ensure that our jobs continue to exist.

This means learning new tricks, taking advantage of the latest technology and also feeding the audiences desire for more radical content.

Film and TV productions are no longer limited by high-quality production either. Nowadays, content is king! In the new age of YouTube and other video streaming websites, people are far less concerned about the standards to which it is produced and are far more interested in whether the content catches their interest and imagination. This is a huge challenge for the old school thinkers in the professional industries, who insist that every film or TV show must be A1 quality. This is simply no longer the case.

Granted, we all like to sit and watch a beautifully shot, very well-made film and we always will. But, a new wave of film-making has emerged. This seemingly started in the 1990s, when the producers of the film *The Blair Witch Project* totally broke all the mainstream rules. The film was shot on a normal, low grade, video camcorder. It was not the quality of the pictures that held the audience's attention, but rather the storytelling. Also, it can't be ignored that the amount of money saved by shooting this film at low cost resulted in vast sums of money being made in profit from the return. Incredibly, the production budget was around $500 thousand, but the film went on to make $248 million worldwide. This gorilla-style film-making makes total economic sense. To respond to this new era, directors, producers and crews are challenged to hone their art down to the bare essentials – which for those used to a healthy budgets is an interesting exercise. In fact, this new wave of film-making is proving a challenge to the whole TV and Film industry.

It's only a matter of time before a film totally shot on an iPhone is released, and why not?

The platform upon which we watch TV and films is also changing. The TV is gradually being replaced by the computer. The founder of Apple, the late Steve Jobs' dream was to see the home computer becoming the centre of each household. Already we are witnessing the world's reliance on email and the insurgence of social media (Facebook and Twitter etc.) taking over how we communicate with each other. From the other side of the world you can talk to your family via Skype and see their faces, just as if you were in the same room as them. You can set your TV recording box via your mobile phone from the train on the way home from work. Local bank branches are closing due to the simplicity and convenience of internet banking. The sound system in your home can be controlled by your smartphone and you can even order your groceries online and have them delivered right to your door. The computer revolution is well under way.

We have already seen the impact of this revolution on the music industry, which has seen an enormous transformation over the last decade. People no longer buy vinyls or CDs (apart from a few passionate collectors). In fact I don't own any music anymore, as I pay a monthly fee to have access to Spotify's library of pretty much all commercial music ever made – I stream and download to listen to my favourite tracks.

This change is rapidly coming to TV. I rarely watch live TV

these days (apart from rugby internationals). The large majority of my viewing is recorded or sourced from an 'on demand' service. I no longer have to wait for my favourite show to come on after the news... I can watch it now... and pause it when I fancy a cup of tea. TV is on its way out and the computer/monitor/smart TV is taking over. The industry is forced to respond to this.

Broadcasters seem nervous about the threat of the unknown. They are desperately attempting to transform their shape, move with the times, harness the opportunities available to them, but can they adapt or change quick enough?

The dot com phenomena may appear to be levelling out, but there is still a long way to go for the likes of my industry. Interesting times we live in.

A few weeks ago I was invited into the Google offices, here in London, to teach a group of their most successful YouTube 'Vloggers' (video version of writing a blog/diary excerpt). I was asked to run a teaching session for six hours, at which I was at a loss as to what to say or do for that length of time. I am easily good for two hours, but six is a lot of time to fill. When I arrived I was met by a group of about fifteen people, aged between eighteen and twenty-three. They were great characters and I could easily see that they were 'go-getters', finding great success on the web. For the first hour I decided to let them tell me about themselves. They each logged on to the web, showed me what the kind of 'Vlogs' they post and we then talked a bit more about how they had produced what we had seen. I was incredibly impressed. Some methods were very simple; a camera balanced on a shelf in their bedroom, filming while they stood and spoke about their lives, dreams, fears and social gossip etc. Some were comedic, cooking 'peanut butter and Nutella cookies' and other inventive recipes. Others were very profound and really quite advanced in their creativity and production. Such a wide range of talent, and by their large number of hits/viewers and subscribers, they are obviously scratching the audience where they itch. It was fascinating.

Eventually, I ended up showing them a few tricks of the trade regarding lighting and the basic operation of their cameras etc. However, I told them that I refused to be like a piano teacher, who comes to teach a kid who desperately wants to learn to play, by teaching them scales and enforcing rules – that is likely to dampen their natural passion. Yes, I may be the 'professional' Cameraman with twenty years' experience, but these guys hold the key to the future of web broadcasting. Our golden rules of camerawork can act as a good foundation, but with these new platforms for expressing their talent and their lives – they have a blank canvas upon which to paint.

Also, within TV we have so many compliances (technical regulations, advertising limitations, quality standards etc.) to adhere to, it can be incredibly restrictive. But, on the web, there are no rules and regulations to stop them. I applaud Google who are a very forward-thinking organization. They are embracing and harnessing the energy and enthusiasm of these young pioneers. They are also rewarding them with monetary incentives from the advertising revenues their posts attract. Some of these figures have the potential to match an average salary! I want to encourage these young creatives and I'm so excited to see where they will lead us to in the future.

Having said all this, TV is not dead yet – thankfully.

When seeking to effectively communicate your message through moving pictures, the principles of film and TV programme-making still apply, so it is definitely worth knowing at least the basics.

These days there are streams of young people who seek a career in TV. The modern transparency in production methods has only increased the desire to work in the industry – which is very appealing when seen as an alternative to a 'proper' job. However, I always say to those who ask me, "How do I get into TV?" that it is important to realize how the industry works and what really goes on behind the scenes – as it's certainly not all glamour.

So, what is the process for making a TV programme?

We start with the idea. This can be thought up through a conversation between friends at the pub, or it can be manufactured through a professional 'Development Team' employed by a Production Company. Either way, if the idea's not good, it won't fly.

This idea (ideally adopted by a TV Production Company) is then written up into a treatment/proposal, usually no more than on a single sheet of A4 paper. This treatment is then sent to the relevant 'Commissioning Editor' of a TV broadcasting house (BBC, Discovery Channel etc.). Each broadcaster will have multiple Commissioning Editors who work in teams covering specific aspects of the networks output, e.g. Entertainment, Factual or Documentary programming.

Now the waiting game starts.

The Commissioning Editors are often snowed under by treatments for new shows and will work their way through each one in time. However, if your connections or channels of communications are good (i.e. they know you) then it is possible to get a quick response.

As you can imagine there is a long line of bureaucratic processes that have to be adhered to within such large organizations. Bosses have to be won over, programming schedules have to be worked out, and of course budgets have to be considered.

It is common for a Commissioning Editor to like an idea, but want to see what it would actually look like on screen. So, they would negotiate a small budget for the Production Company who would then go off to make a 'Pilot' or teaser of the idea (meaning they would actually shoot the idea in basic form, enabling the broadcaster to visualize/test the concept before committing large sums of money).

If you are lucky enough (sometimes seemingly a miraculous event!) to win a commission for a TV show, then the really hard work begins.

The Production Company will then enter a series of negotiations regarding the financial budget for making the TV series. This usually works by the broadcaster asking the Production Company, "How much is it going to cost you to make this show?" The reply will be a sum total of a very carefully worked-out budget. Line by line it will estimate the costs involved and will of course try to ensure making some profit along the way. This budget will then bounce back and forth between the two parties until eventually they agree on a figure.

The Production Company will have added in a percentage of the budget as a 'Production Fee' (their return for the effort) and the originator/writer of the original idea/concept will also be offered a small percentage.

When the legal contracts are signed and the bank accounts are set up, the new production will be given a 'green light'. All systems go!

Only now will the Production Company allocate specific personnel to the production.

A 'Head of Production' or 'Line Producer/Production Manager' (HP, LP or PM) will oversee the administration of the production. 'Executive Producers' (EP) and 'Series Producers' (SP) will start to develop the team who will actually make the show. Executive Producers will take the ultimate responsibility for the production and will normally have a direct line of communication to the Commissioning Editors. Producers will be the managers, who will oversee the project and steer from the helm. This production team will also recruit 'Assistant/Associate Producers' (AP) to add an extra pair of hands to the workload.

Soon after this infrastructure is set up, a 'Director' will be brought in to lead the creative side of the story-telling and the filming process. They will normally have at least one 'Researcher' who will assist them, and carry out a lot of the basic work. This will free up the Director who can then concentrate on planning the shoot, which includes choosing the crew they will want to work with.

The choice of crew is often left to the Director, as they will usually know a Director of Photography/Cameraman that they have worked with before, or know of one who has the most appropriate experience for that particular filming assignment. Ultimately, when employed as a Freelancer to recruit your own team, due to your reputation being on the line, everyone chooses to work with 'known quantities', who are usually friends. Hence, the famous media industry saying, "It's not what you know, but who you know."

As the Director and the Director of Photography/Cameraman work very closely in telling and illustrating the story, it is the Cameraman who is seen as the senior technical crew member. They will usually be the technical department 'go to' and speak on behalf of the crew as a whole.

Note: On some bigger staged shows each department will be likely to have their own 'supervisors' for each role – Lighting, Sound and Camera etc.

Due to this senior role, the Cameraman will usually choose which Sound Recordist and Camera Assistant he wants to work alongside on this particular job. Crews that have worked together tend to be a tight unit and know instinctively how each other work. This creates synergy and harmony on productions, and so, familiar crews are encouraged – it just makes sense.

Once the lengthy process of preparation and logistics of the shoot are nailed down (budgets/dates/schedules/Post(Edit)/ filming locations/crews/Presenters/Contributors etc.) within a few months, the first day of filming will arrive.

A location shoot will normally consist of the following personnel:

Production Team:
Director
Assistant Producer
Researcher
Runner (junior extra pair of hands on set)

Crew:
Cameraman
Soundman
Camera Assistant

The way a shoot is run will go something like this:

The whole team will arrive on location. While the Sound Recordist and Camera Assistant are setting up kit, the Cameraman will join the Director to discuss what they are wanting to achieve. The Director will explain what he or she wishes to say through the film and will offer suggestions of how they envisage this being achieved. The Cameraman will then add what he or she thinks will work, making some more suggestions and often stating what is achievable with the kit, in the time that they have. This discussion will be fairly quick and normally they will see eye to eye on most ideas, working as a team.

The Presenter will be mic'ed up (using a wireless radio microphone) while the Cameraman will be shown the script and both he and the Director will work out what action the Presenter should follow.

It's definitely worth noting here the truth about the role of a 'Presenter'. Years ago you used to have pure Presenters, who did just that. These days, most hosts of shows were formally experts in their field, e.g. Gary Lineker – Footballer, Lauren Lavern – Singer, Stephen Fry – Actor, Bear Grylls – Soldier, Mountaineer and Explorer. It is the credibility of what they have previously achieved which gives them the authoritative position from which to comment/present on their subject. Lots of young people dream of becoming a Presenter, yet when you quiz them as to "Why?" the usual answer is, "Because it will make me rich and famous." Or, "It will help me make a difference in the world." Yet, to this I say; you are far better off being famous first for something you do very well, so concentrate on becoming a professional at that first. And if you really want to make a difference in the world through TV, then become a Director of Producer, because they are the ones who pull the strings. Presenters are ultimately the puppets and mouthpieces for the higher powers that be. They are there to be the face and 'present' the facts.

Back on location, the Director will then spend time with the Presenter of Contributor (presuming there is one) while the crew will finish off preparing the appropriate kit to achieve what has been decided. Meanwhile the Runner may be sorting out breakfast or coffee for the team, while the AP could be prepping the next scene or location so the team can move straight on and save time in the schedule. This ensures everyone's time (which is expensive) is productive.

Soon everyone will be ready and the filming will begin.

The Cameraman will press 'RECORD' on the camera, at

the same time calling "Turning over" (stating he's pressed RECORD). After a few seconds, allowing some head room (enough space for the Editor to cut in or out) the Cameraman will call "Camera's at speed" (stating that the camera is now rolling/filming), following that the Sound Recordist will call "Sound at speed" (indicating that he too is recording) and finally the Director will call "Action"... you know the rest.

At the end of the 'take' (when camera and sound have started and stopped recording – forming the 'Clip'), the Director will say 'Cut' and look at the Cameraman to ask if it was a good take. The Cameraman may well rewind a bit of the clip, to spot check his exposure, focus etc. After checking that the Sound Recordist was happy with what they recorded, he will give the nod – yes. If everything went OK and the Director and Presenter are happy with what was said and the delivery of it, then we all move on to the next scene. And so, the day carries on in this pattern, recording various scenes and clips.

Depending on where we are (city or remote location) decides on how we will eat on the shoot. Sometimes we'll have sandwiches on the go, to regain time in the schedule, and sometimes we'll have a sit-down meal for our break (which is becoming increasingly rare these days). If you are out in the wilds, someone on the Production Team would normally have pre-arranged food to be carried out or made for us. You must have heard the saying, 'an army marches on its stomach'? Well, no truer words could explain the importance of feeding a TV crew. More than anyone on location, we will be the ones working very physically hard – lugging heavy equipment on our shoulders and kept constantly busy, often while others have a breather. This is not a complaint, just a fact and that is why we are well paid for what we do.

Personally, I am like a car – if I run out of petrol, I jolt for a little while and then stop! Yet, if you keep me fed and watered,

I will happily keep going for hours on end. It's become a regular occurrence when I meet a new Director for the first time, for me to warn them: "If I go quiet or start getting grumpy, please don't take it personally – just feed me!" There are many Directors whom I've worked with over the years who will vouch for this.

At the end of the day's filming, the Director will call "Wrap" (end of shoot) when we can all go and get some well-earned rest. But first, the Production Team will have a meeting and start prepping the following day's shoot. Meanwhile the crew will be downloading the days 'rushes' (clips of footage and audio files) to external hard drives, cleaning and tweaking any of the equipment that needs attention and putting our batteries on charge for the next day. Only when this is all taken care of will they go and run a bath to soak their aching muscles (assuming of course, that this luxury is available).

It is here that you have to consider this whole process being played out anywhere in the world. The more extreme the location and the less controlled the environment means that there are far more elements that need to be considered.

Some Production Teams and crews have to work in a huge variety of conditions, from the snowy Arctic to the sweltering Sahara Desert, from the lofty heights of the Himalayas to the grass savannas of Africa. Not your run-of-the-mill office job!

I know of many crew members who say they would love to do this sort of extreme work, but I only know a few who could actually handle it.

Without doubt, Travel Documentaries and Adventure TV shows are great fun to work on as you certainly get to experience some amazing locations around the world. But, in reality it is not a holiday, nor glamorous, and is often very tough.

For these more extreme filming assignments, you have to rely on an experienced team who 'walk the walk' rather than 'talking the talk'. Over the years, I have been on too many remote shoots with people who have talked themselves onto the job, yet with no real understanding of just what they are letting themselves in for. Sadly, they end up hating the shoot and we, who are more experienced, end up carrying them. To be brutally honest, we have enough to do looking after ourselves, without the burden of looking after another. The best crews work closely as a team and each individual has to take responsibility to pull their own weight.

Working and living in remote locations means many aspects of your working day can be very different from what you are used to.

GENERAL LOGISTICS

Where are we going? How long are we going to be there? Who's coming? Who do we really need? How are we going to get there? Where are we going to stay? What are we going to do? Where and what will we eat? Where can we get fresh/safe water supplies? What will happen in an emergency? How will we get home?

Working overseas in remote settings throws up a multitude of questions. Yet, as well as these general questions, there are the more specific issues. For example: As a film crew, we have lots of specialist, very expensive equipment. We will need somewhere to keep this (be it a building, hut, tent or a vehicle). Every day and night we will need to be charging batteries, so if there's not a main supply of electricity close by, we'll need to take a generator with us. And so, the list goes on.

ACCOMMODATION

I have slept in numerous tents over the years. One tent was pitched at 5,000 metres up a mountain with a troop of over four hundred Gelada Baboons, in the Simien Mountains of Ethiopia.

On another shoot, a far larger tent housed my crew mates and I who slept shoulder to shoulder, like a can of sardines, to keep warm in -30°C icy temperatures, deep inside the Arctic Circle. Once in Africa, we decided to forgo the tents altogether due to temperatures of +40°c at night, and slept under the stars for a few weeks.

If you are not lying on a sleeping mat or on the floor, the other option is of course a bed – although some beds do not live up to their luxurious expectation. I have shared beds with many others around the world, yet not romantically as you may be led to think… Rats (Laos), cockroaches (Indonesia), bed bugs (Africa) and big spiders (Australia). Not quite so sexy.

FOOD

There is fun to be had, trying out different foreign cuisines, but when you are on a job you also have a professional responsibility to be fit to work. On location, I tend to eat conservatively and always avoid salads, un-bottled water (without a seal) and anything that might debilitate me. I tend to eat a lot of carbs, well-cooked fresh meat and fish. Far from the risk of having 'Delhi Belly', this cautious diet will often result in me becoming constipated. Yet, at the end of the day, you can always do what the mathematician did... work it out with a pencil! Just kidding – it may take a while, but it'll exit in it's own good time.

Having said all that, along the way, I have tasted some of the more unusual dishes: camel, puff adder, turtle, kangaroo, crocodile, and dog's penis (I wish I was joking!). Some of these were an inquisitive taste, some was the only food we had available to us and some (like the dogs appendage) were part of a tribal ceremony and it would have been deemed an insult if I hadn't partaken with the elders. And just in case you wondered, yes - it tasted like chicken.

TOILETS (ONE OF MY FAVOURITE SUBJECTS)

I have a plethora of fantastic 'toilet' stories, from the wild to the bizarre, from the gross to the glorious. In fact a compilation of these stories may well become my next literary project. But, as you can imagine... no matter where you find yourself, in remote villages, developing world towns/cities or out in the wilds, there is no escaping the call of nature.

Over the years I have experienced the best and the worst toilets in the world. And despite being potty-trained as a boy, I have grown to love pooing in the wild (often a far better option to where everyone else and their pigs congregate!). I have shat from the edge of mountains, sunk aqua turds back into the watery abyss, and I must rival BP for laying my fair share of cable over the landscapes of the world. It has been a joy, but only due to methods carefully developed over the years: Urban – simply don't breathe through your nose. Wild – find two rocks (shoulder width apart) for your feet and a strong, well-rooted stick to hold on to while crouching. The best tip of all is to wait until you are absolutely desperate, then whichever predicament you find yourself in, you can guarantee it will be quick.

(I'll save the other top tips for my book – hopefully available soon in a bookshop near you.)

SECURITY

This is a very serious matter. Occasionally you are fortunate enough to have security professionals travelling with you. Other times you are left to your own common sense and streetwise experience. There are tips that I have picked up over the years – in a hotel... leave a light and the TV on when you are out of the room, as well as making sure the 'Do Not Disturb' sign is on your door. If you are out and about... always make sure your kit is well insured, so if you get robbed at knife point, you can simply give them the camera. You can always easily replace it. Stay in a group of people opposed to wandering off on your own and if in doubt, always play it safe.

VEHICLES

There can't be many forms of transport that I haven't travelled on over the years. Yet, statistically 'travel' is almost certainly the most dangerous aspect of any journey around the world – particularly on the roads. There is far more chance that you will have a road traffic accident than have your plane fall out of the sky, so particular caution must be taken on all road journeys.

A lot of driving accidents abroad happen due to our natural instincts when behind the wheel. Due to driving on opposite sides of the road in varying countries, under threat or in a panic, our instinctive self-defence action will be to steer off the road. However, if you are on the opposite side, this will make you drive into oncoming traffic. Always keep your wits about you when driving overseas and try to inspect the vehicles before you commit to travelling in them.

TRANSLATION

While travelling, if English is your native language, you are fortunate, as these days many people around the world speak a degree of English. Yet, this can also make English speakers very lazy when it comes to learning other languages, because you can tend to get by without the need. If you happen to find yourself in a foreign land, where everyone speaks a foreign tongue without any English – you can still succeed, but you will have to be creative. In the past I have had whole conversations through sign language (not official 'signing' as with the deaf, rather just pointing with my finger and drama-like actions – lots of flapping arms). In such times I have also found a useful application for my art studies, by drawing pictures of chickens and noodles in restaurants etc. Practical use of the game 'Pictionary' seems to work well, is often a fun challenge, and is usually received with good humour.

Fortunately I speak English, but I am also fluent in Australian!

CULTURE

Cultural customs can easily be lost in translation, so in order keep yourself out of trouble, you should do your research before arriving at a location. For example: Some customs will say that touching someone's head will cause great offence. In some lands the clapping of your fist can be incredibly rude (with stark sexual insinuations). Certain cultures and religions require a strict dress code, usually for women, such as the covering of your head, or a skirt that covers your ankles etc. To enjoy your visit, stay out of trouble and get the most from people. Remember, to some degree "When in Rome..."

CURRENCY

In this day and age, dealing with money overseas is actually very easy. The large majority of Europe use Euros, so that makes life easier and the usability of your cash seems to go a lot further. Credit cards have been a game changer, although the computer age has also brought with it a threat of hacking and cloning of bank cards. I tend to always carry a credit card when travelling, but try to keep it for emergency use only.

Gone are the days of the 'Travellers Cheque' or the need for currency converters. By far the best way of getting local currency is to use a reputable cashpoint/ATM machine at the airport on arrival. This way you also get an automatic, trustworthy exchange rate from your own bank at home, with little if any commission charges.

WEATHER

This is one of the more obvious aspects of travelling overseas, but must be taken very seriously. Heat exhaustion can kill, as can hyperthermia caused by the cold. Both cases are highly likely unless you have the right clothing. Covering your head in the hot sun will help stave off heatstroke (which can be incredibly unpleasant). Also, regularly sipping water will keep you hydrated which is essential to health and comfort in a hot climate. In the cold, the famous statement that our bodies lose 90 per cent of their heat through our heads is actually an 'old wives' tale', however simply wearing a warm hat, gloves and insulated footwear will help you save you an enormous amount of heat.

I always try to carry enough clothing for every eventuality, as I have experienced on more than one occasion when travelling to a 'hot' country arriving to find very cold and wet weather. If you are unprepared, you can soon find yourself in trouble.

HEALTH

Not all countries around the world have the same hygiene standards as the developed nations. So, to remain free from sickness and disease while travelling through such locations requires good personal administration and a large dose of common sense. Golden rule number one: Never drink water from the tap. Always wash your hands with soap after visiting the toilet or before eating (these days there are great anti-bacterial hand gels, which you can use without the need of water – it just evaporates into your skin). Watch where you store your toothbrush. Before you travel, check with your doctor to see what inoculations (jabs) or anti-malarial tablets you may require. If you are given tablets... don't forget to religiously take them.

WILDLIFE AND INSECTS

It is obvious that animals can offer some sort of threat, especially when cornered or feeling threatened, so generally give them a wide berth. Don't attempt to stroke or pat a stray dog on the head, or cuddle a seemingly friendly monkey, because you may get more than you bargained for. Having said this, insects are more likely to cause the real damage... especially mosquitoes. Mozzies (as they are usually referred to) can carry malaria which is hugely prevalent in many developing countries, as well as diseases such as Dengue Fever (otherwise known as the 'bone crushing disease', as its symptoms makes it feel as if your bones are literally being crushed). Anti-malarial tablets won't completely protect you from catching malaria, but it will give a boost to your immune system if attacked. The best prevention from any insect-carried disease is to not get bitten in the first place. Wherever possible it is sensible to cover exposed skin, especially at dusk and dawn. Long-legged trousers and long-sleeved shirts may hamper your tan, but rather that than risking very serious illness. On your face, hands or other exposed areas of skin, you should apply 'Mozzie Spray', which comes in varying degrees of strength. In the past, while filming and living in jungles, I have used Mozzie Spray with 100 per cent Deet (chemical) which over a couple of days disintegrated my plastic watch strap due to its toxicity – this strength should only be used in the most extreme conditions and applied with great care. I love the fact that 'Quinine', which is a natural ingredient of gin, is said to be an effective deterrent to mosquitoes. That is the best excuse any traveller could need to drink plenty of gin and tonics.

Add all these elements to the normal working day schedule and you are in for an exciting ride. Working in an uncontrolled, foreign and often hostile environment increases your workload tenfold... now you see why it's not a holiday. Having said that,

I wouldn't change it for the world. Give me a mountain over a studio any day of the week.

While on location in these extreme environments, you may be dealing with large groups of people, who are enthralled by seeing a TV crew in their village. You may find yourself sat in a 'hide' for hours on end, waiting for a monkey to turn up in the tree opposite. You may be strapped in, standing on the skids of a helicopter, hovering 50 metres in the air, while filming your Presenter abseiling to the ground (no prizes for guessing which Presenter that is!).

Remember, most of what you see the Presenter doing we also have to do balancing heavy cameras on our shoulders.

There is every chance that you will be working from literally sun up to sundown. No one will be keeping a check on your working hours in the wilds, as after your shooting day has finished you have to go back to camp and deal with all that requires. Eating, washing and just existing in a camp takes a huge amount of effort, compared to the luxuries of home or a nice hotel.

As touched on before, some people are cut out for this more extreme work and some aren't. Some operators specialize and focus on one genre of filming: Wildlife, Documentary, Drama, Entertainment, Multi-camera or Studios etc. However, there are a number of us who work across most disciplines of camerawork. By doing this you may not get the super-specialist jobs, however you do become generally more employable, because you can turn your hand to almost anything. The more strings to your bow, the more adaptable you are.

The fact that I shoot everything from *The X Factor* to Bear Grylls' TV series means that I have a very broad client base, who can often offer work all over the calendar year. For me, each January and February (traditionally the quietest times of the year for crews) is spent working on *Britain's Got Talent*. This is a gift for those of us fortunate enough to be involved, because while we are busy working, others remain sat, waiting for their working year to begin. In March there is often an overseas shoot/series happening, which will serve as a good stepping stone to the summer. The summer months are always full, due the UK Production Companies making the most of the long days and good weather. Then in autumn, there are usually a couple of bigger series starting, which have been lined up throughout the year. These large series (like *The X Factor*) will often run right up to Christmas, which is when you'll take a month off to relax and recuperate.

In between filming assignments you may well have a number of weeks off, and so it is important to try and be as productive as possible. This is when I concentrate on physically training hard and writing etc. It is always good to be fit and ready for the next job, and other activities, such as writing books, can create another income and also more working opportunities. Even more strings to your bow. It is important to use this time wisely and make the most of the rare opportunity for 'routine'. As well as fitness training or trying to be creative, I also spend a lot of time catching up with friends, many of whom are also in the industry. Although genuine friends, these could in theory also be labelled as 'clients'. Seeing that the TV industry is founded on contacts and friendships, time spent with your friends is a wise investment of time.

Finally, it has been said that there is a 'media type'. I remember being told very early in my career by a friend who was a nurse that it was OK for me to work in TV, because I am a media type. At first I took objection to this label, but then she went on to explain what she meant by it...

Most people feel happy, safe and secure and in their life's

routine. They know where they work, when they will be there, how much they will be getting paid and when. They know how much holiday they get per year and work with the same faces every day. If you have the responsibility of a mortgage or family to provide for etc. I can easily see how this would be appealing and reassuring. However, we media types nearly all work on a Freelance basis. We have no guarantee of work and when we do work it's likely to only last for a matter of days, weeks or a few months. We can rarely plan ahead in our diaries, due to simply not knowing where we will be, or when. This proves very challenging to our social and domestic life, as parties, celebrations and weddings etc. are frequently missed due to the nature of our work. We do get paid relatively well, but we are likely to work a lot less than the average person. This tends to balance out. Certainly until you are established as a Freelancer and have a good base of regular clients, you are flying by the seat of your pants. Some people are cut out for this, though many are not.

Personally, I love my job. I have grown used to the unexpected and find freedom in not being tied down to a more structured work life. The truth is... I would do it for no money at all, but for goodness' sake, don't tell anyone!

3

THE HOTTEST PLACE ON EARTH +56°C

FEATURING: KATE HUMBLE

At the northern end of Africa's Great Rift Valley lies an area unlike anywhere on earth. The Danakil Desert in Ethiopia, reputably one of the most inhospitable places known to man, where volcanoes and earthquakes continually rip the ground apart, spewing lava and noxious gases. It is also the homeland of the Afar tribe, once renowned as the fiercest tribe in Africa. The Danakil is, officially, the hottest place on the surface of our planet – and we're going there!

The initial contact was made through Expedition Media (an online Adventure TV database, that I was, at the time, joint Director of) who received a call from a Production Company called Lion TV. Lion had just been commissioned by the BBC to make a television series called *The Hottest Place on Earth*. The series was to be filmed on location in the furthest, remotest reaches of Ethiopia, Africa.

Even starting to think about organizing a shoot in such a

remote and hostile location was overwhelming. Trish (Production Manager) was responsible for pulling a team together, in order to make the series happen, no small undertaking. With years of experience in TV production she knew that in order to successfully pull the project off, there would be no substitute for a team of people who really knew what they were doing. She had heard of Expedition Media on the grapevine and so thought she would give us a call.

Following a number of conversations, it was soon clear that a handpicked few of us were the right people for the job. Not only could we provide the necessary crew members (all who had experience of working in remote locations) but we could also connect her with companies like Remote Trauma, ex-military experts in security, remote medicine and Health & Safety. We also suggested that she should speak to our friend and colleague Rupert, whom we had previously worked with on *Escape to the Legion* with Bear Grylls. In our informed opinion, he was the perfect man to take the lead on this project. Expedition Media subsequently became consultants on the project, and in a matter of days Rupert had been hired as 'Series Director'.

Rupert categorically agreed that the crew and wider team should be handpicked but also should have experience of working together. If we were going to pull this epic challenge off, we would need a full team effort and complete unity.

Over the following weeks a number of us received calls from Richard (Expedition Media) pre-warning us that we should expect to be receiving a call from Trish at Lion TV. He took this opportunity to describe to each of us about what the job entailed, so that we would be prepared when we spoke to her.

As tipped off, one by one we received the call and readily agreed to take our part in this exciting new expedition.

Some weeks later, many hours of research, recruiting and

meticulous planning culminated in a meeting being called for all the crew who would be going to the Danakil. We met at the Lion TV offices in Chiswick, where we took over their boardroom. Rupert led the proceedings and welcomed us to what was without any doubt going to be the experience of a lifetime.

Looking around the room, we were a motley-looking bunch, many of whom turned up on motorbikes, so were dressed in protective clothing and could have easily been mistaken for a group of motorcycle couriers. Yet, despite the ramshackle look, we were a very strong unit who had worked together over several years on various other projects such as *Escape to the Legion* (set in the Sahara Desert), *Survivor* (Panama and Borneo) and also UK series, such as *Bad Lads' Army* etc.

After the initial introduction, Rupert then passed over to Alex who heads up Remote Trauma. He then started to advise the group on what to expect, what and what not to wear (particularly stating that due to rebel groups operating in the area, any military or combat clothing was not advised). He hammered home the health issues of operating in such an extreme environment, in temperatures that could reach 50° centigrade. This, including the need for a strict routine of taking on liquids. We were advised that we would need to consume a minimum of eight litres of water each day or we would risk serious and very dangerous dehydration, especially when physically working hard. The instruction was given in a very serious tone, as the Danakil was a very serious place. There were looks passed around the room, as the message hit home.

Richard, the Camera Supervisor, brought to the discussion what kit we were going to be using and urged us to consider what challenges our kit would face. With the extreme heat and unpredictable working conditions, we tried to pre-empt how the high specification camera and sound equipment would hold up.

This was completely unknown and so the discussions began on how we could best prepare for all eventualities.

The team assembled consisted of:

Series Director – Rupert
Assistant Director – Duncan
Associate Producer – Max
Producer Director – Justin
Producer Director – Katie
Richard (Roo) – Camera Supervisor
Me – Cameraman
Lee – Cameraman
Shirley (real name Mark) – Sound Supervisor
Lloyd – Soundman
Pete – Soundman
Mutley (real name Pete) – Camera Assistant
Ben – Camera Assistant

It really was the 'Dream Team'.

A few weeks before deploying for Ethiopia the whole team attended a Remote First Aid and Hostile Environments course, run by Remote Trauma. This training was essential due to the fact that we would be operating and living literally two days' drive away from the nearest town that you would consider 'civilization', which may or may not have a reasonable medical facility. On our team we would have Alex, an ex-Royal Marine paramedic, as well as Mukul, a Medical Doctor. Yet, if for some reason they couldn't get to us immediately, we would all need to know how to deal with an emergency, including multiple casualties, in the interim period.

Normally on a shoot of this nature, we would have great backup and a solid extraction plan in place, should a serious medical emergency take place. But in the Danakil, the only helicopter in that NE region of Ethiopia was currently being used to bomb the Eritreans. So, we would have to be self-sufficient until we could drive the casualty out. This was of course not ideal, but a risk we were all aware of and agreed to take.

The purpose of the 'hostile environment' aspect of the course was to prepare us for any firearm, explosives or kidnap situations. Recently in the Danakil region there had been a foreign group who were kidnapped by Eritrean rebels, exactly where we would be going. Fortunately, after tense negotiations with the Ethiopian security forces, the victims had been released unharmed. We were told to make no mistake in remembering that this was a very serious, volatile and dangerous place.

On the course (held in the conference rooms and vast grounds of a stately home in the Home Counties) we were taken through practical workshops, including driving cars through a wood and being shot at. I have to admit, this was a lot of fun (not forgetting that this was only role play). Yet, for me the most startling enactment was driving up to a makeshift rebel roadblock/checkpoint.

Alex's ex-military staff acted very convincingly as hostile foreign militia. We were taught to be aware of your surroundings and always have your hands visible, on the dashboard or seat in front, in order to show the rebels that you weren't reaching for a weapon or phone etc. We were urged to keep calm and look for signs that may help diffuse tension – for example, if one of the guys was wearing a football shirt, mention that you like football too. Ultimately, other than a few more tricks of the trade, the idea was to stay calm and not pose a threat.

I was sat in the front passenger seat and Producer Director (PD) Katie was sat in the rear seat. Driving us was another of

Alex's staff who was acting the role of a somewhat unreliable local driver – all scenarios that could highly likely take place on location.

As our 4x4 approached the roadblock, our driver started to show signs of stress and panic. This was not ideal as we wanted to keep everyone calm and non-threatening. Armed rebel guards surrounded the vehicle as the man in charge beckoned for our driver to open his window... he did as the man asked and handed over his papers.

As this was happening, the other guards were taunting Katie and me, which (even though it was an enactment) was actually very intimidating. We stuck to what we were being taught and kept friendly, calm expressions on our faces and just did as we were told.

The rebel leader then asked our driver to step out of the car. He was then taken away from us out of sight. We were now by ourselves. The main man then came round to my window and started to question me. He was able to twist and turn everything I said in order to make me sound guilty of something, so I just stuck to my brief and played it all very cool. At one point he got quite aggressive and started shouting. This was very unnerving, but with all my focus I still tried to stay passive. Seconds later, from nowhere our driver walked over and got back into the driving seat. He shoved his papers back into his jacket pocket, started the engine and drove off. We had passed the test. Or, so I thought...

Coming out of character, the driver then asked me how I thought it had gone. "Fine," I said. "It was quite intimidating, but I think we managed to stay calm and passive." "How did Katie do?" he asked me. "Great," I said as I smiled and turned to look at Katie, but to my horror she had gone!

By causing a distraction they had focused all my attention

on the main man, while the other guards quickly and silently opened the back door and abducted Katie. I knew absolutely nothing about it.

The point had been very cleverly made and although it was quite chilling, I had definitely learned my lesson. Keep fully aware of everyone and everything. Returning to the group, I gave Katie a big hug to apologize for letting her be snatched.

Alex was quick to add that no one had failed. There were numerous case scenarios that could have taken place and there is never a textbook "right or wrong" way of dealing with them. The course is there to equip you with tips and techniques on how your actions can help the situation and help look after each other, as well as yourself.

No matter how good or bad a student you are, these lessons and lectures become very real and your attention becomes very sharpened when you are about to head off into a real-life hostile environment. Yours and others' lives could be on the line.

Another practical lesson we learned was how to run away from gunfire. I guess one's natural reaction is to just run away, no matter where. But, we were taught that often the sound of gunfire ricochets off different surfaces. Unless you can clearly see the gunman (which is highly unlikely) you will have no idea where the bullets are coming from. This means it is possible for you to run straight towards the gun, thinking you are escaping. The correct method is to run in a zigzag line (which is apparently harder to aim at) towards the greatest means of shelter you can find. It was interesting, though worrying, to hear that most high velocity guns these days can shoot straight through brick and mortar. Your best option for cover from gunfire is behind the engine of a car (although this may only offer a small area of protection and also may move). Or, the number one option is a mound or ridge of sand or soil. In these materials the bullets are slowed right down, which is obviously why firing ranges are always backstopped by huge walls of sand.

The practical exercise for this drill was for the group to stand in the middle of the side lawn of the manor house. It had been drizzling with rain all morning, so the grass surface was wet and we were all stood wearing waterproof jackets. Without warning there was a sudden explosion of gunfire! In a flash, we all went sprinting off in all directions, zigzagging our way over the lawn as the gunshots continued to rain down on us. Some just headed further down the lawn, one or two dived behind a nearby wreck of a car and others disappeared into the woods. It was incredibly disorientating and they were right, you had no idea where it was coming from. I immediately turned on my heels and sprinted in the opposite direction to the main group in a zigzag pattern, through a bush and into a cluster of trees, and I just kept on running.

Hilariously, poor Justin's legs seemed to move far faster than his body, so he went shooting off at speed and then slipped flat onto his back and went skidding over the grass like a panicked penguin.

I guess ultimately it is more of a matter of luck than skill to dodge a bullet. But, at least we now had some educated idea of what would offer safety and what wouldn't.

On top of the firearms, explosives and kidnap training, we were also taught Remote First Aid. This entailed learning primary care of a casualty while in a remote setting, including how to deal with trauma caused by an accident or incident. In the UK and most other Western countries, when involved or coming across an accident with casualties, the first thing we should do is call for an ambulance and the emergency services. However, in serious cases, it is often the first few minutes of your actions (before the emergency services arrive) that can save or lose a life.

So, how should you act when you are in an area where there are no ambulances or emergency services to call upon? It's all down to you.

In my opinion, it should be mandatory for everybody to attend such a course. Whether you are at home in the UK or abroad, in remote locations or even a city, these first-step actions can save lives. Remote Trauma taught us methods of how to remember the steps to take. For example: D.R.A.B. (Danger, Response, Airway and Breathing).

Danger: Make sure you are not going to be in danger when helping the casualty, or you could then have two casualties on your hands – you being one of them.

Response: Check the casualties' response when you speak to them. If they are screaming, moaning or groaning this is actually a good sign as if they don't respond they are likely to be unconscious and in a more life-threatening state.

Airway: Making sure their airways are open (nose or throat) will decide if they can breathe or not. If there is a blockage, you need to clear it. There are various techniques for this, such as jaw thrusts etc., but even just tilting back the head can open the throat and thus the airway.

Breathing: When the airways are open, to stay alive the casualty needs to keep breathing. Variations of CPR are taught these days, but ultimately the heart needs to keep beating and the lungs working.

I personally find all this fascinating, so I was sat in the lesson like a sponge, soaking in all the information. However, there was one question that I was confused about so I asked Alex. "I have heard that you should never move someone in case they have a spinal injury. Likewise, if the casualty has a (motorcycle) helmet on, is it true that you should never remove it? What do you say?"

He calmly and decisively replied, "Yes, if you have to move the person you put them at risk of further spinal injury etc. Yet, if you and they are in danger, it may be necessary to move them to safety, despite the risk of further injury. Also, if they are not breathing you need to remove the helmet, because if you don't keep the airways open the casualty is likely to die anyway!" A simple straight answer.

Ultimately, no matter how good the teaching, a course can't teach you what to do in every worst case scenario. However, with some clever pointers and basic techniques the hope is that if you ever find yourself in such a critical situation you will instinctively be able to do something to help. As the course instructors repeatedly said, if someone is dying, trying *something* is better than doing nothing at all. You and they just might get lucky!

Packing your bag for this type of trip is always worth taking your time over, and packing a bag too heavy was not an option, as space would be tight. We all had the allowance of one personal holdall each. Bearing in mind the vast amount of technical camera and sound equipment we would be taking, this was all we could afford in the way of personal items. Also, we would need to limit the amount of kit we were going to have to physically lug around for the next month.

Unlike when we filmed *Escape to the Legion* in the Sahara Desert, this time we were told categorically to not wear any combat fatigues or military clothing. Previously, in the Sahara Desert, we had found army clothing to be the most comfortable and practical, although, on that occasion, as our subject was based around the military, we could get away with it. In the

Danakil, army clothing would be like wearing a big red and white target on your back during hunting season, or would at least cause an unhealthy interest from the rebel groups in the area. This time we stuck to our lightweight camping trousers, shorts and shirts.

Having said that, there were two military items of clothing that we were allowed to take – desert boots and sweat rags. From experience we knew that the US Army issue lightweight desert boots were the best. They are light to wear, keeping your feet aired and importantly giving you good ankle support. Sweat rags are just that, a two-foot long piece of lightweight cloth which can be used as a sweatband, bandana, towel, general cloth etc. One of the cheapest yet most useful items of kit one can take.

A limited amount of toiletries were packed, as these could easily waste valuable space, we each took great care to only take what was essential. I had to take enough contact lens solution and spare lenses to see me through our time away, but the rest was limited to roll-on deodorant (takes less space and lasts longer), toothpaste, toothbrush, P20 UV sun protection, a razor and small bar of soap. The fact was, we knew that en masse we would all smell. So, unlike working at home, this wasn't an issue. In fact, scented deodorant can often cause unwanted attraction from mosquitoes and other unwelcome insects. In this rare case, smelling of BO could be a benefit.

We would always have to be conscious of hygiene, as germs would rapidly lead to debilitating sickness and diarrhoea, which is the last thing you want when sharing a camp in the middle of a hot desert environment.

Along with these items, I also packed the all-important 'medicines' Tupperware box, in which I put a month's worth of malaria tablets, rehydration sachets, anti-inflammatory pills, Immodium, antihistamine and Strepsils etc.

For 'Personal Kit', all I took was a head torch (with spare batteries), my trusty Leatherman multi-tool and my wide-brimmed Stetson hat to keep the sun off my head. Also worth mentioning is one of the best travelling secrets of taking a few 'comfort items', which can dramatically raise morale when the going gets tough. Mine are nearly always PG Tips tea bags (nothing like a cup of British tea!), a can of tuna (which can pretty much survive in any environment) and a small bottle of Tabasco (which can spice up the dullest or most revolting dish).

As there were going to be so many of us on this expedition team, I figured it would make sense to buy a holdall bag that would stand out from the rest. That way I could keep an eye on my bag and when we stopped to make camp, I wouldn't be searching through the pile of bags to locate mine. I found a medium-sized North Face bright green holdall, which was super-robust and also had shoulder straps like a backpack – this was perfect. When packed and fully loaded, I then took a permanent marker pen and wrote 'MUNGO' in big thick black letters on every side of the bag, as this would make it even more easily identifiable and tell others whose bag it was.

All in all, the preparation for the trip by the whole team was considered, professional and thorough. As we were nearing our departure date, we all felt well-equipped and in good shape, ready for our adventure of a lifetime!

The Heathrow departure hall was the first time we had all met together since the initial meeting and the Hostile Environments course. As we gathered, with our loaded trolleys like a circle of wagons from an old western movie, spirits were high, banter flowed freely and our excitement was palpable.

It was here that we first met our 'Talent' (industry term for the Presenters/Experts who would be in front of our cameras).

Kate Humble, a very familiar face from various BBC TV series, would be our main Anchor Presenter. Her role was to get stuck into the whole experience and link the items with the experts who would be leading studies of how the extreme environment of the Danakil Desert affected the people and animals who sustain a life there.

UK Scientists/Experts:
Steve Leonard – Veterinary Surgeon (animal expert)
Dougal Jerram – Geologist & Volcanologist from Durham University (earth & rocks expert)
Mukul Adarwal – Medical Doctor (human physiology expert)
Mountain Safety Experts – Mark, Andy and Iain (rope work and crew safety etc.)
Steve – Dougal's technical assistant

The commission of the TV series was a joint venture between the BBC and the Discovery Channel, so we also had two American representatives joining us: Adventurer – Richard Weiss and his colleague, Sue.

It is always slightly overwhelming when large TV crews and teams arrive at the airport. There is always a phenomenal amount of kit and, on this occasion, also a lot of people. I guess it's something that one gets accustomed to, but from experience you also know that these relative strangers will soon become good friends. You are about to be sharing a unique experience together, that in the future only those who were there will truly understand.

After a relatively painless nine-hour flight, we landed in the Ethiopian capital, Addis Ababa in the hot mid-afternoon sun. Greeted by the driver of a good-sized minibus, we were taken straight to a local hotel. With the whole team gathered together we soon took over the entire hotel building.

Fortunately Ethiopian time is only two hours ahead of the UK, so our body clocks were pretty much unaffected. However, the temperature was a different matter altogether. Set at an altitude of 2,300 metres (7,546 feet), Addis was the perfect stop-off for our first day, as it was a lot hotter than the UK, yet was still dramatically cooler than the Danakil Desert.

We were given the rest of the afternoon and evening off to acclimatize to the heat, but also to get our heads around the fact that we had been transported to a completely different world.

We spent some of this time off at the hotel, sorting and checking all our camera equipment to make sure it had arrived in one piece. As we were flying further north the following morning, there was no point in unpacking it all, so we took off to find some food and a cold beer in a local bar.

Stepping outside of the hotel, we were faced with a very busy main road, full of traffic, which led like an artery deep into the sprawling city. The noise was as deafening as the multitude of colours were blinding. The thick air was full of dusty dirt and the heat swirled around us as each passing vehicle busily rushed by.

As a small group of us were crossing the main road, a local man, with a friendly smile and a pretty good grasp of the English language, latched onto us. "Hello, hello. Welcome, my friends. Where are you from?" At first we tried to ignore him, as the British seem so accustomed to do on the streets of London, but like any experienced street hawker, our nonchalance did not discourage him in the slightest. Once we had dodged the cars and crossed the road successfully, he was now walking right beside us. The British stiff upper lip can only remain rude for a while and eventually one of us returned the conversation. "Thank you, we are from London, England."

"Ah... England, this is very good. Let me help you, where are you going?" said our self-appointed new friend.

"Just going over to the bar for a drink," we said.

"My friends, you must come to my brother's bar – it is very close and you are most welcome." His English was actually very good and he was relatively smartly dressed, so we decided to cut him a break and visit his brother's bar at least for a quick beer. There must have been eight of us walking down the road, following the local man as he chatted away to us.

A few minutes later he led us off the main road and down a smaller road. We were then steered down a narrow alleyway. When we left the tarmac of the pavement, at this point a few of us were becoming a bit twitchy and whispered under our breath to one another that this wasn't a great idea and we should turn around and head back. Yet, as often happens in a group of eight or so guys, we dare not show any fear. So, naively we cajoled each other along. We figured that if we stuck together we'd be alright as there is relative safety in numbers. After all, he seemed like a good guy and it would be terribly un-British of us to refuse his hospitality.

There were several more twists and turns down dirt floor alleyways, lined by bamboo-walled fences, until he eventually ushered us through the door of a very basic concrete-walled house. As we all filed in, we stood in what seemed like a large reception room of someone's private house. As our host disappeared to find his 'brother', we just stood and looked around for the non-existent bar.

A minute or so later the man appeared again, as jovial as ever. This was when it struck us that he hadn't gone off to fetch his 'brother', but rather a couple of girls who he then offered to us. So, that was the catch – he was a pimp who wanted to provide prostitutes for us. Without hesitation, we all turned and walked out of the house, despite the man's protests for us to stay. As we walked out and hastily navigated our way out through the labyrinth of alleyways leading back to the main road, we berated ourselves saying how disappointed Alex would be if he saw how quickly we were duped into the honeytrap. As with all events involving a bunch of guys, later over a beer, we managed to have a good laugh about it.

However, when settled into a proper bar/restaurant, we realized that it was sad how the man immediately saw Western white men and thought that they would be wanting to spend their money on prostitutes. Still, we survived what could have been a lot worse and we had learned our lesson. From now on we would keep our guard up, as taught.

The following morning it was an early start. Since before sunrise the main road outside the hotel had steadily grown in noise and the hustle and bustle of people commuting to work, while others shouted to sell various colourful garments. This was all interlaced with trucks spewing out smoke and makeshift taxis blowing their horns, which, from my experience, made up an average, stereotypical African city scene.

We were up, despite it being two hours premature for our body clocks. We sorted our personal kit bags out and then headed outside to the minibuses which would transfer us all back to the airport.

Despite being blurry-eyed, spirits were high and there was a real sense of wanting to get on with the job in hand. There was plenty of the usual crew banter flying around, mostly to do with people farting in the bus or the like. Although seemingly childish, yet it was this sort of banter that would get us through some of the toughest times on this trip, plus it was unashamedly amusing. One thing is for sure, the British are not short of wit, and crew banter in full flow is second to none.

As mentioned before, arriving at any airport with a large group of people and an unbelievable amount of flight cases, bags, boxes and tubes is stressful. Add to that a hot, bustling African airport and it's nothing short of hellish. Having said that, despite the ensuing chaos, our Fixers (locals who are employed to deal with our logistics and translation etc. – effectively Tour Guides) did a sterling job and made checking onto our flight relatively painless. Within a couple of hours, the team and all the kit were in the air, crammed into a small, very heavy-laden aircraft, heading north.

A few hours later, we touched down at Mekele Airport in the North East Highlands. We were aware that here, all our months of planning and preparation was about to be put to the test. Now there was no turning back.

We poured out of the small airport like a tsunami of people and kit. I don't think the locals quite knew what had hit them. Outside in the car park were several Toyota Land Cruiser 4x4 vehicles, lined up like a modern camel train, waiting to be loaded and led off.

As we came through the doors, we noticed that Richard (Camera Supervisor) was not looking great. He had lost all his colour and looked as though the life had been drawn out of him. He admitted to feeling very rough and subsequently disappeared behind one of the vehicles and vomited. Not a good start. The poor guy was mortified to have come down with something before we had even started. But, this was no sign of weakness as almost all the team were to find out. This was just part and parcel of being in such an alien environment.

With one man down, this is where the established friendship and close unity of our team came into play. Without questioning, we all rallied around and covered off all that had to be done, so that Roo (Richard's nickname) could lie out on a back seat of one of the cars and rest. Having shared the camera supervising role with Roo on many occasions, I took over for the time being and prepared to shoot the first opening piece to camera with Kate (Humble).

The first shot of any documentary is always a little nerve-wracking. Not that I hadn't done it hundreds of times before (by this time I'd been filming for well over fifteen years). But, when you have just landed somewhere remote and you are building your camera kit for the first time following an arduous flight, you just have to hope that it all still works. On top of the technical side of things, you also have the Director breathing down your neck, anxious to also make an impression. For the fresh Presenter, it is also time to break the ice and get something down on tape. No pressure, then?

As 'Shirley' (my designated Sound Operator) plugged his sound mixer cable into my camera, I looked through the camera viewfinder and lined up what I thought would be a good shot. Usually the Director would watch the shot through a monitor, but not wanting to disrupt the unpacking of the 4x4s, Rupert said that he trusted me, and so we went for the first take.

The content of Kate's first piece to camera included the statistics and facts of our expedition. Our team comprised of twenty-five Scientists, Adventurers and Specialist Camera Teams and fifty Ethiopians in our support team, including Drivers, Fixers and Translators/Guides. On top of all these people we also had over 2,000 kilogrammes (two tons) of equipment.

As I held the shot steady, Kate effortlessly executed the first take. Sometimes even the most seasoned Presenters can require a number of 'takes' to get all the facts and inclination right. But, Kate was technically superb and I was quick to say so. As Rupert called "Cut", I said, "That was amazing. Humble, the one-take wonder!" She laughed. Just for safety, in case of some digital drop out or something distracting in the background etc. we did one more 'take'. Again, Kate smashed it out of the park.

Shirley and I were thrilled, as we had been told earlier that we were going to be seconded as Kate's crew for the duration of the shoot. If her presenting skills were this polished, we were in for a relatively easy ride.

With the first shot 'in the can', we finished loading up the vehicles and prepared to head off on our adventure.

Shirley and I kept our camera and sound kit out, as we were going to have to film the journey along the way. This is often the most tiresome bit of filming, as it requires racing ahead, hopping in and out of the car as the convoy drives past. Mutley (Camera Assistant) and Duncan (Assistant Director) travelled with Shirley and I. Each vehicle had a handheld radio (walkie-talkie), so our Jeep would be able to drive ahead and communicate with each driver in the convoy, when to stop and wait. Once we were set up for the shot ahead, we would call them on.

We tried to vary the shots from low, wide and close-up shots. We shot with the camera resting on the side of the road, as the gnarly tyres drove past in close quarters. Other times we would stop the convoy and race ahead for a good few kilometres and find a high vantage point from where to shoot. Mutley would then put the camera on a tripod and change the wide angle lens to a long lens. When we were ready and I had the camera rolling, Duncan would call, "Go, go, go!" over the radio and in sequence the distant convoy would start to snake its way through the heat haze, towards the camera. The shots looked stunning.

We had 120 kilometres to cover on the first day, which in normal terms doesn't sound much, but driving through African towns and villages is far more demanding that simply zooming down a motorway. Not only is the traffic chaotic and the road surface punctuated with potholes (some of an alarming size) but on top of the bouncing and swaying around from your local driver slaloming his way around the craters, you have the oppressive heat and dust. We would use the air-conditioning whenever possible, but this would mean having the windows up to allow the AC to be effective. This would then result in the car interior filling up with thick dust from the holes in the footwells and other gaps. The compromise was to have the windows partly open, which meant you had to endure the heat, but at least you could breathe relatively clean air.

Such conditions meant that we had to carefully judge when the shot was worthy of holding us all up for fifteen minutes or so. From experience, we knew that is was better to try to nail as many shots as soon as possible, in order to keep moral up and people on your side. Often we would just drive for a number of hours without shooting in order to eat up the kilometres.

Later in the journey we left the tarmac road, and hit gnarly dirt roads/tracks. This was when the going got tough and our speed dramatically decreased. To convey the story of our journey, this change of road surface was seen as an important transition of our expedition, leaving civilization and heading off deep into the remote, barren wilderness. From this point on we would not see tarmac for over three weeks.

To film this transition, I managed to squeeze myself halfway out of the rear window and sit on the car's door frame. From this vantage point I would be able to track some of the other vehicles as we drove side by side. This was hard work, trying to keep a relatively steady shot while being thrown around, but what was worse were all the dust clouds created by the other vehicles in our convoy. In a matter of just a few minutes I was covered in sandy, red dirt from head to toe. It was a good shot though, so well worth the effort and discomfort.

It was a long, hot day and it was over eight hours later before we eventually arrived at our first camp location in the dark. Here we were situated at the bottom of the Highlands, right on the edge of the Danakil Desert. Any eight-hour car journey is exhausting, but when most of it is off-road, it is shattering. As the convoy of 4x4s pulled up, one by one the doors opened and the passengers practically fell out of the vehicles, absolutely exhausted. We had made it, but we were very tired, hot and hungry.

With only the odd spot of artificial light, we couldn't really make out any details of exactly where we were, but what we could see reminded me of a scene from an Indiana Jones movie. Although it was dark, there were areas dappled in occasional sweeping moonlight. The area appeared to be wide and the ground was quite flat, similar to a dried-up riverbed. Small scattered groups of people, with the occasional shape of a camel, could just be made out as they huddled together, and silhouetted by their camp fires. Underfoot was thick, dusty sand. The air was still, with not a breath of wind. It hung thick with dust. The first thing that hit us when we left the security of our vehicles was the intense heat. The rumours were true... it was like standing in an oven.

To the right of where our vehicles had parked was a slight incline where there was a long table set out, with twenty-five plastic chairs lining it. The table was lit by staggered candles, and despite being in what seemed to be like a sand bowl, it looked surprisingly inviting.

Not far from the table was a fire, which a couple of locals were crouched over, cooking up soup and pasta. Strange as it may seem, having a picnic set up in such a wild, inhospitable location, we needed to get used to it, as this was to be our experience of home for the next three weeks.

Unloading the vehicles was always a chore, but the sooner you started, the sooner it was done. Then you could get some food and get your head down for the night. One by one we all grabbed our personal bags. As planned, my green holdall stood out well, despite being covered in thick dust from being strapped to the roof of the 4x4. As I patted it down, I thought how nice it was to get it 'christened' and not looking so shiny and new.

It was too hot to sleep in tents. So, our advance support team had laid out twenty-odd camp beds for us to use. Using our head torches, we each found a bed, and threw our bags on to claim it before returning to the dining table. While the majority of us got stuck into the food, which was basic, but undeniably good, Steve (the vet) was skulking around the camp area with an ultraviolet torch. More interested in the food, we pretty much ignored him, until he piped up and shouted that he had found a scorpion. It turned out that the area surrounding the camp was crawling with them. Steve quickly added that if we were stung by one, they wouldn't kill us, but it would hurt like fury. So, he would advise us to not wear sandals and to take extra care when going to the loo in the night.

Steve Leonard is a funny guy. He's tall, handsome and has an infectious personality. He speaks with a broad Yorkshire accent and jumps at any opportunity to pull a prank. Yet, his joking aside, he is a talented, successful Veterinary Surgeon who has appeared on a number of TV series. Steve was recruited onto the team of scientists to explore how the extreme environment affected the wildlife in the Danakil. What animals do the local tribes keep and how do they keep them? On top of that, it would be interesting to see how his Western veterinary medicine would compare to their ancient methods. Maybe there would be the opportunity to share his knowledge and help them?

I immediately warmed to Steve as it was clear that he was a 'grafter' and just wanted to be one of the boys, which he soon was.

Poor Roo was still feeling ill, so he got some liquids down his neck and hit his camp bed earlier than the rest of us. Unfortunately for him, the whole team had previously agreed that if anything happened to us along the way, which could illustrate how remote and tough it was, then we would be filmed. So, while feeling like death, he had a camera shoved in his face as Mukul (Team Doctor) checked him over by torchlight.

Having known him for many years, I could see how this pained Roo. There is an unmentioned, somewhat macho competitiveness amongst crews and to be the first 'casualty' was not a label that any of us wanted to carry. However, we all knew that this expedition was incredibly extreme and sickness, diarrhoea or injury could happen to any of us, at any time. In a way, despite the humiliation, I think maybe Roo was lucky to get his major bout of illness over early.

With food in our bellies and plenty of water on board, each of us retired from the picnic table to our sandy camp beds. Going to bed on this first night was somewhat of an experiment. Should we take our clothes off, to keep cooler, risking insect bites and sunburn in the morning? Or keep covered up and sweat our way through the night? I opted for the half and half approach, as I took off my trousers, but left my light safari shirt on. Taking my boots off I was careful to stretch my socks over the opening, to deter any eight, six or no-legged creatures making them their new abode. Along with my head torch I carefully placed them within arm's reach by my bed, so if I had the call of nature during the night, I would know exactly where I'd left them. As I switched my head torch off, I lay back on the thin mattress, pulled the sheet up to my waist and stared into the vast, pitch-black sky. I could hear the muted sighs, groans and snores of others settling down in their outdoor beds. Soon, I drifted off to sleep with a real sense of relief that we had made it thus far. I was also aware of a fluttering of excitement in my stomach of what adventure lay in store for us the following day.

Opening my eyes the following morning, I awoke to a scene like that which one reads about in the Bible. Multiple men, with dark complexions, dressed in their long robes were flaying sticks, with which they prodded their camels. One by one the 'desert ships' (camels) reluctantly rose off their knees with a slow creek into a standing position, their flat hoofs puffing down on the bright sun-bleached sand. The "Yip" and "Holler" from the camel herders were occasionally replied to by a throaty growl and roar from their lanky beasts.

Even though the sun had only just shown its crown over the barren hills that encircled us, its warmth was menacing, as if to warn us of the extreme heat that would punish us once it was blazing, high in the sky.

There were random stirrings from the beds of our camp. Some people just lay there, savouring their last chance of sleep and rest before having to wake up to the reality of the day ahead. Yet, each of us knew that it would be favourable to make the most of the early cooler conditions. I shuffled up to my elbows and then swung my legs over to the sand below. There was a thin covering of sand all over my bed and me.

One or two of our support team, to my right, were already busy hovering over the fire, preparing a basic breakfast of eggs and bread. I blearily reached down and found my boots where I'd left them. I picked them up and knocked them together to displace the sand, before tentatively removing my socks from the openings. Turning them upside down and giving them a good shake and more knocks, I waited to see if I had any unwanted guests. Thankfully they were empty.

I have always been a morning person. Once I'm awake and on

my feet I get a rush of life and start chirping away, much to the annoyance of my more nocturnal colleagues.

So, once up and dressed, I started to go around the beds and shake those still snoozing, cracking some friendly jibes as I went.

Before too long we were all up, dressed and squaring our kit away.

Breakfast was set and we began our morning ritual of taking our malaria tablets and guzzling down a Berocca multi-vitamin soluble tablet.

Having made the first cup of British tea from my precious stash supply of tea bags, I stood, holding my plastic mug, and surveyed our surroundings. Where we had camped turned out to be the gateway to the Danakil Desert. This was effectively the start of the camel motorway that started up in the green Highlands and led all the way out across the desert lowlands. The desert, as flat as a billiard table, stretched out for kilometres on end, looking just like a dried-out seabed. The camel herders would depart from here, leading their camel trains, some numbering over fifty of the long-limbed, humped creatures. Their journey would take them snaking through the wadis and out onto the desolate daunting landscape that would lead them to the famous Salt Mines of Dallol. This journey would entail a full day's walk and, due to the blistering heat, most would risk the threat from bandits and walk through the night to avoid the hottest parts of the day. I noticed that most of the camels that had rested here were being loaded up with huge slabs of dirty-looking salt. These groups must have walked through the night, arriving in the early hours, and were now preparing to continue their journeys back up into the Highlands. To think that only two days ago we were in London was quite mind-blowing.

Once we had all taken some eggs, bread and jam for breakfast, we were called together by Duncan. We stood around a tarpaulin sheet that had been laid out as we were given instruction by our medics Alex and Mukul. As every part of the expedition was to be filmed, Shirley and I got rigged up and covered this talk on camera.

They told us that this is where the serious business starts. Placed on the sheet in front of us were 'bum bags' with two bottles attached to each unit. While mobile, especially on foot, these were to be our source of water that we should be constantly taking on board. Whenever necessary we could refill our bottles from plentiful supplies carried in the 4x4s or on our camels. Dehydration out here would not just give us a bit of a headache, it could kill us! They reminded us that each day we should be looking to drink no less than eight litres of water. At times the heat would be so great, especially before we acclimatized, that our bodies would sweat to cool down, but here the sweat would evaporate before we even noticed it. This could fool us into thinking that we were not losing liquids and this could be extremely dangerous.

We were told to take a 'buddy' (partner) with whom we should work with to make sure that each other was taking on enough water and looking OK. It made sense for each Cameraman to 'buddy up' with his Soundman, as these were the people that we would be spending the most time with.

The best proven method of staying hydrated was to constantly sip water all day long. If we were thirsty, we were already on our way to being dehydrated. We would also keep an eye on our 'buddy' to make sure they were sipping, and if we saw any signs of grumpiness, mumbling, confusion or erratic behaviour we should tell a medic immediately. At this, while still filming, Shirley and I looked at each other and sniggered. Shirley always mumbles and acts confused and I, especially when hungry, become grumpy and erratic. We wondered how we would know the difference.

One of the most telling ways of seeing whether you are dehydrated is to look at the colour of your urine. You should always aim to be peeing champagne opposed to Tetley tea. This, I said, Shirley could check himself!

Joking aside, this was a great way of making sure that each of us were being looked out for, but it also made the team work together. It was continually stated, 'Out here there are no heroes!' Meaning, if you feel out of sorts, unwell or have stomach problems etc. don't hide the fact, trying to be tough, because the consequences could be severe and end up affecting others as well as putting the whole expedition in jeopardy.

Everybody gave due attention and then picked up their bum bag and went to fill the bottles with water.

After sorting all our kit, which was then transferred from the 4x4s onto our own camel train, we were set to go. The mission for the day was to enter the vast wadis on foot, which would lead us onto the outer rim of the great expanse of the Danakil Desert. When on the edge of the desert we would carry on walking north to our second camp. This would be our launch site from where we would walk out into the heart of the Danakil to see the Salt Mines the following day.

As we left the safety of our camp, we were joined by two armed men who would act as our guards. Both were carrying old but well-maintained AK-47 assault rifles. One took point, at the front of our line, as the other took the rear. This was a stark reminder that we were not only entering a natural hostile environment, but also one that was man-made.

It was unbelievably good to be moving, especially on foot, finally putting into practice all that we had trained for. We had talked and constantly thought about this for the last few months back in the UK. Personally, I was on fire! Overly excited, skipping around with the smaller Canon camera, tabbing ahead,

I would race to get shots of the team walking out through the heat haze, flanked on each side by the huge sandstone walls of the wadi. Every now and then, Shirley and I would look for high ground to scramble up in order to shoot from a different, more interesting angle.

Surprisingly, on the route out through the wadi there was a small stream of water that had found its way into the wadi, running down from the foothills of the Highlands. At one point we had to cross it. Some went for just splashing through it with their desert boots being submerged up to the ankle by water. I paused and watched Andy, one of our specialist climbing team, to see how he would approach the crossing. He splintered from the group and walked a few metres downstream to find a spot where he could hop over it. Using a dry spit of sand in the middle he hurdled over the water and retained his dry boots. Shirley and I followed suit. It wasn't long before those with wet feet started to complain of rubbing and blisters. From experience, if you don't know how best to do something, watch and copy someone who does.

We walked for hours, all being mindful to keep taking on water. Sipping away, you never felt as though you were taking in enough water, but neither were we getting thirsty. Every now and then we would stop, take a breather, refill our water bottles and have a light snack. The pressing thing that we noticed, especially on these breaks, was that there was nowhere to shelter from the sun. Again looking at those who know what best to do, we noticed that our camel herders would rest by crouching down in the shade of a camel's shadow. We followed suit.

Everything was going well, except that we had been moving slower than anticipated. Even though it was undoubtedly tough going, spirits were still high. Along the way we had been stopping and filming short pieces to camera, such as Kate talking to Dougal about how the mighty slopes of the wadi showed clearly how the rock formations of the area were constantly on the move. The content of the film so far was strong and on camera it looked as dramatic as it was actually being there. Walking in the heat was tiring, but it was the stopping to film that really slowed us down. Having said that, we had to allow for this, as after all that was why we were here in the first place.

The original idea was to press on hard and try to make our camp in Hamadella, about 45 kilometres to the north. To walk this distance in normal UK conditions would be no trouble at all. However, due to the heat and all the filming, as the day wore on we knew that this goal was unrealistic. We had only covered around 18 kilometres by the time the sun started to drop and this meant that we would have to find camp elsewhere. Not long after this realization, we found ourselves walking alongside a dried-out riverbed; this seemed like a reasonable place to spend the night, so we stopped there.

As we had been caught short on the camping plan, we simply had to make do with what we had. Fortunately, our camels had been loaded with a contingency plan in mind. The local Fixers set about making a fire and getting some food on the go, as the rest of us looked around for a flat spot of ground to make our bed. There was always a race to find the best spot of ground and so the banter started again. Clearing rocks and stones from the man-size rectangle of dirt which we were to call 'bed' was to become part of the routine on this trip. When sleeping, we crew tended to stick quite close together as we knew that to sleep in close quarters was safer, but also a bit more of a laugh.

We were tired from the day's walk and our first real exposure to the heat, but as we sat under the stars that second night, we talked and laughed. Eventually we lay down, trying to make ourselves as comfortable as possible and fell to sleep. On the bright side, with temperatures at night still in their mid 30°C, at least we knew we would not get cold.

Bearing in mind that each day the sun would set around 7 p.m., once you've sat around talking for an hour or two after supper, you would almost certainly be going to bed by 9 p.m. As we are conditioned in our normal lives to sleep for around seven to eight hours at night (if lucky!) this meant that we were all rising way before the sun at around 5 a.m. The following morning this proved to be a real benefit. We had a long day's walk ahead of us, and the sooner we got going in the cooler temperatures, the better.

After a light breakfast, along with our buddy, we filled our all-important water bottles and religiously took our malaria tablets etc. As soon as the camels were loaded and the packs were on our backs, we started walking again... and what a walk it was.

Before long, the vast wadi walls decreased in height until we were left on the flat, barren, sandy landscape that we had envisioned. Don't by mistaken, it wasn't like the image of the Sahara Desert that you may have, with huge, undulating sand dunes. This was literally like a completely flat seabed, as if someone had just pulled the big plug out of the ocean! Underfoot the sand became hard and at times cracked as you walked over it, like baked mud. Dougal informed us that hundreds of thousands of years ago, where we were walking actually *would* have been a seabed.

It was quite overwhelming when you looked across the seemingly never-ending desert landscape. There was absolutely nothing for as far as the eye could see. We were told by our Fixers that the small bump on the distant horizon was in fact a huge volcano mountain, a fact that at first was hard to conceive.

The morning was pretty much taken up by walking, so we could cover some serious ground. If we were going to cover 30 kilometres, it would take us around ten to twelve hours, so we would have to ease up on the filming. Having said that, there was one shot that I refused to let go.

As we skirted the edge of the Danakil desert there was an amazing view of where the flat, ancient seabed starkly met the vertical mountains of the Highlands. In front of this awesome panoramic view ran one of the main tracks favoured by the camel trains. As the line that we were walking on took us parallel to that track, I saw from each direction two very long camel trains heading towards each other. I figured that if I could have the camera on a tripod ready in time, both camel trains would pass in close proximity. This would surely make an epic shot, when zooming out to reveal the vast mountains behind.

Shouting to Ben and Mutley to "Grab the legs!" (tripod), I quickly looked for the best spot to set up the camera. Spreading the legs of the tripod, I kept watching the camel trains, desperately willing them to cross, as I hoped would happen. Setting the spirit level bubble on the tripod to the centre, to level up the frame, I then zoomed the long lens onto the spot where I estimated that the camels would pass. Adjusting the focus to that position I quickly practised a zoom out to see what my end of frame should be. If it worked to plan, this would surely be a monumental shot!

The rest of the team carried on walking as we stayed in position, patiently waiting. It was only a few minutes later before my prediction came to pass. The camel trains met right on target! It looked beautiful, as due to the camels' long necks, they almost looked like paperchains being pulled in opposite directions as they passed one another. The sight was mesmerizing. I held my breath, to keep my movements on the camera steady, and then gradually put some weight on the servo rocker button, which in turn slowly zoomed the lens out. It worked perfectly and almost certainly stands as one of the better shots of my career. When the shot had passed, with a "whoop" of celebration, I stopped the camera recording and quickly disconnected it from the tripod. I carried the camera and one of the boys took the legs, as we jogged to catch up with the group.

Around midday, the hottest time of the day, the temperatures were soaring into the high 40°C. Still we kept plodding on, sipping and walking, sipping and walking.

Before arriving in Ethiopia, we had been told about a natural phenomenon that occurs in this region. It is called 'The Gara' – the Wind of Fire. We had yet to witness this for real; that was until early in the afternoon of the third day. There is no better way to describe the feeling of the Wind of Fire than to imagine you are walking against the airflow of a giant hairdryer – literally! Walking directly against it almost gave you the feeling of claustrophobia, as no matter what you did, you couldn't escape the incredible heat. It enveloped your entire being. It was intense, and made walking so much harder. Yet, it also gave us a thrill that we were on a truly amazing, hardcore adventure.

It ended up taking us fifteen hours to reach our destination. It was dark by the time we eventually saw the lights of the remote Ethiopian military outpost of Hamadella. It was here that we would camp for the night. We walked into camp physically exhausted, but to our delight the advance support team had once again set the picnic table. Unlike the first camp, this time there were no beds, just thin mattresses to lay on the ground again. While we still had an ounce of energy, already as almost a matter of routine, we each went straight to the pile of bags, and found our own. We then grabbed one of the mattresses and quickly picked a flat spot of ground, with the least rocks as possible.

We were so hungry that anything would have pleased us, but to our delight our travelling cook had made a huge bowl of pasta with a goat meat sauce. Even though we were completely knackered, the energy rush from the food relit the fun banter and again we laughed our way into the evening.

Before we bedded down, Alex, who had been scoping out our new location, called us together. He said this military outpost was literally the last line between us (Ethiopia) and the Eritrean border. There had been brutal open warfare between the two countries over the last decade. Despite the hostilities recently ending, the situation was still extremely volatile and alarmingly fragile. Only a year before we were there, a group of British tourists had been kidnapped right where we were camping! "So be alert."

He then added, "If you need to go to the loo in the night, please make sure you walk that way (pointing behind us) because if you walk *that* way (pointing in front) you will be shot." There was no need to tell us twice. He had clearly reminded us all that this was certainly not just a 'walk in the park'.

Unfortunately for me, it was minutes after this talk that I had the rumblings of my first 'call of nature'. Seeing that there was only a small brick one-room building where a soldier or two bedded down, it was obvious that there was no such thing as a toilet out here. However, there was likely to be a designated area for such occasions, so I asked one of our Fixers where one would go to the toilet? Completely matter of fact, he said that if I walked 20 metres back down the track and crossed over, there was a gully which was used for that sort of thing.

I reached into my day sack and picked up my toilet roll. Adjusting my head torch, I set off back up the track. This event is never something you look forward to in the wilds (unlike at home) but at some point it's inevitable, so when you receive the call, you just have to grin and bear it. The secret that I've learnt is just make sure you *really* need to go, then it's over in a flash.

Having walked around 20 metres, I crossed the track and saw

the gully as the Fixer had mentioned. I stood on top of the gradual drop and shone my head torch down into the darkness. To cut to the chase, it looked as if it had been used as the 'designated area' by not just a few soldiers, but rather a passing army! Literally every metre there was a pile of someone's crap. Some piles had a stick poking out of the top (the preferred method of 'wiping' for the local) but there was also the occasional 'flag' of loo roll flapping from the pungent peak. Taking a deep breath, I gingerly took a step down, being desperately careful where I lay my feet. No matter where I looked, as I tiptoed around, I couldn't find enough space to do what I needed to do. By now, the foul stench started to drift up into my nostrils, and having being baked in the sun all day, the flies that were nestling down on *their* warm mattress were disturbed into flight and buzzed all around me. It wasn't great.

I consciously started to breathe through my mouth, in order to prevent my nose from smelling. After a good few minutes and a step formation worthy of *Riverdance*, I found my window of opportunity in a clearing of around one square metre. Without going into further details, fortunately it was over quickly and mercifully it was a 'Bollywood Ending' (very clean and often with a teary end). Job done.

Being a typical bloke, when I got back to camp, while rubbing my hands with sanitizing gel, I gave a detailed description of my last few minutes. Eyebrows were raised and heads shook, but I also managed to win a few laughs.

With a weight off my mind, I lay on my mattress under the stars and drifted off into a deep sleep.

Mercifully no one was kidnapped or got shot while going to the loo overnight. It was the usual early rise and before we knew it, we were heading off on our two-hour walk to the Salt Mines of Dallol.

It was like we were moving across the surface of another planet altogether. Walking was easier, as underfoot it was nice, flat, well-baked, crusty, salty sand. However, the heat reflected off the ground was full-on, like the sunlight bouncing off snow, the scene was blinding to the naked eye.

The first sign that we were approaching the salt flats was a break in the distant flat horizon. To the eye, you couldn't quite make out the details, but you could see a bustling, dark line of movement. The closer we got, we could start to make out figures of men and camels moving around, seemingly busy at work. When we were very close, the scene before us was of biblical proportions, with hundreds of men chipping away at the ground with very remedial tools. This was Dallol, where the locals had been mining salt for multiple generations.

Standing at 120 metres below sea level, the scene appeared unchanged from exactly that which you would have witnessed in this place 2,000 years ago. The nearer we got the more amazing it was. Some of these men led the camel trains out, while others worked all day long, out in the blistering heat.

As part of documentary, we filmed Kate and Steve getting involved, trying their luck, mining themselves. The method was to chip, with a flat-headed hatchet, around an area of the salty ground. Exaggerating the existing cracks they then pushed wooden poles under the lip of salty crust, in order to lever the large sections of the surface up. From there someone else would take over, taking a smaller flathead hammer and cutting the block of salt down into squares approximately 50 centimetres square, each weighing one kilogramme. To be that accurate with no tape measure or scales, just a free swinging hammer, was a real skill, honed to perfection over many years of practise.

When a number of salt slabs were piled up, a camel would then be loaded with the blocks and when laden to capacity, they would once again make their return journey to the distant markets of the Highlands.

We were told by a senior man that each one kilogramme block would be worth five pence, but would sell for ten times that in the market. The workers themselves would get paid a maximum of two pounds (British Sterling) per day, for a brutal twelve-hour shift slaving away in this, nature's oven.

Filming this scene in the most intense, exposed heat of the trip thus far was incredibly taxing. Those who weren't holding cameras or sound equipment held umbrellas over us as we filmed. It was here that we noticed that even under these conditions we didn't pour with sweat all over our bodies. It was too hot for the sweat to even show; it simply evaporated the minute it appeared. I had never experienced heat like it.

These men spent their working lives out on the salt flats, digging, hammering and lifting all day long. For us, a few hours was all we could take.

After the gruelling hours filming at the Salt Mine, thankfully, it was time to head off and travel to our new location, Kusra Wad in Afar land.

The journey to our next point of interest was nothing short of eventful. Having reconvened with the convoy of 4x4s, it was a welcome break to sit down and get driven, despite the dust clouds and the violent bouncing around. We were soon going to find out why the locals used camels to get around the desert. Despite the obvious cost of owning and running a car being so far out of reach for a local, even if they could afford a car, it simply would not survive in that heat and environment.

Our drive to the village of Kusra Wad should have only taken us four hours. Yet, after two and a half hours on the go, we had only covered 6 kilometres. This was due to the sand changing in depth and one minute being hard, the next minute deep and soft. But the heat also affected the vehicles, which they didn't like at all. We literally spent the entire day pushing cars out of sandpits and waiting for steaming, stalled cars to cool down, all the while feeding our precious water supplies into the parched radiators. It was again exhausting, which everything seemed to be out there. Yet, with grit, determination and stickability, we eventually made it to the village, which was to be our new base camp.

The Afar tribe are reputed to be one of the most ferocious tribes in the world, and they were going to be our hosts for the next fortnight.

Their reputation for being as hard as nails was partly due to the fact that they can exist in this, one of the most punishing environments on planet Earth. Yet other factors contribute, such as the way their warrior men file down their teeth into sharp points, which gave them the aggressive look of a shark. Also, famously, during an attempt by the Italian Army to conquer the Afar land (which they failed miserably to do) when the Italian soldiers were caught, their testicles were cut off and the Afar warriors wore them hanging around their necks!

To be honest, as we arrived we were completely unsure as to what kind of welcome we would receive. Once again, by the time we had finished another epic journey, we arrived in the dark. As you can imagine, we were very relieved to be greeted by a full village turnout, boasting large smiles, harmonious singing and jovial dancing. We filmed our welcoming committee by using the 4x4 headlamps for light, which worked adequately.

It was here that we were reunited with Katie (Producer Director) and Max (Assistant Producer) who had already been out living with the Afar for the last week or so. Their job was to go ahead, as a forward party, and befriend the Afar people. Winning their hearts and minds would be critical to the success of our documentary. As well as this, Katie and Max would spend their time researching what we should and were allowed to film. This was no small task. Not only had very little filming been done with the Afar people before, but as they were strict Muslims, it would also, in theory, be very hard for Katie to gain respect from the strictly male elders. The Afar culture dictates that the men and women live completely separate lives. Most of the time the women live in one hut, while the men live in another. The women work, making food, building and maintaining the mud huts, looking after the kids and fetching water (often a mammoth task, entailing walking vast amounts of kilometres each day, with full animal skins on their backs). The men, on the other hand, looked after the camels... who pretty much look after themselves. You get the picture.

We weren't at all surprised to find that Katie and Max had done an astonishing job at preparing the way for our arrival. The Afar Chief, Golissa (his name meaning 'frightening' in Afar) was completely sold on the idea of having us all there and in fact had even given us special permission to film with the women, which was staggering. It was great to see these two again and it was nice to have fresh faces to talk to. As you can imagine, following their tough few weeks, the feeling was mutual.

That night we enjoyed another dinner from the famous picnic table and this time, as this was to be our new base camp, we had the offer of army-style canvas tents. Not wanting to appear ungrateful, we attempted to go into the tents and make them our temporary homes, yet the temperatures were so high, it was far too hot. The tents were subsequently relegated to being our kit stores and walk-in wardrobes.

As we were growing accustomed to it, we continued to sleep under the stars each night.

In this base camp, which was situated on what was a sandy,

shrub-scattered area of land, things were far more organized. Compared to our last few rough nights, it felt like a posh Shangri-La hotel. We had two 'long drop' dug-out toilets, with makeshift wooden box seats (relative luxury). We also had two canvas walled showers, where there actually wasn't a shower, but you could go in with a shallow bucket of water and have a basic wash in privacy. All that was missing was the mini-bar! On that note, most of Ethiopia is Muslim where alcohol is not usually drunk. There was no alcohol in the Afar region, which is probably wise considering the heat. I can't imagine what a hangover would feel like in 50° heat!

As the nights went on, it was amazing to witness how quickly our bodies started to adapt to the extreme temperatures. It was only a matter of a few more days before we would wake up shivering at night if it dropped to 35°. At home you would have trouble sleeping in that heat. The human body is incredible.

Now we were established at base camp, life became slightly more routine. We crews were designated to different assignments, in our different teams. Shirley and I were with Kate and Katie. Roo and Lloyd with Rupert and Dougal. Finally, Lee and Pete were with Justin and Steve. Every morning we would all wake around the same time, get some breakfast, then prep the camera and sound kits before leaving camp for the morning's work. Justin took Lee and Pete to spend the day with Steve, who was going to spend time with the Chief, Golissa. Filming a taste of the Chief's life, like all the men in the village, they just spent a lot of time sitting around talking. Yet, it was actually very interesting to see how Golissa handled his leadership of the village. The highlight was watching him sing to his beloved camels, which he did every morning to set them at ease.

A few days after arriving at Base Camp, a splinter group consisting of Roo, Lloyd, Alex, Rupert, Dougal and the climbing team, went off for about a week. They were to travel many kilometres up-country, on their own excursion, to explore an incredible earthquake fissure.

Two years previously, locals said that there was a "vast crack in the earth", which apparently opened up overnight. This fissure was so remote that it's only ever been mapped by satellite and no one had ever ventured inside it. This is exactly what they set out to do.

It took them days and days of driving to reach it, but what they found was literally breathtaking – a vast tear in the ground, literally the size of a small valley, which had torn open in an estimated twenty-four hours. As Dougal brilliantly summed up, "This is the stuff of Hollywood!"

As they had been delayed getting there due to a dispute about camels that were going to have to carry their kit up to the fissure, the team were now under time pressure to do what they had set out to do. On arrival at the natural phenomenon, the climbing team wasted no time in rigging up a rope system that would send Dougal and his equipment down into the guts of the enormous fissure. There he aimed to create a 3D scan of it. This would be a scientific first, and so they were all very keen to achieve this.

Due to earthquake and volcanic fissures emitting noxious gases, many of which are dangerous, if not lethal, while testing the rope system Mark (Mountain Safety Expert) wore a full-face oxygen mask and also took a gasometer to check the gas levels. As Mark was lowered down, he had only got halfway down when his gasometer went berserk! The alarms told him that there was H2S (Hydrogen Sulphide) in the air. This is the worse type of gas that can kill a human in just one breath. They say that the last thing you smell is rotten eggs, then you die.

Mercifully Mark was wearing the oxygen mask, because if he hadn't, the fissure would have claimed its first victim.

Needless to say, the remaining safety team got Mark out of there immediately.

The poor fissure team were bitterly disappointed and, following a tough discussion, it was decided that it was simply not worth the risk to lower Dougal down into the unknown. If he was down there and his oxygen mask slipped or failed, he would be killed. No science experiment is worth that. All the effort of getting there and not being able to complete the task in hand was heart-wrenching. To his credit, Dougal continued to be upbeat about the situation and cracked on, successfully creating a fabulous scan of the fissure from the top ridges. He is incredibly passionate about geology and for him just to witness this extraordinary fissure in person was enough for him.

Once that was done, the team travelled back down to the vehicles and spent the next few days exploring other points of interest in that area.

Meanwhile, back at base camp, we were covering our own stories:

Steve, Justin and his crew continued to look at the Afar animals and see how they had physiologically adapted to live there. This involved them spending a day with Golissa's son, who was aged around six years old. Despite being so young he was solely responsible for the Chief's precious herd of goats. He would shepherd them all day long and lead them to scavenge on what little vegetation they could find. After a while it was too hot for the crew to continue chasing the goats around, so Steve strapped a GPS tracker onto one of the goat's backs. At the end of the day they returned to find the goat and picked up the data from the tracker. It showed that the little goat had covered over 12 kilometres in its quest to find food. Interestingly, the little goat continually stopped and started, to save energy and reduce its body heat. On top of that it was seen that (unlike most goats) this one was relatively selective about what vegetation it ate. By only selecting the best fruit or plants this meant it received the most nutrition from its limited menu. This is how the goat has adapted to be so hardy and thus so important to the likes of the Afar people, as a constant and reliable source of milk and meat.

Later that week, one evening, while walking back from the 'ablutions block', Steve was sure that he had heard a pack of jackals (small wild dogs) in the scrub nearby the camp. He thought it would be fantastic to set a bait at night and catch them on film, using our infrared cameras. Justin agreed that it was good idea. Steve then suggested that it would be worth staking them out first, to make sure they were in the area to save wasting the crew's time and effort. Again Justin agreed. What Justin didn't know was that Steve had an alternative plan up his sleeve.

Later that night, he and Justin disappeared out of camp and into the scrubland. Steve told Justin to go in one direction as he went in the other, but reminded him to be very careful. Jackals could be extremely dangerous, especially when cornered or frightened. So, off Justin went, gingerly stepping his way through the scrub bushes, being very quiet and careful. Meanwhile, in the dark, Steve quickly ran and hid in a bush in the direction which Justin was heading.

Over the years, Steve (being Steve) had perfected imitating the growl and vicious bark of an aggressive small dog... it really was very convincing.

You have to bear in mind that this was quite an unnerving place to be; it was pitch black, Justin was by himself, quite a distance from camp, and could at any minute come face to face with a pack of wild, aggressive dogs!

Steve's patience was rewarded and eventually Justin headed straight towards him.

As he approached Steve's bush, Steve started to growl. Justin stopped dead in his tracks and let out a muted expletive. Steve stopped. Justin's breathing grew heavier as he stood frozen in his position. Steve growled again, only this time increased the length and volume. Justin jumped and then froze again... emitting another expletive. A few seconds later, Steve let loose and erupted into a frenzied barking fit. At this Justin jumped about 2 metres in the air, screamed out "$%*@!!!!", and in a storm of flaying arms and legs, he sprinted out, through the bushes, back onto the track and, like Forrest Gump, he just kept on running. As he ran, he repeatedly shouted and swore, which grabbed our attention back in camp.

Running up to meet him, to see what on earth had happened, we found Justin as white as a ghost and swearing as if he had Tourette's. Before he could regain his breath and really explain what had happened, we heard howling following behind him – although the howling was not from dogs, but by Steve who was crying and howling with laughter. It was a very funny night but now with the stage set, everybody became a little bit paranoid and started to look over their shoulder, waiting for the next prank from the vet.

Fortunately Justin saw the funny side of Steve's prank, and the next evening decided to bravely go in again, this time with a crew, and set the bait in front of the infrared cameras. At this point poor Lee and Pete had both gone down with sickness, so they were having to stay in camp and rest up (I was about to say 'stay in bed', but alas there were no beds.). This was not a nice place to be ill, so you felt even worse... no beds, little shade from the sun, and certainly no escape from the festering heat. Sheer misery.

So far, Shirley and I had kept well, so Justin asked if we would mind coming out to help. Well, it's not as if there was anything good on TV that night (!) and it sounded like fun, so off we all trudged, into the darkness.

By red torchlight, allowing our eyes to retain as much night vision as possible, we found a good spot by a thorny bush where we laid some goat meat as bait. We then carefully positioned two infrared lamps about 3 metres on either side of the bait, hiding them in surrounding bushes. We then backed away about 30 metres, where we found a good place to sit and hide. With the camera trap set, it was a waiting game. We all sat on the ground and made ourselves as comfortable as possible, while huddling around a small monitor from which we could also press RECORD when they arrived. It was a proper stakeout and was actually quite exciting. Who knew what animal may come along, wandering into our camera trap?

Steve whispered that the jackals would be so aware of our presence that we would have to be extremely quiet. Not only would they hear us, but they would also smell us... the minute he said that, someone let off an enormous fart, at which point we all erupted into laughter like naughty schoolboys. Well, that had blown it. Now we would have to settle back down and wait for the dust to settle, hoping that the raw meat would overpower the smell of the fart and entice the jackals back in.

The problem is, when you get a bunch of blokes together, no matter how old you are, when you get the giggles, you just can't stop. It was like being in a library when everyone else is quiet, you just can't keep control of your hysterics. Thankfully, we were all in a funny mood that night, so no one really cared, but every few minutes, as everyone was desperately trying to keep dead quiet, someone would eventually guffaw and snort out another sniggering convulsion. It was quite brilliant and a very welcome light relief from the usual intensity of the Danakil.

After about an hour of waiting (and silent giggling), miraculously our patience was rewarded. We quickly pressed the RECORD button, as on the right-hand side of our little monitor screen we saw a nose appear and then a pointed ear. It then disappeared. Our interest was now acutely focused back on what we were doing. Suddenly from the right side again came a medium-sized, inquisitive jackal. We couldn't believe our luck and in the faint glow of the monitor, all our faces lit up into beaming smiles.

He scurried over to the bait, smelt the meat and then stood, attentively looking around to see if he was under any threat. Seconds later another jackal appeared, rooting around in the background. In a flash, the dog nearest the bait snatched a section of the meat and darted off into the surrounding bushes. The footage we were getting was fantastic and better than we had hoped for.

After that little episode we waited for another hour or so and had a few more sightings of the pack. We estimated there would have been about five jackals in total. It was amazing to see these highly elusive, nocturnal hunters in so much detail. What a great night's work. We had loads of fun doing it, and on top of that we got some cracking results.

Before packing up the camera trap, we needed to film a short piece to camera with Steve explaining what we were doing. We did this with Steve walking forward, dimly lit by a hand basher (handheld, battery powered light). As I filmed him, I walked backwards. However, due to the irregularity of the ground, I asked Shirley and Justin to guide me. Having done this many times before, Shirley held onto the back of my belt. As he led me backwards, he walked forwards. On the other side, Justin put his hand on my shoulder. Yet, he also walked backwards. Halfway through Steve's piece to camera, Justin tripped on a low shrub plant and went flying into the air and landed flat on his back. That was it, we all collapsed into laughter again!

After this event we affectionately nicknamed Justin 'Calamity', as he seemed more than a little accident prone. We absolutely loved him for it and all the great entertainment he provided us with. A brilliant Director, top man and a good friend.

In between all these different events and stories, life in camp carried on as normally as it could. It is all too easy to skip over the details and miss reading between the lines, but living in a camp out here was truly hardcore. We lived like a vagrants, with no beds, no proper washing facilities and, as you can well imagine, it wasn't long before we all stank. The only consolation to this was that we all smelt bad together.

This is one aspect of these sort of expeditions that I actually really like, not necessarily because I like to be dirty and smell (at home I am quite the opposite, thankfully), but more because it's a real release from the clinical, over-sanitized lives that we lead in the West. On top of the freedom of living rough, there's even more freedom being away from mobile phones, computers and televisions – something that I think we need to bring into check more often in our lives back home. Out here, our days and particularly our evenings were spent talking to people and reading. Time well spent.

Everybody on the team had their specific jobs, each as important as the other.

Duncan (Assistant Director) was like the father of the family, who brilliantly organized all the logistics that went on behind the scenes. People like him are the unsung heroes of such expeditions. I have worked with Duncs for many years, all over the world, and we get on very well. On every shoot, especially of this hardcore nature, there always comes a time when you need to 'vent' frustration, because things are tough or not going the way they should be. Over the years I have often played as Duncan's venting partner. We would go and find a quiet spot and just rant away for an hour or two, after which you always felt much better.

However, one of the only things that Duncan was not so good at was being disciplined at regularly drinking his water. I'm not sure who his safety 'buddy' was, probably Rupert, who was now a few days drive away. Due to this fact, once or twice Duncan went into full physical meltdown. As we had been warned on numerous occasions, dehydration out here was sudden, severe and dangerous. Duncan's body reacted by going into violent spasms of full body cramps. Anyone who's experienced cramp in your foot or leg knows just how painful it is, but imagine that happening all over your body at once. It was horrific! The only remedy was to get liquids into him as quickly as possible. We did this through electrolyte drinks (such as Dioralyte), and one time our medics even gave him an intravenous saline drip. After a few of these attacks, he finally learnt that they were easily avoidable, but you had to drink your water.

Those of us back at base camp would always stop for lunch, which was always laid on the long picnic table, which was situated under a free-standing awning, offering shelter from the sun. Every meal time was a battle with the incessant flies that couldn't believe their luck. I'm sure those flies would never have tasted the heavenly sweetness of strawberry jam before our visit, and it must have made the usual diet of camel or goat dung seem incredibly bland. We were their new best friends. Unfortunately, the relationship was not reciprocated.

Still working on the buddy system, we would all share whatever each other needed.

Hygiene was a priority in base camp, but people were regularly falling ill through the seemingly unavoidable germs that were revelling in the hot conditions.

Over our two weeks spent there, most of the camp fell ill at some point.

A few days in and Mutley dropped. The strange thing about his illness was that he wasn't properly sick like the others. He just wasn't himself. He would quietly mope around the camp and he didn't want to admit that he was ill, but he was completely devoid of energy. He knew what he had to do, but he actually physically didn't have the energy to do it. He just spent hours feeling rough and sleeping.

Max had a terrible time with his stomach and relentless diarrhoea. On the opposite end of the spectrum, I spent a lot of the time constipated. This was probably due to the need of more water in my system, as well as a lack of vegetables in our diet. I would go and sit on the 'long drop' wooden seat for what seemed like hours. As these makeshift loos became increasingly soiled and rancid as the days went by, it wasn't a nice place to spend any length of time. As I would walk back into camp, on a number of occasions I passed poor Max as he was going for the tenth time that day. We would look at each other and both silently shake our heads, though for completely different reasons.

It may seem vulgar to talk about these subjects, but when you are actually out there, because of the 'buddy' system, it is actually very important to share what is going on within your body.

The only person who seemed to get away scot-free was Katie, who seemed to just breeze through the whole experience. She was labelled as 'Super Woman'.

After lunch we would all tend to sleep. No matter how well we slept out under the stars at night (in which generally we slept very deeply), when it came to lunchtime, we had been up for hours and seeing that we wouldn't be asked to work in the midday sun, we would all find a spot of shade, grab a mattress and get some zzzs. If there was a wind blowing which blew sand in your face, we started to build walls of bags and kit cases around our heads, which worked very well. It wasn't until later in the afternoon, when the temperatures dropped a little, that we would get back to work.

The highest temperature measured on the base camp thermometer was 56°C (132°F)!

Every now and then we would hear a holler from the cook's tent, as a few of the locals had seen a 'Dust Devil' approaching. This is a spinning thermal wind like a mini-tornado. These Dust Devils varied in size and some of them were big and alarmingly powerful. They became an almost daily occurrence, so we became a little blasé about them.

However, one day a huge one blew straight through our camp!

The great swirling wind tore one of the big green canvas army tents completely off the ground, even though it was fully pegged down. We watched in amazement as the tent spun up about 15 metres in the air, while spinning its way across the scrubland. After this display of power, every time we heard the local warning cry, we would get to our feet and carefully watch the Dust Devil's journey... willing it to simply pass on by.

On another day there was a general strong wind blowing over the camp. This was kicking up a lot of sand. So, in order to stop the camera kit tent filling up with sand, I ran over and quickly started to unleash the ropes that held the rolled-up canvas window flaps that covered the light mesh windows. As I was untying the last flap, as the canvas rolled down it unveiled an enormous white camel spider about the size of my hand! It was not so much the spider itself that made me jump and squeal, but more of the surprise to see it there. Those who were sitting by the table turned at my scream and then burst out laughing. One by one they all came over to have a closer look at the huge creature that would not kill you, but could give a nasty, painful bite. Now we knew that these huge spiders were in our camp, far greater vigilance was taken over the tents, our boots and bags.

Sometimes ignorance is bliss.

During our final week in Kusra Wad, Steve was running camel clinics and Dr Mukul ran health clinics. Villagers from all over the region heard on the grapevine about this and so took the rare opportunity to bring their sick animals and children to see if they could be helped by the Western doctors.

Meanwhile Kate, Katie, Shirley and I focused on the harrowing story of the Afar women.

Afar women have no freedom of expression, as their lives are completely suppressed by the dominant men. In order to spend time with the women and film their day-to-day lives, we needed to gain access to them, but this caused many difficulties. Due to the separation between the sexes, there were strict rules in place that prohibited men from mixing with the women. This was an issue for Shirley and I, which meant that in theory we wouldn't be allowed to enter the women's hut or area.

This is where the brilliance of Katie and Max's ground work really came to fruition. Partly because of Golissa's trust in them, but also I think due to the fact that Steve and Mukul were helping his people so much with their medical clinics. Golissa eventually gave us special permission to interview the women on camera, which was unprecedented.

Despite gaining his permission, he would only allow Shirley and I to enter the women's hut, which meant that we would be short of a translator (all our local translators were men). This seemed like an unsurpassable problem, that was until Valerie Browning turned up.

Valerie is an Australian nurse, who for many years now has

served, taught and lived amongst the Afar people. She has particularly been working within the Afar community trying to eradicate female genital mutilation (more commonly known as female circumcision) which was rife in such areas of Africa.

No longer a young woman, she has dedicated her entire life to this role and even ended up marrying an Afar elder. Sometimes when travelling the world you meet extraordinary people – Valerie was one of the best.

As Valerie not only spoke fluent Afar, but also completely understood their complex culture, she was perfectly able to bridge the gap between Kate (Humble) and the local women. As you can imagine, for the local women, it was strange and nerve-wracking enough having two big white men in their hut, let alone being filmed by a huge camera at the same time. Understandably, at first they were very reluctant to speak.

Not too long after entering their hut and spending time just allowing them to get used to the strange situation, they started to warm to our team. Fortunately, most of the men who had gathered outside to see what was going on had grown bored and so started to disperse. This was when some of the older women started to really open up.

Kate, very sensitively, interviewed them about their lives, how they dealt with the dangers of childbirth and also how they dealt with their sexual relations with the men etc. Not long at all into the relatively freer conversation, it was clear that some of the remaining men outside had picked up on the fact that the subject of sex (which was a strictly taboo subject among the Afar) was being talked about. So, they firmly made their presence known. Once again, out of fear, the fearful women retracted into their shells again. The atmosphere around the hut grew heavy and you could have cut the tension with a knife. As the men were becoming more and more agitated, we decided that it was wise for us to stop the interview and filming. Shirley and I left the hut and Kate and Katie shortly followed after us.

Kate was bubbling over with emotion and was incensed by the way that the men were bullying the women. It was such a stark difference to how women are treated in Western culture. We started to film an interview with her to capture her immediate thoughts and reaction. Within a few sentences she broke down into tears and wept out of frustration. While filming this, both Shirley and I admitted to shedding a tear. It was really very moving.

Kate is well known on television for being a well brought-up, very attractive, intelligent and capable woman. She is strong, and I think she quite likes that fact. When we first talked as a small group about her role of getting under the skin of the plight of Afar women, one of the things that she stated was that she would definitely not cry on camera. The reality of the situation that we were deeply engrossed in obviously proved too much. It's important to say that by asking such questions we weren't seeking to judge or add drama, but simply wanting to represent these women's lives in an accurate way.

Leaving Valerie to wisely diffuse the situation and reassure the women in the way that only she could, we left there to visit Mukul at his health clinic.

The whole trip was now hitting a deeper level of emotion and this was only going to continue.

As we entered the hut where Mukul was seeing his patients, it was stiflingly hot. There were loads of people crowded in to the small hut, built out of mud and reed, which only had one flap to enter and exit from. Shirley and I, both pretty tall, squeezed our way through the tiny doorway, dragging our heavy, cumbersome camera and sound kit after us.

Twisting and turning our bodies to find space to sit, I then raised the camera onto my shoulder and started to record. In this humid atmosphere, sweat poured down my face and I could feel the torrent of salty liquid pouring down my back.

The family that became the main focus of our story had walked over five hours to see the doctor. With an incredible gentleness and sincerity that he is blessed with, Mukul began to examine a little toddler boy, called Sayid. Shortly after he had started, Valerie was able to join us again, keen to make the most of having a Western doctor on hand. Through Valerie's translation, Mukul asked Sayid's parents if he ever got short of breath while running around. "Yes," the parents replied, "he will walk from here to the door (only a couple of metres) and fall over." Mukul listened to the little boy's chest through his stethoscope and then turned to Valerie and said that he could hear a very loud, clear heart murmur. Valerie's reaction was one of shock. He then explained to camera that Sayid's heart was not working efficiently enough to push blood around his little body, so it's as if he's jogging all the time. Without treatment, he would certainly die very young.

Mukul was distraught that with only his limited medical field kit, there was no way that he could effectively treat the child.

For us, as Westerners, it is hard to comprehend what it must be like to live where there is no real hope should you or one of your family have a serious medical condition. However, in the remote world of the Afar, death is never very far away. This is just a fact of their tough existence. On this occasion though, all hope was not lost. Valerie happened to be travelling later that day to Logia, 500 kilometres away. She told us that in Logia there is a hospital that would be able to treat Sayid. Luck was certainly shining down on this family today.

The next problem was that Sayid's parents had never left their village, so were terrified at the thought of going so far away. At first they said that they couldn't go, even when Valerie explained to them that this would certainly be their only chance to save little Sayid. Still, they could not be convinced. The situation was desperate.

It wasn't until Valerie explained to one of the elders of the village, who was a relative of the family, the seriousness of the situation that there was a breakthrough. In Afar culture, as we knew all too well, the men rule. On this occasion this proved to be a positive thing, as the elder then ordered the young man and wife to go with Valerie and get Sayid the treatment that would save his life.

It was upsetting to see the parents so distraught and scared, yet they obediently did as they were told, gathered their few possessions together and carried Sayid over to the 4x4.

At the vehicle, Kate said a tearful goodbye to Valerie. This wonderful woman had made a huge impression on us all in the short time that we had spent with her. With that, we filmed as the 4x4 drove off, with Valerie and the family on board, into the sandy distance.

We later heard from Valerie that the family had actually never been in a car before, which proved just how big a deal this was for the couple. Apparently, within the first few minutes of the drive, they all suffered from travel sickness caused by the strange motion of the vehicle. This was a tough, yet amazing story of lucky Sayid.

There is one more story worth mentioning that happened in our last week still in base camp. We had all been invited to a local Afar wedding, although the wedding itself is not what the story is about. This is one of the greatest stories of fate that I have ever witnessed.

As we all left base camp in our 4x4s for the overnight visit to the wedding, we drove over very rough terrain for over four hours (something we were getting quite used to by now). Like our initial journey to the camp, our vehicles struggled with the extreme conditions. Yet, typical of our luck, it was when we were truly in the middle of nowhere, when we hadn't seen a hut or any sign of human life for hours on end, when our 4x4 began to stutter and stall. Our hearts sank. The local driver kept nursing the engine for another few hundred metres until eventually it completely packed up. The extraordinary thing was *where* the vehicle came to a halt. It stopped literally outside the only mud hut for miles and miles. As we waited for support from the other vehicles following way behind, we got out to stretch our legs.

As you can imagine, we were hardly on a busy route where vehicles regularly passed, so the people who lived in the hut were astonished by what had turned up on their doorstep – not only the huge Land Cruiser jeep, but also a load of strangely dressed white people. Remember, Afar land is certainly no tourist trap.

The head of the family unfurled the flap of the hut's door and stuck his head out. Our local driver greeted him and explained that we had broken down and were waiting for help. Noticing us, the slightly bewildered man spoke up and asked the driver if we had any medicine. We had better than that, we had Doctor Mukul and Steve. It's a fact that Veterinary Surgeons have a wide range of medical training, but choose to specialize in animal physiology.

The man then asked if they would go in and see his son, who was very sick. Of course, it was the least they could do, as we were likely to be there a while anyway. Not wanting to overwhelm the family, only a few of us followed Mukul and Steve inside. The hut was dark, hot and very smoky. It took a little while for our eyes to adjust to the darkness, but as they did, there on the floor, sat on a reed mat, was a woman with a very small, incredibly thin and sick-looking little boy. It really was the scene of the all-too-familiar heart-wrenching 'charity' video. The toddler was literally just skin and bones. You could practically make out his entire skeleton, and his rolling eyes were sunk into his little skull. Mukul's face dropped, as he was not entirely sure that he would be able to help a child who was so far gone. Still, he lovingly crouched onto the floor and examined the boy.

One of the first things he realized was that the child had little potted burn marks all over his body, so through our driver (now acting as translator), he asked the parents what they were. The answer was horrifying. Part of Afar traditional medicine is to burn the skin of the sick, in order to banish the evil spirits.

By no fault of their own, this was what they had been brought up to believe, so there was no judging them for this. Mukul sensitively carried on with his examination.

To his astonishment, Mukul diagnosed that the child was critically dehydrated, to the extent of being extremely close to dying. In fact, he said to us, that the boy may only live for a few more days, if that. He wasn't entirely sure whether he could help at this late stage, but there was no question that he would try.

Mukul returned to the vehicle to fetch his medical kit. Returning into the hut he sat, looked at the little figure on the ground, and started to search for a vein. The idea was that it would be best to put the boy on an intravenous saline drip and get large amount of liquids into his system as quickly as possible. Finding a vein proved almost impossible as his little body was so desperately thin. Interestingly, Steve suggested that there was a method that they sometimes used with animals when you couldn't find a vein and that was to go in through the groin. Mukul said that he had heard of this, yet had never had to do it. So, with still no luck finding a vein, they had no other option but to try the groin.

The child was so far gone that he didn't even flinch when the needle went into his parched skin. The bag of liquid was attached to the tube and then Mukul explained to the parents that when this bag was empty that they should attach this other one that he would leave with them.

We knew that the following day we would be returning this way, so Mukul said he would drop in and see how they were getting on. The parents were still totally overwhelmed by the whole goings-on, but were immensely grateful for the help.

Outside, we stood for a few minutes more, talking while the car engine was being fixed. Mukul was very moved as he told us on camera that the truth of the matter was that the boy would likely not make it through that night! This left us all very quiet and sombre as we reflected once again on the harshness of life out here in the Danakil.

Minutes later, the engine was running again and we headed off to the wedding.

The following day, as promised, we retraced our route in order to visit the family again.

Getting out of the car, we half-dreaded hearing the result of what had happened to the child overnight. Mukul and Steve went into the hut. This time we respectfully stayed outside. The mood was unusually, but understandably, quiet. A few minutes later the door flap opened up and Mukul, Steve and the father, carrying the child, came out. We had to take a second look to be sure of what we saw. The boy looked completely different... he had put on so much weight as his body had guzzled up the much-needed fluids. He actually looked pretty healthy. His cheekbones had disappeared back under plump cheeks and his face had morphed back from being gaunt and ghostly to the look of a normal Afar child of his age. It was a miraculous transformation. Needless to say the parents were again overwhelmed, only this time with joy and gratitude. All of us who witnessed the event were deeply moved and elated.

Mukul was thrilled, but very humbly was quick to state that

all he did was very simply get liquids back into the child's body. But, what *was* miraculous was the fact that yesterday we broke down right on their doorstep. If our engine hadn't stopped, we would have driven on by and the boy would almost certainly have died.

One of the problems that caused the boy's rapid deterioration was violent diarrhoea (an extremely common problem in the developing world), so Mukul left the family with some drugs that would help the boy's recovery and also reminded them of the importance of finding as clean water as they could.

This whole event was truly amazing and one of my highlights of the whole expedition.

On our last day back at base camp in Kusra Wad, we said our goodbyes and thank yous to all those locals who had generously shared their lives with us over the last two weeks. It had been a real privilege to gain such an insight into the Afar way of life. It was sad to be leaving Golissa, his family and the village behind, but was also nice to be moving on to a new change of scenery.

Soon we were heading off to hook up with the splinter group again, before facing the climax of what would be the final leg of our epic expedition, climbing to the summit of the famous Erta Ale volcano.

Our convoy of 4x4s drove east this time, to the foothills of the distant volcano.

As we approached the foreboding dark mountain, in the distance we saw a huge cloud of dust which was being kicked up by the other convoy of vehicles. Drawing up side by side, the horns were honking and arms were waving from the windows. In the wasteland at the base of the volcano we all jumped out of our 4x4s and shook hands, hugged and exchanged stories of what we had been up to over the last week. Smiles were plastered all over our faces and being reunited, our spirits were soaring.

The convoy, once again at full strength, headed off towards the dark grey foothills. Within an hour or so, we left the dirt and sand that we had become so accustomed to, and our tyres seemed to revel in the grip and firmness of the black volcanic rock that now formed our track.

It was like leaving one sandy planet and entering another made of rock. The further we twisted our way up into the foothills, the more the environment dramatically changed. Eventually we reached the spot where we were to build our final base camp. This is where we would spend the night, before setting off on foot, to scale the summit of Erta Ale – also known as 'The Smoking Mountain'.

This new camp ground was built on a tough, half-rock and half-dirt surface, which was a most welcome break from the sand. Not only that, but we were surrounded with sporadic trees, adorned by tufts of long grass, the likes of which we hadn't seen for over two weeks. Despite having a very early start the following morning, that night we stayed up later than ever before, chatting away and laughing about funny things that had happened while the others were away. There was a real 'end of school' feeling in the camp.

It was around four-thirty in the morning when we left camp. We had an 18-kilometre climb to the summit ahead of us and it was imperative that we broke the back of it in the coolness of night.

With all our kit prepared the night before, we almost literally got up from where we had bedded down and started walking. As it was dark, we all wore our head torches and for the first hour or so I filmed on the small Canon camera, using its infrared setting. It was great to be walking again and seeing that this was the last part of our expedition there was a noticeable spring in our step. We shot some great footage of our kit carrying camel trains, numbering forty-five, their eyes being highlighted in the green and white coloured infrared footage. As a group, we set off at a steady pace and managed to sustain this for most of the climb. Shirley and I were on first filming shift, so we were darting past the walkers and the camels to run up ahead and get shots of them all passing by. Operating in the coolness, beating the sun to the break of day, seemed like a real novelty and a very welcome relief.

As the sun wearily woke up and started to raise its fiery head, it was soon Roo and Lloyd's turn to take over. When they did, Shirls and I were able to just enjoy the walk, carrying only our bum bags on our waists and day sacks on our backs.

Along the winding route, that traversed its way up the back of this vast volcano, Dougal was quick to point out what he called 'zits'. These were large bits of rock that had literally been pushed up by volcanic activity to make a huge lump. He likened it to a spot or zit. He also took great pleasure in pointing out 'bombs', which were large rocks, sat within a smashed hole of cooled lava crust (like a stone being thrown into a piece of meringue). He explained that these rocks would have been expelled, spat from the mouth of the volcano, flying high into the air and then landing with a bang where we saw them today. As he explained this to us, you could see members of the team nervously looking into the sky and half-expecting one to rain down on us any minute. Considering the distance of many kilometres that these rock bombs had travelled, this was quite a daunting thought. Volcanoes are dangerous places and should be treated with the upmost respect.

Many hours later, we arrived at the barren, rock-strewn summit. By now the sun was high in the sky and considering our gain in altitude, it definitely felt as though we were much closer to it – as it was considerably hotter up here. As we walked up to the edge of what looked like a crater, our breath was taken away by the sight before us.

Erta Ale has three craters at its summit. The northern crater is huge, probably about the size of a small town. It appears to have sunk about 50 metres into the ground and the surface that forms its interior is a massive expanse of nothing but grey/black cooled lava. At a number of points where the surface had cracked and broken, it bellowed sinister noxious gases, which appeared to be as innocent as just white smoke. Reminded of the team's fissure experience, we knew that this place was a 'wolf in sheep's clothing'.

The southern crater, which we were now standing high on the edge of, was a little smaller than its neighbour. It also had sunk down a good 30 metres and was made up of the same charcoal black lava surface, which resembled a very burnt, giant meringue. The main difference between the two was that this crater led out for a few hundred metres to yet another small crater. From what we could see from our vantage point, the third crater was only about 50 metres wide in diameter and appeared to disappear into what can only be described as an abyss. Rather strangely, from the small crater we could hear what sounded like crashing waves! The kind of sound you would normally hear along the coast, certainly not up here on the top of a dry, barren volcano. It was quite bizarre and somewhat unnerving.

As we waited for the forty-five camels to arrive with all our kit, we were told that the ground where we stood was going to be our main camp for the next two nights. As the camels arrived in dribs and drabs, we set about getting the three large cameras out and setting them up to start filming. Meanwhile, the Mountain Safety team skilfully climbed over the edge of the precipice that we were perched on, down onto the dark meringue surface below. There they set about trying to find a safe route for us to be able to walk across to the smaller crater. We watched as they bravely took steps over the layers of crust, never knowing how thin the layers were. These could at any minute crumble under their feet and drop them into who knows what? This was totally unchartered territory.

Before they put their full weight on their leading foot, they would stamp down to see if it cracked, which it often did. Effectively they were walking on eggshells with a potentially lethal yolk. In order to remember where their safely checked route was, they covered their tracks with snap light glow sticks. This way we should also be able to see the safe route clearly once the sun had set too.

It wasn't long before we were ready to film and by now we could see that the climbing team was just small figures in the distance. We stood and watched as they skirted their way around the distant small crater. They had done a brilliant, very brave job.

With all three big cameras fully rigged up, Roo, Lee and I took up different positions to film our team of experts arriving. One took a wide shot, another the close-up and the third a super-wide shot. By doing this, we hoped to portray just how vast and dramatic this summit was.

With the cue of "Action" shouted by Rupert, the team, who had backtracked 10 metres or so, turned and walked up to stand on the edge of the precipice, overlooking the outer crater. Standing in their positions they gasped and whooped at the scene in front of them (just as we had on our arrival). They then set out and talked about what the mission was for the next two days while up there.

The mission was ultimately to take another 3D scan of the

smaller crater, which had never been done before. This would be a 'scientific first' and would allow the science and geology community of the world to have a new insight into how the earth was moving and shifting over the years. That's what it sounded like to me anyway, although to be honest, I was more interested at that point in keeping my shot steady, the horizon level and my focus pin sharp. The bit of chat that really caught my attention was when they mentioned that in order to execute the best, most accurate scan possible, they were going to have to attempt to get Dougal and his equipment down into the belly of the crater itself. Now this, I thought, would be fun!

Happy with what he heard and saw, Rupert shouted, "Cut!", at which we stopped recording and took the heavy cameras off our shoulders. The next scene was going to be filming the team of experts walking out over the treacherous surface below to see the small crater up close. This of course meant that to film all this we camera and sound teams had to go first.

By now the climbing team had returned safely and were ready to guide us crews out onto the menacing meringue. As we stepped into our climbing harnesses, we were all given professional, heavy-duty gas masks to wear. Should we smell or start coughing on any gases we were to put these on immediately. One by one, our harnesses were checked over by the safety team, which was mandatory. As this happened, we were instructed as to which route we should take, according to where we needed to be positioned for our best shots. Typically our filming positions of choice were not going to be on the 'safe route', so each crew would be 'spotted' (looked after) by a member of the Mountain Safety team.

As with all filming of this nature, we camera crews tend to focus on our shots, rather than where we are putting our feet. The climbing team would therefore watch our feet for us and shout or grab us if we were about to put ourselves in grave danger.

The real success of a Mountain Safety team working in the television industry is understanding that the camera crews have to sometimes push the boundaries of safety in order to get the required shot. It is those Safety Experts who understand this fact and facilitate what we need to do in the safest way possible who get asked back. There was no fear of our current safety team not being willing to take high risks. They were all greatly experienced and highly skilled professionals, whom we literally put our lives in the hands of, without question.

To get down the cliff upon which our camp was perched, we had to carefully descend down a sheer, slender, rocky track which the climbing team had kicked out of the rocky face of the wall. They had bolted into the rock a number of anchor points upon which rope was threaded through karabiners. This gave us some kind of handrail on our way down. Safely nursing our large, heavy cameras and sound mixers down this was pretty tricky. Fortunately, we all made it down without incident. Even 'Calamity' (Justin) made it down in one piece.

Now we were on a level with the luna-like landscape before us. What we could see close up was the very unstable, fragile and unpredictable surface. Also, from here the crashing sound that we'd heard from the top grew louder and sounded more and more like a raging sea. What on earth was it? To say that at this point we felt safe and happy would be an outright lie. This was no disrespect to our safety team, but what lay before us surely had to be one of the most hostile natural environments on planet Earth.

We took our first steps very gingerly, being mindful, whenever possible, to stay rigidly on the clearly marked, tried and tested route. As your boot went down you could hear the crumble and crunch. Some of the ground underfoot was solid and stable, but most of it was actually not. As we started to venture off the tested ground to reach our camera positions, every now and then our feet would punch clumsily through some of the thinner parts. When this happened, your foot would crash through until it met a thicker, firm layer, often as deep as 30 centimetres below. Whenever this occurred, there was always a 'heart in your mouth' feeling, as you desperately hoped that you wouldn't be the one to stumble upon a cavernous bubble that trapped you in a bottomless black hole. Seriously, this was no place to fool around. This was completely unchartered ground and anything could be lurking below our feet.

With the help and guidance of our safety team, eventually all three crews were in place. We signalled by using walkie-talkies that we were set and ready to go. This time Rupe's call came over the airwaves, "Turn over please all cameras..." (start recording). In succession, we each buttoned on and replied, "Camera one is at speed" etc. (confirming that our cameras were rolling). "Thank you cameras, standby... and... ACTION!" Again, all in our separate positions, one on a long lens, one wide and the other taking a profile wide shot, we all filmed and followed the 'Talent' as they followed the safe route, previously marked out.

Before they could reach the small, mystery crater's edge, we held them just far away enough so they couldn't see in. We wanted to film their reactions as naturally as possible. However, despite them not being able to *see* anything, there was no doubt that they could hear the ever-increasing sound, 'Whoosh', 'Crash' and 'Boom!' Strange oceanic sounds. They stood stunned, half-mesmerized and half-terrified at what lay before them. This gave us crews the chance to quickly move into our final positions for the big reveal.

Roo and Lee took off with their soundmen to positions further around the crater's edge. Shirley and I were to be the ones closest to the team as they stepped up to the edge and then looked down into the crater for the first time. I was to capture both a profile shot and then a P.O.V. (point of view – what they were seeing). In order to do this we would need to be situated as close to the edge as possible.

Before finally finding my resting spot for the camera and tripod, to quench our growing fascination of what was down there, Shirley and I went over to take a peek over the edge.

To say that what we saw was breathtaking would be both literal, but also a gross understatement. As we stepped close to the very edge, a huge waft of heat rushed up and pushed us backwards. It was like 'The Gara' (Wind of Fire) times by ten. We both reeled back, shouted, and gasped in both surprise and horror.

Now knowing what to expect, we edged forward again. It felt as though we had opened a huge oven door and the heat was searing our fragile human bodies. The sight before us I shall never forget for the rest of my life. We were standing right on the very edge of what was like a giant black cauldron. Beneath our feet was a drop of about 50 metres, down to what is best described by the Afar people, who call it 'The Gateway to Hell'!

Deep inside this crater was a large shelf of more dried lava which led to the side where yet another smaller depression stepped down. In this dip was an open, active, sea of black, bright orange and fire-red lava. This deadly pool, which measured in diameter around 20 metres, splashed and bubbled, bright orange, pure liquid lava. It literally splashed and gushed in waves as the poisonous gases forced their way from the centre of the earth and through the surface of this 1,000°C boiling soup. The surface kept breaking and bursting; the gases blew like the desperate gasps of a drowning man. It was, without a shadow of doubt, the most terrifying sight I had ever laid my eyes on. In the truest sense of the word – awesome.

We were totally dumbstruck and had to consciously pull ourselves together before turning our minds back to the job in hand. Andy, our designated member of the climbing team, anchored some heat-proof rope away from the edge, which he then attached to my climbing harness. This allowed me to manoeuvre the tripod closer to the foreboding, craggy edge in relative safety.

Normally I would attach a safety line to the camera and the tripod, but with limited lines available, on this occasion if my camera fell, so be it. There was no way I was going in with it!

As I positioned myself on the 'wrong' side of the camera, standing between the camera and just a few inches from the sheer drop, great plumes of noxious gases came charging up the cliff by my feet. Almost instantaneously both Shirley and I started to choke. We quickly fitted our gas masks. This was not a sensible place to be standing and the sooner this big reveal shot was done, the sooner we could move to safety and fresher air.

Fortunately it was only seconds later that all the cameras were in position and the call to action was heard over the radio. As we filmed the team walking up and seeing the sight that we had just witnessed, I suddenly realized that the intense heat was radiating through the rock and penetrating through the soles of my boots. So, while I filmed, I literally had to alternate lifting my feet up off the rock in order to be able to remain standing there.

Not surprisingly, the team's reaction was similar to ours, disbelief and being almost frightened by the power of this, the world's oldest active lava lake.

Roo and Lee shot the revealing wide pullout shot and the view from the opposite side of the crater. Put together, along with my profile and P.O.V, the edited sequence was truly awe-inspiring.

Minutes later "Cut" echoed out from the walkie-talkies. Without a moment's delay I picked up the tripod, with the camera still attached, and pushed it away from the edge. I had never been so glad to finish a shot before.

There was plenty more fun to be had at the Gateway to Hell over the next few days, so we all made our way back across the lava meringue and back up the cliff to camp.

The truth is, the camp was hardly the safest of places to be either, but after what we'd just witnessed, it seemed like the safest place on earth.

The problem we now faced was that it was now around midday and the heat of the sun had become a real issue. This place was completely unrelenting. All filming was called to a halt, as on the summit there was literally no shade at all. Even the camels, who carried our kit up, had to return back down the volcano as there was absolutely nothing alive up there for them to eat, so not even camel shade was available. With a concerted team effort, we all concentrated on creating our own shade by using some old tarpaulins and odd ends of rope. Before too long, we had created a low-slung, Bedouin-style tent. It wasn't pretty but it worked. Following some food, made by the local chef who had brilliantly constructed a makeshift kitchen nearby, we all took a long, well-deserved siesta.

It had been a long, hot, exhausting day, yet before the sun went down it was imperative that we made the usual effort to find our personal bags. We would need to sort our kit out, and especially find our all-important head torches, before the blanket of darkness was pulled over us once more. The safety team wisely made a point of rigging more snap stick glow lights to along the edge of the cliff. One night when you go for a pee you risk being shot, the next you potentially fall 30 metres to your death! After spending some time in such a place as the Danakil, these potentially dangerous factors soon become quite matter of fact. By this point in time, we had already been living in the hottest place on earth for almost three weeks. There was nothing more that could surprise us... or so we thought!

At night, in the safety of our camp perched high on the cliff's edge, we could no longer see the lava field below that separated us from the Gateway to Hell. However, we could easily make out the bright red glow of the active lava lake, which was illuminated against the contrast of the black of night. It was a beautiful sight, although, as we lay in our gravelly beds on the ground, with our eyes shut, we were still constantly reminded of our sinister surroundings by the ever-present splashing and booming echoing from the never sleeping, hellish pit.

As usual we slept in small groups, although as flat ground was at a premium up here, we all lay in fairly close proximity to one another. We had become so accustomed to sleeping out under the stars that we would fall into deep sleep within minutes of resting our heads. One by one we all slipped off into our own world of fiery dreams.

It was a matter of only a few hours later when I felt my shoulder being shaken by a hand. I jumped in shock and quickly spun around while opening my eyes to see who was touching me. To my relief, it was Alex. Before I could ask him what he was doing, I heard lots of people choking. In his cool, calm voice, Alex told me that the gasometer alarm was going off and that we would all have to get up and move further down the volcano. I went to grunt my recognition of the message, but then started to choke myself. I watched through strained, bleary eyes as Alex quickly did the same to everyone. He really is a good bloke, I thought, and thankfully a light sleeper while bearing the responsibility of all our safety.

In the faint moonlight, zombie-like figures could just be

made out, staggering around and tripping on rocks. These shapes cursed as they lifted their thin mattresses and a few of their belongings, all the while choking on the foul, dangerous air. A few hundred metres down the slope, Alex referred to his gasometer and gave us the thumbs up, saying that we should be safe to sleep here. So, like kids who had been sleepwalking, we pretty much dropped whatever we were carrying, lay on the spot and fell straight back to sleep. Throughout the night the odd cough could still be heard.

The following morning we found out that dear old Alex had stayed up all night, in order to watch over us and the gasometer. A true hero!

If the blazing sun, immense heat, dangerous rock falls or the lava itself didn't get you... it would be the lethal gases. We drew the conclusion that Erta Ale certainly did not welcome any of its intrepid visitors.

The next day was busy. We were already on a bit of a back foot due to the broken night's sleep. One or two had fallen ill again overnight and I noticed that my 'buddy', Shirley, didn't seem quite himself. It wasn't his mumbling, he always did that. He wasn't being grumpy, Shirley rarely is. It was more that he just went really quiet. I kept asking him, "Are you alright, Shirls?" to which he would mumble, "Yes, yes, I'm fine, thanks." But I knew him well and it was clear that he wasn't fine. As previously instructed way back, before heading off from our first camp, I went and told Alex that Shirls seemed out of sorts. Alex and I agreed that it may just have been a rough night, due to the moving and coughing, but we would keep a special eye on him.

The day carried on, much as the day before, traversing over the lava landscape, filming various experiments and interviews. Dougal, who was really the main focus up the volcano, was

Man Vs Arctic

Another day in the office with Bear

The A-Team (crew with Bear Grylls)

Hottest Place on Earth crew convoy

Roo and special camera cover

The salt mines

Mungo and Shirley

Dougal's triumphant volcanic lunge

On the edge of the gateway to hell

Sailing into Darwin, Australia, having survived the stormy crossing of the Timor Sea

Ural sidecar, Georgia

We made it to Australia! Alive and kicking

The finish line - Sydney, Australia

Airport hell

Freddie Goes Wild – Beer o'clock - Tanzania, Africa

Goat dispatch

Camp logistics

Satellite phone & battery chargers

Filming the bow wave – Borneo

Team photo – Arnhem Land, Australia

Searching for orangutans

Leeches feed on my leg

Messy work in the jungle

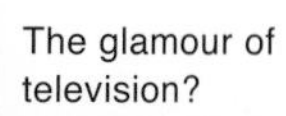

The glamour of television?

filmed by crews on staggered shifts throughout the day. We covered him setting up his expensive, state-of-the-art scanning equipment and attempting the huge task of creating a 3D scan of the outer crater of the Gateway to Hell. Later that day he moved closer to the smaller crater and managed to take a successful scan of that too. He did this from the top edges that we had first stood on the previous afternoon. This whole process took pretty much the whole day and it wasn't until supper when we all crowded around his special rugged laptop and viewed his day's work. It was fantastic to see the scans and showed us a great example of what amazing technology is now available to scientists. Which is just as well, because in science, there is still *much* to learn.

That night, Shirls was still out of sorts. So, as we kicked the rocks away from our bedding down site, I asked him again how he was. Finally he admitted that he had been "shitting through the eye of a needle" all day and also the previous night. Shirley is a quiet, reserved chap, and unlike me who wants the world to know about my bowel movements, Shirls preferred to just suffer quietly. At least with this knowledge, Alex and I were able to make sure that he got more rest and took on plenty of liquid, including Dioralyte. Often under these circumstances, in such conditions, a problem shared is a problem halved. As we settled down for the night, I enjoyed ribbing him about his covert excursions to crouch behind an unfortunate rock and together we made jokes about how hard it was up here to find a pot to piss (through your arse) in etc. It was horrible for him, but as with everyone else who had been sick, he stoically soldiered on.

Mercifully the second night was gas-free, apart from of course the odd camp bugle, which was always blamed on the chef's cooking!

Unsurprisingly, we woke to yet another glorious day of bright sunshine and punishing heat. Not even the weathermen could have gotten *this* forecast wrong! The only saving grace was that all being well, this was our last day of filming.

The plan on this final day was to spend the morning lowering Dougal and his equipment into the lower hellish crater, to attempt part two of the scan. Once down on the lava shelf, he would do the scan and then, finally, attempt to throw a temperature probe into the fiery lava lake itself. In the afternoon, we would pack up camp, rendezvous with the camels and make our descent back down to the original base camp in the foothills.

After a makeshift breakfast we filled our water bottles, prepared our camera kits and put on our climbing harnesses, making sure to attach the gas masks. Before we knew it, we were all back on the perilous path over the lava field and arriving at the hellish cauldron.

We three camera crews resumed similar positions to the first day's filming. Though thankfully, this time I didn't have a profile shot to do. This meant that I was able to place my tripod and camera a good 2 metres back from the edge. Andy made sure that I was tied in again, just in case. Shirley and I now had some waiting to do before the others had reached their positions.

This time, most of the real action was going to be happening on the other side of the crater. So, I had a long lens attached to my camera, which enabled me to film what those directly opposite couldn't see happening below them.

I only knew what actually went on over there, having seen the footage afterwards. But what I did know was that everything seemed to take an *extremely* long time.

One of my favourite moments from the rushes of that far camera position was when Dougal, who was fully rigged up in his abseiling harness and helmet, was just going over the edge of the far crater wall. As he leaned out, putting his weight onto the abseil rope, he looked up and said to Kate and Steve, "Smoke me a kipper; I'll be back for breakfast!"

He then lowered himself all the way down to the upper shelf of the inner crater. I filmed his every move from my high position around 50 metres away on the other side of the crater.

Abseiling down alongside Dougal went Rupert, who took the small Canon camera to film him at the lava level and also Steve (Dougal's assistant). Before any of these guys had abseiled down, Andy, from the climbing team, was the unsung hero and descended first to test the rig and check for lethal gases. Having paved the way for the others, Andy now patiently waited at the bottom.

For the remaining hours of the morning (which felt like days!), the four guys meticulously carried out their work. The heavy scanning equipment was lowered down by rope and they carefully walked around the treacherous volcanic shelf. Without any doubt, the stakes were high. It was far more likely deep down there that one of them could easily walk over a thin volcanic tube that could swallow them straight into the fiery pit below. When they started to walk around, it was nerve-wracking to watch from above.

There have been many times when I have been filming something thinking this could be disastrous, but this time there was an added, almost sinister feel to it. The pit was so volatile and other-worldly that it felt as though we were almost tempting fate.

Deep in the crater, Dougal and his assistant Steve worked hard, as Rupert filmed them and Andy watched over them all.

Meanwhile, we all stood high up on the cauldron lip above. The hours slowly ticked by and we were all roasting in the unforgiving sun. After a while, hunger, thirst and the general discomfort of standing up on our rocky ledge got to us. Whenever it appeared that the guys below were flapping around, Shirls and I started to shout down into the crater "Come on, Dougal, get on with it!" As the time went on, the abuse from above became far more fragrant. Fortunately, they couldn't hear us over the splashing and wheezing of the lava lake. This ended up becoming quite amusing, so we upped the abuse more and more to try and make them react.

Once that game died a death, we went back to silently stewing on our perch. It had been literally hours now that we had all been stood out in the searing heat. We were frustrated because we knew we had limited time allowing us to still be able to make it down the volcano later that day.

Eventually, the scan was complete – thank God. So, while Steve and Andy dismantled the equipment and started to get it raised back up to the team above, Dougal finally donned his 'space suit', which could withstand stupidly high temperatures. What with the surface of the lava he was walking on and now wearing a special white protective suit, complete with helmet, he literally looked like an astronaut.

Rupert took up a filming position on Dougal's level, as the rest of us filmed from high above. Dougal began to walk cautiously towards the hissing and spitting lava lake. This was without doubt the most dangerous part of the entire expedition. No one knew just what would happen from here on in. He had a safety line attached to his harness, but even that would be of little use, should he fall into the lake. Dougal was literally risking his life to throw the temperature probe into the bright orange, bubbling lava. If successful, again this would be a scientific first, so the cameras were rolling and the pressure was on.

Closer and closer he tentatively edged towards the shelf's lip. Up above, we and our radios fell silent. We all focused our attention on making sure we were filming what was about to happen. Dougal was a matter of 1 or 2 metres away from the edge when we could see that he was pulling out the probe and positioning it for the throw. Over the radio microphone monitor we heard him say, "Here we go... one... two... THREE!" With that he threw the probe underarm, all of 5 metres! It fell down towards the lake, but fell short by a long way and then got snagged on a rock. The throw was worthy of that more commonly seen at a primary school sports day. Seeing that the probe was now snagged, his one attempt at this was blown. Mercifully, from where Dougal was standing, he couldn't hear the jovial cursing and laughter that rained down from above. I hasten to add that the ribbing we gave was all in good fun, as no one could take it away from Dougal that he had balls of steel to even be down there. I'm not sure if I would have fancied taking that risk, just for the sake of science!

Thankfully, all was not lost. Dougal had still achieved a 'first' for science by executing a magnificent 3D scan from the inside of the oldest active lava lake in the world. Despite the crap throw at the end, the whole team's effort had ended up being well worthwhile.

As "Cut" was called, we were finally able to move away from the edge of the crater and then carefully make our way back to camp. Through our training we tried to concentrate on being careful, as this was the time when accidents were most likely to happen, when we relaxed, tired and relieved that it was all over. Even though there were only 'final interviews' to shoot, we knew that we couldn't switch off from all the dangers that still surrounded us.

A couple of hours later, we were all safely back in camp. It was now early afternoon and we were all completely knackered, not only physically, but also emotionally. It was so hot, and we were keen to break camp and get moving on our long descent down the volcano. But, as always, another challenge raised its ugly head.

The complexity of abseiling the team in and out of the small crater had made us run quite a few hours behind schedule. This resulted in our water supplies, which had been carefully rationed, running out. This was not just unfortunate and uncomfortable, but also extremely dangerous. We were told that the water that we had remaining in our bottles would have to last until we reached base camp at the bottom of the volcano. Some had more than others, so the team were careful to share evenly what supplies we had left. With the 18-kilometre descent still ahead of us, this would be tough. At least this time we were heading downhill.

Some of the camels hadn't yet arrived at the top and we were keen to start getting people off the volcano, so the team split in two. The first group descended, while the others stayed with the valuable kit to make sure it left the summit safely.

Now that the team had massively decreased in numbers, the camel herders, who had returned to the summit that morning, saw this as an opportunity. To cut a long story short, they knew that they had us between a rock and a hard place (literally). So they, and their forty-five camels, decided to go on strike. They said that they would only bring all the kit back down the volcano if we paid them more money. Tired and thirsty, our tempers began to fray. Long discussions with the herders became heated, that was until one of them cocked their AK-47 rifle. At that point, we knew that we were fighting a losing battle. We finally agreed to pay more, and for the sake of a few extra hundred dollars, it certainly wasn't worth getting shot for, but the blackmailing smarted.

In retrospect, when not in the predicament of being stranded in 45°C heat on the summit of a volcano in Africa... you can sort of see their point. Wanting to squeeze more money from the rich Western film crew. Put in the locals' situation with an AK-47, I may well have tried it myself.

It was a few more hours until we eventually left the summit in the mid-afternoon heat. It was now a race of time, to get down as quickly as possible. Those of us in the remaining group made sure that we had our head torches close to hand, as the chances were we would finish our descent in darkness.

The journey down was tough and seemed never-ending. Yet, as we knew the shoot was now officially 'wrapped' (ended) we managed to dig into deep reserves of banter and witty humour which kept us amused and entertained until we finally staggered into base camp.

The advance party had kindly prepared bowls of water and soap for us to freshen up in, plus there was piping hot, fresh food waiting in pans. Although better than the chance to wash, or even the delicious food, was the ample supply of fresh bottled water. Never before had it felt so good to get some water down our severely parched throats.

The usual boost of energy from food soon kicked in and the atmosphere in camp was understandably jovial, as the whole expedition had proved to be a complete success. The science experiments had been ticked off. The filming had been challenging, but we had in the can some truly epic footage. Yet, most of all, with all credit to Alex, Duncan, Mukul and the Mountain Safety team, we were all alive and in one piece.

Looking back at where we had been and what we had been up to, the odds were highly stacked against us. This was truly unchartered territory, upon which we faced some of the most extreme elements of the natural world, and we had made it through. Professionalism and attention to detail, coupled with teamwork and friendship, had succeeded. What a great achievement by all.

Even though we slept very well that night, we were acutely aware that we were still a number of days away from civilization and we weren't quite out of trouble yet.

Early the following morning we loaded the 4x4s and began our exodus from Afar land. The journey out would take us over two full days of driving, the majority of it off-road. As always, it was hot, dusty and very bumpy. For those who were still sick, it must have been horrific. Soundman Pete was particularly ill over these two days and his car had to constantly pull over, allowing Pete to go and crouch in the bushes. He continued to push liquids down his neck, but his body's system just couldn't retain it. Slipping into serious dehydration, the companions who travelled in the car with him grew very concerned.

That night, after a brutal drive, we camped in a sort of makeshift rural motel (the term 'motel' used very loosely). A few stark, concrete buildings were situated in a walled compound, which encircled a few decrepit, very basic rooms. In these rooms were beds. Yes, proper wooden beds. These were the first actual beds that we had seen in over three weeks. It was funny to think that we had only been there for three *weeks*, because it honestly felt like *months*.

We were as excited as kids at Christmas, laying on the beds and sighing out loud, as you do when you're slipping into a hot bath. It was luxury. Miraculously, there were enough beds for the whole team. However, having grown so used to sleeping outside, one by one we all started to drag our beds out of the rooms and into the dusty, dirty courtyard. We felt much happier back out in the open air, and there under the stars we slept in our real beds.

The owner of this remote, rural establishment couldn't believe his luck. He probably hadn't had any business for months (if not years) when suddenly a huge convoy of 4x4s full of dirty, smelly, bedraggled Westerners rock up and ask to rent all his rooms for the night. To our astonishment and delight, he disappeared for a while and then returned with a crate of Coca-Cola bottles and even a few beers! This was a moment we had been dreaming and talking about for weeks. The taste of the beer was that night pure amber nectar.

Aside from all the revelry of having a few drinks, the consolation for the poor few who were sick was that at least they got an early night in a real bed.

The next day we were back in the vehicles. The further we drove, we noticed that the temperatures were getting lower and even becoming quite pleasant. The welcome sensation of cool air helped us to bear the seemingly never-ending drive, which was finally rewarded by hitting tarmac. Again, like the beds, the joy of these experiences cannot be underestimated. To be driving on a smooth road meant no dust, no bumps and most importantly that we could dramatically increase our speed. We could now gain more ground and make our way back to civilization quicker.

Even with almost half a day on the asphalt roads, frustratingly we still couldn't make Mekele. So, we had to stay yet another night out. This time we were put up in what appeared to be a school building complex, where we had no option but to sleep in rooms, which took quite some adjusting to. Sleeping outside, no matter how hot it was, you could feel even the slightest breath of a breeze. Imprisoned back within four walls felt terribly claustrophobic.

It was on this night that poor Pete really hit rock bottom. His dehydration had now advanced into a raging fever. So, Alex and Mukul spent a great deal of time at his bedside. They even took some of his blood to perform a malaria test, which fortunately was negative. He was plied with more liquids and some drugs that were available from the medics.

Fortunately the next morning Pete was looking a lot better. He still had dodgy guts and remained very weak from his ordeal, but it looked as if the fever had passed during the night. Even though we were now touching the outskirts of real civilization, our Western bodies were still so vulnerable to this foreign land.

Two and a half days after leaving Erta Ale, we finally arrived back at Mekele Airport. We checked in our filthy, war-torn luggage and said our thank yous and goodbyes to our team of local Fixers and drivers.

The short flight back to Addis Ababa was mostly spent looking at the back of our eyelids.

Before catching our flights and returning to the UK, we had one more night to spend back in the capital city of Addis. We checked back into the same hotel we spent our first night in, where we all retired to our individual rooms, with the plan to meet up for supper later that evening.

Entering my room, I threw my bag onto the ground. It landed, making a large cloud of Afar dust. This sanitized, pristine room was a whole world away from where we had spent our last three weeks. As I ran the shower, I thought of Golissa and his family still out there, living how they and their ancestors over many generations had before them. That was *their* world, but *this* is mine.

I practically peeled my heavily soiled clothes from my body and left them in a rancid pile on the floor. Walking into the bathroom, I sat on the toilet. I didn't need to go, but I just sat on it because I could. Following that pleasure, I stood and sat in the blissfully hot shower for the longest duration that I had ever showered before. It took me about three attempts to properly wash the grime, dust and dirt from my skin and then out of my matted hair and beard. I then spent about half an hour cutting my long stubble with my Leatherman scissors, before even attempting to put a razor to it.

A few hours later I walked out of that bathroom, feeling and looking like a new man.

That evening, we all sat at a long table in a nice restaurant and enjoyed a celebratory meal and some sensationally cold beers. The expedition was officially over.

Arriving back into London Heathrow Airport, we were delighted to be met by the Lion TV Production Team, including the big boss himself – Richard. In all my years in the business, I had never been welcomed home by a Production Team. Normally I was just greeted by a mini-cab driver holding my name up on a handwritten sign. Not only had they formed a welcoming party, but they also distributed to each member of our team a fancy bottle of champagne. A lovely, thoughtful touch to show their appreciation of our hard work.

Leaving the terminal to walk to the car park was another huge shock to the system. It was mid December and the temperatures were freezing. The contrast from where we had lived for the last three weeks was certainly extreme.

When I finally arrived home to my flat in Wandsworth, I had to turn the central heating up to full power, but even that wasn't sufficient. So, I had to go and put more layers of clothing on. Having acclimatized to life in the hottest place on earth, our poor bodies would now have to readjust to the cold, bleak British winter. I sat on my sofa, wrapped in clothes, wearing a hat and my Ugg boots, thinking about where I had just been and all that we had shared and seen. There was no doubt that I was living life to the full!

It was a very cold, but very merry Christmas.

4

IRELAND TO SYDNEY – BY ANY MEANS

FEATURING: CHARLEY BOORMAN & RUSS MALKIN

It was midweek and I was at home when my mobile phone rang. The display said 'Unknown Number'. Who could this be? Hitting the 'Accept' button, I had no idea just how big answering this call would be, or the truly once in a lifetime opportunity it would offer me.

"Hi, is that Mungo?" said the girl. "My name is Jo and I'm calling from Big Earth Productions. We made *Long Way Round* and *Long Way Down* and we're looking for a Director of Photography (Cameraman) for our next expedition and we've found your CV and would really like to meet you."

Long Way Round and *Long Way Down*, I thought to myself... this was the call that all cameramen who work on the adventure circuit wanted to receive.

"Hi Jo. Thanks for the call. Yes, I'd love to come in and meet with you." I knew this could be a golden opportunity.

Jo then went on to invite me to meet them at their office/

warehouse in Avonmore Road, Olympia, London. I had seen this place on television, which acted as the HQ base for the *Long Way Round* and *Long Way Down* TV series, where Ewan McGregor (Scottish-born, Hollywood movie star) and Charley Boorman (previous actor) prepared and set out on their epic motorcycling trips.

The back story is that Charley had been acting in a stage play alongside Ewan. Spending so much time together it soon became apparent that they shared a passion for all things motorbikes. They talked about bikes, tinkered with them and dreamed up amazing journeys that one day they could do together. One of those was a trip riding from London to New York (certainly not just a nice ride in the countryside). Around that time, the two boys attended a friend's party where they bumped into Russ Malkin (Big Earth Productions) who, after hearing the grand plan, suggested that they should make it into a TV series and he would be willing to help them produce it. The rest, as they say, is history.

Trip one, the *Long Way Round* (LWR) was a thoroughbred motorcycle expedition. This documentary followed Ewan and Charley as their dream became a reality, as they rode their BMW motorbikes from London to New York. The route they chose was the road less travelled, through Eastern Europe, Russia, Mongolia and then crossing over to Alaska and riding all the way down through Canada, Northern America to finally arriving in New York. Overnight this became an iconic television series and subsequently firmly grounded them both as global celebrity motorcycle adventurers.

Trip two, the *Long Way Down* (LWD) followed on from the success of LWR. This time they rode from John O'Groats in Scotland to Cape Town, South Africa. This route took them all the way down through Europe and then down the whole length of Africa – no small feat.

Claudio von Planta had been recruited as the Cameraman who would join the boys on these first two expeditions. This was one of the most enviable jobs, as he also got to ride a BMW GS motorbike throughout the trips. One of the most amazing facts about Claudio's recruitment for this role was that at the time of being interviewed, he didn't have a motorcycle licence! This was the point at which other Cameramen were up in arms and green with envy. Yet, to Claudio's credit, he subsequently took his motorcycle test (under quite some pressure) and passed.

He was rightfully highly praised for the work he achieved while being on the road. It was no easy task seeing that it was just Ewan, Charley and he, left on their own for the majority of time. He was also heavily featured in the iconic road trip film.

Having watched Claudio's involvement meant that I was fully aware of what a great opportunity this could be for me, not only for an adventure of a lifetime, but also to put my name as a Cameraman on the map (as it had done for Claudio). Being associated with this previously hugely successful TV series could not be at all bad for business.

Within a few days I found myself stood at the door of the famous warehouse. I decided that it would be a wise move to ride my BMW GS1150 motorbike to the meeting, as it would show that I was 'one of them'! With my crash helmet in one hand and my gloves in the other, I rang the doorbell. I was welcomed in by a pretty girl who led me through to a seated area in the main warehouse space. This cavernous space was every boy's dream. It was full of motorbikes (including the actual ones ridden by Ewan and Charley on the previous expeditions), large tool carts, skateboards, a pool table, musical instruments and even a few cars, including the Nissan 4x4 which was used as the support vehicle on LWD. The room smelled of petrol and it wasn't precious, just practical – which in my eyes was perfect.

This truly was the place of dreams for big boys with big toys and I definitely wanted to be a part of it.

Pretty soon I was led into a meeting room where Lucy (Producer) and Jo (Production Co-ordinator – whom I had spoken to on the phone) were sat. A few seconds later, Russ swept in.

Those who know or have met Russ Malkin will, I'm sure, agree that he is a force of nature. He is in his early fifties, although he honestly looks at least five years younger. He is charismatic, vivacious and certainly loves to talk. I was quick to get the impression that Russ doesn't like to hang around. He is a 'do-er' and doesn't suffer fools gladly. This meeting was to suss me out and see not only if I was capable of the job in hand, but as importantly, see if I was a character that they would get on with.

Russ set the scene. The plan was *not* to do another *Long Way Round/Down* as Ewan was busy filming movies. This time Charley was going it alone. In order to make this work, they would have to change things a bit. So, rather than just being limited to motorbikes, Charley would use a whole range of transport. The overall concept was born from a discussion between Charley and Russ while on a flight home from an event in Valencia, Italy. They had come up with the idea of crossing the world (literally) using all different forms of vehicles, synonymous with the country they were in. Travelling from Wicklow, Ireland (Charley's home town) to Sydney, Australia – 'By Any Means'.

Practically, the idea was to scale the team right down. The base in London would still work as the HQ for the trip, but this time there would only be three people on the road; Charley, Russ and one other... the Cameraman. This was obviously the role for which I was being interviewed.

The real issue with a trip of this magnitude was not so much the practical and technical aspects of 'one man banding' (one person filming, recording sound, dealing with the footage/media etc.), which obviously presented lots of challenges, but rather the length of time that this epic journey would take. The Production Team estimated that it would take at least four months to complete. This is where they became stuck with regards to finding a Cameraman.

Having talked through my experience (at the time) of over fifteen years in the job and having filmed in over fifty countries, there was little doubt that I was experienced enough or capable of the camerawork. So, they asked me if I would be able to leave home for four months. Fortunately, I was able to say, "Yes."

There are plenty of good camera operators out there, but the more experienced ones tend to be older, thus being more likely to be married or have family commitments. For people in this domestic situation, to get up and go away for four months just wouldn't be a realistic option.

Responding further to this question, I added, "This is what I do! I think you will struggle to find someone with my level of experience who can just get up and leave for that length of time. There may well be many drawbacks to being single in your late thirties, however, there are also some benefits. I have no ties, no responsibilities and no dependents."

This seemed to be exactly what they wanted to hear. After a bit more discussion about what the intended route would entail and the various modes of transport Charley would be likely to use, I offered my suggestions of how I would film it all. After a short while enough had been said. So, we said our thank yous and goodbyes and I left them to make their decision. Apparently they were seeing a few more people, but they would be in touch very soon.

Leaving the warehouse and returning to my motorbike, I felt that I had done my very best and believed that I was definitely the man for the job. It just seemed to fit. Yet, even though it seemed obvious to me, who knew who was next in the door? It could well be one of my mates. I rode the short journey home, desperately willing for them to choose me.

The next day my phone rang again. It was Jo. I held my breath. She said that they really liked me and were keen that I should now go to the next step and meet Charley. After all, seeing that he and the Cameraman would be pretty much living in each other's pockets for four months, it was crucial that he felt comfortable with whoever they should choose. She said that the following week they had arranged a day for Charley and Russ to learn to sail on the south coast, so could I get the kit together (the same camera equipment that I would choose to use for the trip – should I get the job) and spend the day filming them having their sailing lesson? This would test how I worked, how we worked together as a 'three', and my footage would be sent to the editors, who would comment back on how good I really was. This was a wise move from their point of view and made perfect practical sense. Jo also added that as well as spending the day with them, it would be great if I could also spend a night in their local hotel, so they could spend some social time with me, to doubly make sure we all get on. Of course, I instantly agreed.

My choice for the filming kit was to *keep it simple* (a mantra that I've stuck to all my career). On such a trip the last thing you wanted was to lug around unnecessary equipment. Also, whatever we used needed to be robust and up to the job. So, over the next few days I pulled a favour from Hotcam (TV facilities company – hiring cameras, sound equipment and lighting etc. – whom I had worked with a great deal over the last ten years). I borrowed a Sony Z7 camera and a couple of radio mic's. I also borrowed a Toshiba mini-cam and a 'clam shell' (monitor/video tape recording device for the mini-cam). I managed to fit the main camera and sound kit into a Lowe Pro photographer's backpack and the mini-cam I carried in a separate Peli case. I figured this would show them that I knew what I was doing – minimal kit and minimal luggage to carry.

I know of some experienced Cameramen who point-blank refuse to use a 'small' camera. They are convinced that in order to do the job professionally, you must use bigger cameras and better lenses. I totally understand where they are coming from; however, I firmly believe you should use whatever camera is best suited to your filming task. On this occasion, filming vast landscapes and then being cramped into small vehicles etc. all the while having to physically hand-carry all the kit, I needed a small camera. The Sony Z7 was the best in its class at the time, and would be perfect for the job.

On the day of the 'test shoot' I woke up early and before leaving my house checked through all the kit. It was strange, because what I was doing on this day I had done literally thousands of times before. With a shoot this simple, I could practically do it with my eyes shut. Yet, because I knew I was on trial, I actually felt quite nervous.

As I drove down the motorway, I kept saying to myself, "Just relax, Mungo, be yourself, just do what you do best and enjoy it." I guess it was a particularly strange feeling, because I was not only being tested on my technical ability, but also my personality. I found my peace by thinking, I will just be myself and if I'm right for the job they will choose me and if for some reason I'm not chosen, then it obviously wasn't meant to be. There's a reason for everything, *come what may.*

Having seen Charley on LWR and LWD I knew what he looked like, but didn't have much of an idea of how he would be face to face. I generally get on well with people and having spent most of my career working with well-known people, I've learned to just treat them like normal people – which of course, ultimately they are.

It was still early morning when I arrived at the marina; the weather was overcast, but had that hint of hope in the air that it may brighten up later. I parked my Land Rover as close to the sailing school as I could. A few minutes later another car pulled up and Russ hopped out, shortly followed by Charley. Russ was his usual extrovert self and greeted me with a firm handshake and a big white smile. He then introduced me to a somewhat more bedraggled-looking Charley, who shook my hand with a warm smile. He was a lot shorter than I had imagined, but he had a friendly way to him that immediately set me at ease. Following them into the sailing school, we were met by the staff who offered us tea and coffee. Seeing that I had already been up for hours (having driven down from London) I was relatively awake. I accepted a tea while Charley opted for the more tactical coffee.

Typically not wanting to waste any time, Russ asked if I was happy with everything and then suggested that I got the camera kit set up and pretty much filmed everything that I deemed interesting. He said that he wouldn't offer any suggestions up as it was important for them to see how I worked etc.

Returning from the Landy with the camera kit fully rigged, I walked back into the sailing school building and first found Russ, so I fixed a radio mic to him (mic on the inside of the T-shirt, chest height, and clipped the small, square receiver pack to his trouser belt). I then carried on into the building, filming as I went. I walked down the corridor and into a room at the end, looking for Charley, who I was told was changing into a wetsuit.

With the camera still rolling, I knocked on the door (with my hand in shot) and entered the room. I saw on the camera monitor Charley standing with the rubber suit on, but he was struggling to pull the zip up over his chest. He looked at me and said, "I seem to be struggling to do this bloody zip up!" I continued to film him struggling with it for a few seconds and then interjected, "Charley, you've got the wetsuit on the wrong way round, mate." He had, and when he realized I was right, we both burst out laughing. He then chortled away (as he does) as he stripped off and started again. This was a great bit of natural humour to have captured on camera, and the first of many funny moments that we would share.

Having spent the day filming these two, sailing and capsizing, we ended up in a local hotel, where having freshened up we met for a meal and some drinks. I was pretty confident that I would pass the technical test, but now for the social.

Following a few pre-dinner drinks, we sat down for our meal. After a long day, the pre-dinner drinks had the desired relaxing effect. We were tired, yet still managed to strike up some fun conversation. Russ and Charley bickered and bantered with each other as I interjected and added my boot in where I saw fit. We all got on really well and my desire to be offered the job was ever increasing. This was cemented when Russ said to me, "Look, Mungo, at the end of the day, we just want to go on an amazing trip and have a laugh!" I was sold.

It was a matter of days later when I got the golden call. It was Jo again. "We'd be delighted if you would come on board." *He shoots... he scores!*

I was thrilled. I quickly phoned my family and close friends, who were equally as pleased for me, if not a tad jealous. This was an amazing opportunity that I was very fortunate to have been offered.

Now the real work began.

The next two months were spent busily prepping for the trip of a lifetime that lay ahead. If all went according to plan we would be on the road for four months, travelling 28,000 kilometres through over twenty countries, and using well over one hundred modes of transport.

I spent a lot of time in the Avonmore Road warehouse over the weeks leading up to our departure. This offered the chance to nail down the details of kit and more information about the challenges we would be likely to face. It also meant that I could spend valuable time with Charley, Russ and the team. It was hardly like work, it was really good fun, with plenty of mucking around and drinking endless cups of tea. It was really just planning the details of an epic adventure with new mates – great.

Russ was very much leaving the technical decisions to me. Whatever I wanted or needed, I got. It was really quite refreshing, compared to the usual scenario of kit wish lists being stripped down 'due to budget'. Yet, I could see why Russ was so generous with the budget for kit – by hiring me they were effectively getting three jobs covered in one person: Cameraman, Soundman and Location Director. This was very clever, as adopting this gorilla-style of programme-making (simple and cheap) meant that with a competent operator you could save yourself a whole heap of expenses.

The weeks of prep were very different to normal, as we were constantly being filmed. Due to there only being three of us going on the trip, this meant that I would also be featured on screen as part of the team. This was a new experience for me, but came with its benefits.

The style that LWR, LWD had carved out as a niche was also adopted by *By Any Means*. This meant filming and including all the characters on the road. The story of the expedition would be told from start, middle and end. So, the preparation in the warehouse told the story of how it was all started and set up, including the recruitment of the team etc. This filming would take place all the way through to the point when we set off. Following that the film would then follow the journey of these three characters, which made the viewer feel as if they were also on the expedition.

Currently also working at the warehouse HQ at this time was a Danish girl called Anne. She filmed this prep and was also asked to film the first leg of our journey, when we would leave from Ireland. This meant that we were able to firmly establish on camera that there really were only three of us going on the whole trip. The UK section was the only time you would see Charley, Russ and me on screen at the same time. Following on from this, I would be mostly hidden behind the camera – unless something major happened...

As you could imagine, during this preparation time there was loads to do, not just technically. We would be required to have multiple visas for travelling through the twenty plus countries. To achieve this we needed to hold three current passports each. Due to my normal work, I always hold two current passports, but to have a third was quite exceptional. Thankfully, seeing that we had a legitimate need of applying for multiple visas in such a limited timeframe, we were granted special permission and got an extra one or two each.

There were elements of safety that had to be seriously considered. In the UK we are spoilt with first-class emergency services, who will respond to need within minutes of the call. Where we were going, most of the countries would not have such services. So, if we found ourselves in trouble, we would have to know what to do, and at least deal with the situation the best we could until help got to us.

We had all been on comprehensive First Aid courses at some point in the last few years, but we thought it wise that we should sit a refresher course. Dai (who was on the team for LWD) who is an ex-military paramedic, came in to our HQ to give the three of us a bespoke refresher course. The danger that we would most likely face on the journey, statistically speaking, was on the road. You are far more likely to have a road traffic accident than get bitten by a snake or be kidnapped etc. So, this was where most of the focus was aimed.

It is not ever really talked about, but on shoots it is often likely to be the Cameraman who will be looked to when there is an emergency or crisis. Not that we are anything special, but rather that due to many years of travelling experience and the likelihood of having done number of courses associated with emergency scenarios, we are the ones who should have some idea of what best to do. Plus, we are innately practically minded. This is fine, but my concern on this trip was that if there was only three of us, the chances were that we would all be in the same vehicle at any given time. So, if we were in an accident I was potentially going to be a casualty too, meaning that we would equally rely on each other.

Sat in the First Aid refresher, Russ and Charley didn't seem to be paying much attention at all. Charley spent most of this time on his phone and Russ kept on popping out to do other things. I think they figured that as they got away with it before, they would get lucky again. I was less inclined to think that way, so made sure that I covered all bases and took reams of notes in my little moleskin notebook, which would act as my source of reference for so many facets on this trip. Dai patiently led us through theories of what scenarios we may face and then what the appropriate action/treatment should be. This included practical role plays, such as of one of us having a broken pelvis or an arterial bleed etc.

We were taught, in an emergency, if we were to use a mobile or satellite phone to call for help – we should memorize and use the ETHANE code as a reference to clearly inform about any incident:

E Exact location
T Type of incident (car crash, climbing fall etc.)
H Hazards (fire, rockfall, traffic etc.)
A Access (for the emergency vehicles – clear or blocked?)
N Number of casualties
E Emergency Services required

On a lighter note, Dai mentioned that the most likely ailment to hit us would be 'traveller's diarrhoea'. Often just accepted as a consequence of eating unusual foods in foreign lands, diarrhoea should definitely not be taken lightly. The loss of bodily fluids can rapidly cause dehydration, which if allowed to become severe can result in very serious illness. I then piped up and said, "I had heard that diarrhoea is hereditary..." Charley dismissively shook his head and said, "No, it's not", which I followed up by saying, "Yes, it is... because it runs in the genes!" There was a momentary pause while it sunk in and then Charley and Dai burst out laughing, while Russ just stared ahead with a blank look on his face, saying, "This is not a good start." The mood was lightened as we carried on playing doctors and nurses.

My new role in front of the camera (for at least snippets) meant that I would, for the first time in fifteen years, finally get a share of some of the privileges that are normally reserved exclusively for the stars. For example, all three of us would be filmed (by Anne) riding out on motorbikes for the first Irish and British leg of the trip. A contact of Charley's who makes custom open-face motorcycle helmets, offered to give us three, one in each of our choice of design. Looking through the magazine, we picked the design we wanted printed on the top of the helmet. We also added our name and blood group (which was to be printed on the side of the helmet – another good safety precaution). Mine read 'Mungo O+'. I also got a nice leather jacket and endless amounts of *By Any Means* T-shirts and buffs (neck scarf) etc. It was nice to feel really included.

Having already travelled extensively, all three of us had most of the vaccinations that we needed... or so we thought. Typically there were boosters that needed topping up, as well as new jabs that were required when travelling through certain countries, especially those far less travelled. On this occasion there proved to be a bonus of playing a pin cushion. We were told that there was a new drug out that would significantly reduce the chances of us getting 'traveller's diarrhoea'. We were told that it's not normally given to everyday travellers, but seeing that we were going on such a unique journey and we had a tight time schedule to keep, we could have it if we wanted. Without hesitation, Charley and I accepted the jab on the spot. We walked out of the Fleet Street clinic feeling like we'd been kicked by a horse, but at least now we were fully inoculated.

The two months of prep rapidly disappeared and before we knew it the departure day was almost upon us. I had packed and re-packed my two backpacks to see what I really needed and what could be dropped. What I ended up with was the most impressive and efficient pack I had ever done.

The camera bag held all the camera and sound equipment that I would need for the whole four months. Every four weeks or so a member of the Production Team would fly out and rendezvous with us on location in order to pick up our shot tapes (rushes) and deliver more stock (fresh tapes). Both Charley and Russ would be carrying their own small 'diary' camera, so they could also act as a backup should we lose or break the main camera.

My personal bag was a triumph. For four months I packed

four pairs of underwear, four pairs of socks, four T-shirts, one fleece pullover, one pair of jeans, one pair of shorts, one pair of Blundstone boots, one pair of trainers and a pair of flip flops. Added to that were my toiletries, but that was it. I had never packed so light before, yet when you are forced to narrow down what you take it's amazing just how little you really need.

The day before we left for Ireland, Ewan popped in to see us off. He rode into the warehouse on a beautiful milky green vintage motorbike. It was great to see him, although he admitted that it was weird seeing us all ready to set off and knowing that this time he would be staying behind. He hung around for a while as he and Charley tinkered with his bike, before finally warmly wishing us luck and then zooming off on his bike.

This was it... the fact that we were going off on this epic trip the following day was really starting to sink in.

It is a strange feeling when you are about to head off on such an expedition. You are excited, although also a little apprehensive. You are aware that you are going to be gone for a long period of time and even though you will be on a huge adventure, the rest of life at home will carry on pretty much the same. When saying goodbye to loved ones, you can't help but think that this could be the last time you may ever see them... should the worst happen.

Some people may think I'm morbid for thinking this way, but on the contrary, I'm just being practical. It would be naive, if not irresponsible, to ignore the fact that what we were undertaking was potentially very dangerous or at least dramatically upping the odds of being in harm's way. Before I leave, I always make sure that 'my house is in good order', just in case something happens. This can work out as a positive in many ways; should I get into trouble or injured etc., people at home will know where my important documents are etc. Should the worse happen and I die, everything is in order to pile less onto my family. I would hate to depart from this world without my family and friends knowing how much I loved them.

The next day came very quickly and before we knew it we were on our way to Heathrow Airport to catch our plane to Ireland. It was quite strange, because although in a day or two we would have officially started our trip, our route would actually bring us back through London. So, this first section almost seemed like a false start. On a practical level, this was a great opportunity for us to 'shake' the kit down and see if we were carrying needless equipment or needing to pick up a few extra bits and pieces.

We spent the final night at John Boorman's house in Wicklow, Ireland. John, Charley's father, is one of the UK's successful film directors, with notable films to his name, the likes of *Deliverance, Hope and Glory, The Emerald Forest* etc. He welcomed us all with open arms and it was fun to spend the evening with him, hearing stories about his and Charley's earlier life. At this point Anne was still filming events, which meant that I could actually kick back and enjoy the build-up to the next day. After all, it would be a while before we had another day off.

The following morning we were up early. The weather was typically Irish; cloudy with the threat of drizzle. However, it would take more than the weather forecast to dampen our spirits. This day had been months in the making.

We were all buzzing and raring to go. Following a light breakfast, we headed out to the garage where our three motorbikes sat waiting for us. Charley was on his red custom-built Café Racer, Russ was on his silver Norton Commando and I was on my yellow and white Triumph Trident. Both Russ' and my bike needed a jump start from John's ride-on lawnmower. It was almost as if in their old age their engines were stiff and reluctant to get going. Finally, when all three engines were started, the deep, thundering sound was really quite impressive. Fortunately, John's beautiful house is set secluded within a number of acres of land, which was just as well with the din of noise coming from the old wooden garage. I thought that it must have appeared like something from the movie *Back to the Future* – the garage seemingly shaking with the loud growling sounds, as if it housed a secret and somewhat peculiar science project!

It didn't take long before we were suited, booted and wearing our three smart, matching crash helmets and goggles. After saying our goodbyes, in single file with Charley leading, we set off down the Boorman driveway and onto the country roads of Wicklow. That was it, we had started our journey in Ireland and were heading for Sydney, Australia – *crazy!*

To write every detail of the next four months would take a book in itself (which has already been written – By Any Means: His Brand New Adventure From Wicklow to Wollongong *by Charley Boorman, Sphere, 2009 – available at all good bookshops). So I will mostly just note 'behind the scenes' excerpts from particular stages of the journey that stick out in my mind.*

IRELAND (WICKLOW – KILK'EEL)

The conditions were wet, windy and cold, yet the beauty of the Irish countryside never fails to impress me. I loved just riding my 1971 Triumph in our mini-convoy and secretly revelled in not having to shoot the journey at this point. I remember stopping en route for what I think was one of the best breakfasts I've ever had – a Full Irish Breakfast. The ride to Kilkeel took us a full day and I remember Charley complaining that no matter how 'pretty' his new Café Racer was, it gave him a numb bum.

IRELAND – ISLE OF MAN, UK (SCALLOP TRAWLER)

Filming was handed over to me at this point, and even though we left the fishing port at 'the crack of a sparrow's fart', we were blessed with a glassy, flat sea and a breathtaking sunrise. This was a dream start, as in adverse conditions it would have been hell. Later in the day we caught fresh scallops from the sea bed and within seconds cracked them open and threw them straight into a frying pan in the ship's tiny galley, the freshest possible way to eat scallops. To this day, scallops fried in garlic and fresh chilli's remains one of my favourite dishes.

ISLE OF MAN (TT CIRCUIT)

Here we had the privilege or riding the infamous TT circuit, which is one of the toughest, most dangerous and thus most highly respected motorcycle racing circuits in the world. Joining us on this circuit was the current champion and lap record holder – John McGuinness. This high-speed race literally takes place on normal A and B roads (small, provincial roadways). Riders 'average' ludicrous speeds of 130 m.p.h., reaching top speeds of 170–190 m.p.h. Charley rode a classic Augusta bike, while John rode his factory specification race bike. It was Russ' challenge to attempt to keep up with them, with me riding pillion on the back, filming with one hand as I gripped around his waist with the other. Seeing that I weigh ninety-five kilogrammes, it was unrealistic to expect us to keep up with the other two bikes, so Charley and John raced ahead and then doubled back, to allow me to film snippets of their circuit.

I had fixed mini-cams to each of their helmets and microphones to their jackets, so when they left us and roared off up the road, we would still have footage and audio of what they were up to. On the highest part of the TT circuit, over the downs, Russ and I had lost sight of the two altogether. I leaned over Russ' shoulder to have a peak at the speedometer and we were hitting 95 m.p.h., but still no sign of them.

It may seem strange to say, but as I tucked in behind Russ, I felt as though I was being watched... that strange sixth sense feeling.

Still hurtling along at 95 m.p.h. I glanced to my left and there, literally half a metre away from me, was John's helmet! He had sneaked up on us to spook me out and it worked. I jumped out of my skin. Seeing that he had suitably freaked me out, playful John nodded at me and tore off to the right and opened up his throttle. He shot off like a missile.

Turning the corner at the top of the climb, we saw in the distance John and Charley waiting on their bikes at the side of the road. As we pulled up, they were both laughing. As John had taken off beside me, in seconds he had reached a speed of over 170 m.p.h. at which point the mini-cam had torn off his helmet and was flapping around his back, only remaining attached by the cable. He apologized to me as he handed over his helmet and the dishevelled mini-cam unit. We all laughed, saying we just hoped the moment where it tore off was caught on camera. Thankfully it was. We left the TT circuit with the upmost respect for the riders, but also a definite realization that they must be 'two sandwiches short of a picnic' – *mad.*

ISLE OF MAN – LIVERPOOL – COVENTRY

Next, we hopped on board a huge passenger ferry to cross the Irish Sea. Visiting the bridge of the vessel was interesting. Unbeknown to us, this would become one of many visits to see the Captains of ships over the next four months.

Arriving in Liverpool we sailed past the famous Liver Building. At this point we were cutting it very close to be on time to catch our train to Coventry. When we docked, we had to physically run down the gangway, off the ferry and desperately hail a cab, who then raced us to the station. From the taxi rank we ran again (carrying all our gear and equipment – which proved to be a great test to see how we would cope). Finally, we jumped through the door of the train as the doors were closing. There was a lady standing inside, right by the train door, who was somewhat startled to see three men, carrying loads of bags while filming, dive through the door towards her. She yelped with shock as we burst in, although when she recognized Charley she appeared bashful and pleasantly surprised. Within a few seconds of being on the train, the guard came through the door and told me to stop filming as we didn't have the permission to do so. Normally the Production Team would prearrange permission for filming in all our destinations; however, on this shoot there were so many unknowns, that this just wasn't realistic. Being stopped filming was to become a running theme, although fortunately we soon became aware that it is pretty much only the UK that has gone health and safety mad. I recently heard a great quote: "We used to have death and glory, now we have health and safety!" Says it all.

That night we slept on the floor of the Coventry Transport Museum. Why? Good question. But, after a meal and a few bottles of red wine it seemed like fun. Charley and I bedded down in the same area, near the motorbikes and sidecars, while Russ opted to stay in the reputedly 'haunted' room with the old penny farthing bicycles etc. This was right up his street, as he does have a strange curiosity in all things ghostly.

COVENTRY – LONDON

Since LWR and LWD it had become a tradition that Charley and Ewan would ride into their final destination with a convoy of motorcyclists who joined them for the event. We figured that this time it would be fitting for us to *leave* in a motorcycle convoy. So, the *Motorcycle News* (MCN) magazine, who were firm supporters of Charley, had advertised through their networks that fans of Charley should rendezvous at the motorway services at the Birmingham end of the M40 on this day.

We got up very early, slightly foggy-headed from the previous night's revelries, and were reunited with our three bikes (which had been transported in a van from Ireland to Coventry). Russ and I had to jump start ours again, but it wasn't long before the three of us roared off towards the M40.

It looked as though it would turn into a beautiful day, yet the early morning fog was absolutely freezing cold. As we approached the start of the motorway, with our frozen extremities, we were secretly nervous to see whether any motorcyclists would actually turn up for the convoy. If not, it could be very embarrassing.

Eventually we turned off the main carriageway and onto the 'Services' slip road. We couldn't see anything through the trees and we were dreading seeing only one or two bikes sitting there waiting for us. However, to our amazement as we snaked our way up the slip road and into the car park, there before us sat around five hundred motorbikes and nearly twice as many riders. It was like the scene of something you would be more likely to find at a Superbikes race event. We were all ecstatic and somewhat relieved. I was particularly thrilled for Charley as it meant so much to him to have the support of the motorcycle community, particularly as this was his first solo mission without his superstar friend Ewan. He was stoked.

After a quick pee and a warm cup of coffee, the three of us led the convoy of over five hundred bikes back onto the M40 in the direction of London. With such huge numbers we rapidly blocked all three lanes of the motorway, much to the bemusement of our fellow road-users. I felt so excited, proud and privileged to be playing a key role in this event. The three of us riding at the front looked at each other, whooped and laughed as we looked in our wing mirrors and could see nothing but a sea of colourful, thundering motorbikes, all 'riding out' for us. It was truly amazing and this was only day four.

LONDON

Within a few hours the impressive convoy rolled into the car park of the famous Ace Café on the North Circular Road. As we pulled up, Charley, Russ and I were siphoned off by security staff from the masses into a cordoned-off area. It was there that our next mode of transport sat, a beautiful, iconic, red Routemaster double-decker bus.

The iconic motorcycling hang-out, the Ace Cafcycling hangode of transport sat, a beaut So, most of the Production Team were there fielding journalists and photographers etc. While Charley and Russ were taking interviews I kept myself focused on the job in hand and started to rig the Routemaster bus (which Charley was going to drive to the south coast) with our mini-cam rig. There was a frenzy of Press and large numbers of people, so it had been brilliantly organized by the girls at HQ.

As I was carrying the mini-cam case around the side of the big bus, I felt a hand reach over the barrier and grab my arm. I turned to see that it was Shirley (my dear friend and Soundman) and Trev (co-owner of Hotcam). I couldn't believe it. Both avid bikers, they hadn't been able to join the convoy from Birmingham, but they had ridden out to the Ace Café to see me off and wish me well. I was so touched by their support and also thrilled to have some close friends there amongst the throng of people. As I was chatting to them, one of the Production Team came up and told me that I was needed for a photograph on the balcony via the roof, by the legendary Ace Café sign. The boys and I laughed as I was ushered off for the photo call. This never usually happened to the likes of us. We had been on many hundreds of shoots together, but as crew we always just blended into the background – not today.

Sat on that balcony, having my photo taken with Charley and Russ, for me was a true statement of acceptance. We were in this as a team and a team we were.

Within an hour or so, it was time to head off again. I hugged Shirley and Trev goodbye. It was strange to think that it would be months before I would see them again. Charley, Russ and their families climbed onto the bus. Charley had only a minute-long crash course on how to drive the old Routemaster and, to his credit, he took to it like a duck to water.

Before he drove off I quickly dived onto the bus and set the mini-cam to record. I then hopped off again and got into a car that Lucy (Production Manager) was driving in front of the bus. I quickly picked up my Sony Z7 camera, squeezed my top half through the sunroof and filmed as Charley released the handbrake and rolled the big red bus out onto the North Circular Road. For me this was all very fast-paced and somewhat frantic, but I kind of revel in having to make things happen quickly – which was just as well, as that was how it was going to be for the next four months, so I had better get used to it.

As we headed onto the M25, Lucy and I raced ahead in the car to get on the top of a motorway bridge in order to have a good vantage point from which to film the bus. We pulled off at the Cobham turning and swung around the corner and onto the bridge. I quickly jumped out and stood midway on the bridge and prepared to film. Meanwhile Lucy went to swing the car around, ready for a quick exit. As I saw the bus coming in the distance, I breathed slowly to reduce the movement of the camera. It was a good shot as I filmed it disappear under the bridge, though as

I swung the camera around following the movement of the bus, the camera ended up filming a police car which had pulled up right behind me. The officer got out and asked me what I was doing. I explained about the trip, that Charley Boorman was driving the bus and that we were heading off to Australia etc. I'm still not sure whether he quite believed me or not, but before letting me go, he took my details down in his little black book. That was a first, and hopefully the last.

SHOREHAM

A few hours later the bus arrived in Shoreham and pulled up at the lifeboat station. Charley and Russ, along with their families, jumped out and walked over to the building as I filmed. This was the last time that the boys would see their families, so once I had captured the essence of it on film, I gave them some privacy. At times like this I had mixed emotions, on one hand feeling good that I was a 'free agent' only having to look after myself and keeping life simple, but on the other hand, I wished I had someone to say goodbye to. I was incredibly thrilled when, as a surprise, my old dad turned up at the lifeboat station. Ever the encourager and supporter, this meant a great deal to me. He's the best.

We joined the lifeboat crew and rode on the deck of the large lifeboat as it hurtled down the slipway from the boat shed and into the English Channel. Charley was then allowed to helm the impressive life-saving vessel from Shoreham to Brighton.

BRIGHTON

An hour or so later, we floated into the Brighton Marina where we were met by a Mark I Land Rover Defender. I climbed into the back of the classic, immaculately preserved 4x4, as Russ sat in the passenger seat and Charley took the wheel. The drive to

Dover took us three hours, due to the limitations of the labouring antique engine. In my modern-day Landy the drive would have taken us half that time.

DOVER

We arrived late in the evening at our hotel, situated on the waterfront of Dover harbour; we were absolutely exhausted. It had been a huge day that started way back in the Coventry Transport Museum. Finally we had the chance to rest our weary heads before we left the shores of the UK the following morning.

We rose early and grabbed a quick breakfast, before heading over the road to the beach. On the water's edge sat a 'Laser' dinghy that Charley and Russ were to sail across the English Channel to France. The sailing instructor helped the boys change into drysuits while I busied myself fixing the mini-cam to the boat's mast. Eventually the time came that we pushed the Laser into the cold water and in the direction of France.

The English Channel is one of the busiest shipping lanes in the world, so sailing across it safely is no small feat. Legally you have to be escorted across by a Pilot boat, which I hopped on board and used as a filming platform.

My secret weapon that day was a seasickness tablet that I had swallowed just before breakfast. From previous experience, while filming the Marlin Fishing World Cup in Mauritius, I had learned that when you film on a boat, no matter how calm the sea appears, your eye moves in a very different motion to your stomach. This causes the most terrible, debilitating seasickness. I had learned to plan ahead and not take the risk. Unfortunately poor Lucy (Production Manager), who was also on the Pilot boat, was somewhat green around the gills.

As I filmed the little Laser sailing boat, bobbing about in the mighty sea, I held a shot that included the boat with a backdrop of the famous white cliffs of Dover. This was very poignant for us, as it would be many months before we would be reunited with our homeland. I couldn't help but think of how traumatic it would have been during the Second World War, and particularly D-Day, for those soldiers and sailors who would have had the exact same view, but would likely never make it back. I counted my blessings and silently thanked those who gave their lives for our freedom.

FRANCE – SWITZERLAND – AUSTRIA – ITALY

Arriving on a beach very close to the port of Calais, France was a landmark day for our trip. We had reached mainland Europe and it finally felt like we were truly on our way.

Travelling through north-eastern France was very pleasant. We drove a quintessentially French Citroen DS 21 classic car from Calais to Paris. Despite breaking down twice (which was no reflection on French engineering, but rather an embarrassing lack of petrol), the old car was extremely comfortable.

That night we stayed in Paris at Charley's niece Daphne's apartment, before crossing the majestic city by public rental bikes (more commonly known in London these days as 'Boris Bikes'). To film this I rode on the back of a motorized scooter bike, expertly driven (as only a true Parisian can) by one of Daphne's friends. It was fun and made a great sequence.

Our next departure was taking place in the evening from the grand Paris-Est train station. The final destination was to be Venice in Italy and our mode of transport to get there was the famous Orient Express.

True to fashion we turned up in a dust cloud of pace and pandemonium. We were buzzing from the cycle ride and were all in very high spirits.

The Orient Express train is world-renowned for its luxury and first-class service, so it was no surprise that we would be required to change from our jeans into trousers while onboard. For dining we would be required to wear 'black tie' suits. Fortunately, wherever possible the Production Team back at HQ had prearranged such details along the way. To be honest, I am not a fan of dressing up at the best of times. However, when you bear in mind that most of the clientele who travel on this famous train have spent a small fortune (often a chunk of their life savings) to celebrate a very special occasion or a holiday of a lifetime – the last thing they deserved was a rag-tag crew of three blokes spoiling their once-in-a-lifetime treat. The truth was we had no choice, the dress code is compulsory – play ball or don't ride on the train. In our circumstance, due to the fact that we were travelling so light, all I had was jeans. So, the only option I had was to change, immediately, into my black tie trousers. This provided no end of amusement to Charley and Russ as I wore my black tie trousers, along with braces over my *By Any Means* T-shirt. I looked like a mime artist, which I thought for Paris was actually quite fitting.

Climbing aboard the classic train, we were immediately shown to our individual, superb cabins. We were blown away by the luxury and knew we should savour it while we had it – as it would not last for long. That evening we each stepped out of our cabins, dressed like penguins, and made our way down the winding train to the dining carriage. The scene was unchanged from that of the 1920s. Dozens of couples sat face to face at their candlelit dining tables, the men in black tie and the women in evening dresses. The waiters, also dressed to the nines, gracefully fluttered from one table to the next, while in the corner a pianist sat tinkling on the ivory keys. It was subtly suggested that we should reside in the bar until the second seating. The bar was equally as formal, but with far less people.

Due to the publicity that our show would give the Orient

Express, we were on full complimentary tickets, which included all food and drink. Following an exquisite dinner, we returned to the bar, where all three of us agreed that the comp' tickets were well worth making the most of. Before too long Russ was on the piano, banging out his signature Honky Tonk tunes as Charley and I howled with laughter while playing charades – it was great fun. Thankfully, as it grew late, the honeymooners returned to their love nests and the elderly retired for the night, so only a few other guests joined us. I hope they saw the funny side of it. Due to etiquette, I was not permitted to film following dinner, which suited me just fine – *another drink please!*

I woke the following morning a little heavy headed to a (mercifully) delicate tap on my cabin door. Seeing that the cabin was the size of a generous wardrobe, while still in my bed, I leaned over and opened the door latch. To my surprise and delight it was our butler (yes, really!) who was bringing me breakfast in bed. I knew the boys would be filming themselves over this event with their small diary cameras, so I just puffed the pillow behind my back and sat up. With a magnificent breakfast tray on my lap, I ate and sipped tea, while watching the Swiss Alps pass outside my large window over my feet. It's a tough job, I thought, but someone's got to do it.

The snaking train wound its way through Switzerland and Austria, before eventually pulling into Venezia, Italy. The train station there is situated right next to the start of the multiple waterways that carve out this amazing city built on water. We alighted from the Orient Express and boarded a water taxi, which took us to the five-star Gritti Palace hotel.

Just as we thought the luxurious side of the trip was over, we found ourselves staying in one of the best hotels in Venice, although our schedule, as we were growing accustomed to, only ever allowed us to stay one night.

The next morning we left the hotel very early indeed. We were off to meet a 'greengrocer' who was going to give us a taste of how the infrastructure and logistics worked in order to keep such a city going.

As there are no roads in Venice, just waterways, all the usual service industries have to operate by boat. On the long, sturdy grocery barge we chugged down large and small waterways. Along the way we saw police boats, fire service boats as well as the more mundane yet equally as important delivery boats. I moved up to the bow of our boat to film Charley and Russ taking in all the wonderful sights, as we slipped along.

The one thing no one warns you about are the incredibly low bridges that connect the maze of 'streets' (canals). Given that I am 188cm tall, my head tended to be sticking up and with my concentration focused on the camera and filming, there were a few close shaves (almost literally) when suddenly from the stern of the boat one of the boys would shout, "Mungo, duck!"

One of the great aspects of *By Any Means* was that we wanted to champion those people who do jobs that never really get noticed. Here, our host the grocer would work from three in the morning, sorting out his goods and then methodically delivering them by hand and boat to his regular customers. Despite the beauty of this extraordinary city, it was hard work – so, next time you sit down for a meal in such places, spare a thought for the people who rarely get any credit for working so hard behind the scenes.

CROATIA

That afternoon we were on the move again. This time to a port where we met a high-speed catamaran passenger ferry that would shoot us across the Adriatic Sea to Porec, Croatia.

We arrived in Porec just as the sun, a huge golden ball of

fire, was dipping into the black glassy sea. As we pulled up to our dock I saw the developing stunning shot of the sunset and quickly elbowed my way to the front of the queue of passengers. I was desperate to get onto land, set the tripod up and capture this on film. I don't think I made any new friends in the process, but the shot was well worth it.

Croatia is one of the most uncelebrated jewels in the crown of Europe. It is simply stunning. I first witnessed the Dalmatian Coast with its turquoise blue, crystal-clear sea, dotted with idyllic islands, from the window of a C130 army plane when flying into Split, shortly after the Bosnian war. But the setting we found on this evening was reflective of an exclusive Italian resort, with extravagant private boats moored up in a marina reminiscent of Monaco. A far cry from the former army base on my last trip there.

We were met by two young Croat guys who were providing our next form of transport – a Yugo car. This little car was very similar to a small Fiat. It was originally built by the Russians as 'The People's Car' and for us it was fun to be in something a little more down to earth, following our previous pampering with luxury. Within seconds of driving out of the port area, Charley ran a red light and crunched the gears as Russ, who was sat in the back, gave a running commentary. There was much laughter and we were still in high spirits... unfortunately that was not to last.

After a short overnight stay inland, we carried on driving the Yugo to Zagreb (capital), where we caught a bus to Vukovar, which is situated on the border of Croatia and Serbia.

In 1991, during an eighty-seven day siege, the city of Vukovar was almost completely destroyed during the Croatian war for independence. To visit a town where statistics show that over 4,000 people were killed or went missing, 22,000 were exiled from their homes and 10,000 people were held in Serbian concentration camps, certainly dampens one's mood.

As we arrived, the mood between the three of us was different and sombre. We felt somewhat unnerved by the atmosphere that we found ourselves surrounded in. Even though years had passed since the war, it felt as though there was still a palpable tension in the air. As we stepped off the bus, there was only a smattering of people dotted around. To be completely honest, we didn't feel that welcome. It wasn't that Vukovar was necessarily dangerous anymore, but when such horrors have happened in the recent past, the survivors are still reeling with the pain, fear and trauma of it all.

It is in this type of situation when I have a personal battle against the professional. I have got a job to do. I knew I had to capture our next transit from the bus for the TV programme, but I had to be careful in deciding when it was appropriate to pull the camera out or when to leave it safely stowed away. So, I casually took the camera out and walked to the far corner of the street and quickly filmed the sequence. I was acutely aware that people were watching me do this, and due to the atmosphere I didn't hang around. After an awkward half an hour or so, we eventually managed to find a cab, which drove us to our hotel.

The buildings that did survive the devastating conflict were scarred, most of them beyond repair. Despite the fact that over ten years had passed since the worst fighting, Vukovar was still crippled as a community. Any businesses or industry had failed to flourish, thus leaving the city financially on its knees. There is no need to spell out what effects this has on such a community. What an incredible contrast when compared to what we had witnessed on the wealthy west coast.

Our hotel was still standing, but only just. The front doors were riddled with bullet holes and the interior was, not surprisingly, very basic. We each went to our rooms and freshened up before attempting to find an evening meal.

When I stay in hotels in such unknown and potentially hostile environments, I religiously stick to a few rules, in order to look after myself and my kit. The first thing I always do is check for the nearest emergency exit to my room (a good practice in any hotel around the world – at least in case of a fire). When leaving my room, for a meal etc., I hide the camera kit where prying eyes wouldn't naturally look. I then draw the curtains, turn a few lights on and leave the TV on (finding a channel in the local language – to mask the fact that I'm a tourist). Finally, I always hang the 'do not disturb' sign on the outside door handle, as this gives the impression that the room is occupied. I'm pretty sure it has the desired effect, as I've never been robbed yet (touch wood!).

That night we ventured out into the derelict city to find supper. We walked down the main streets and hardly saw a soul. It was really quite eerie. After a short while, we had heard from someone that there was a small restaurant at the end of a long alleyway. We weren't sure if walking down the dark alleyway was the best idea, but we had little choice. Eventually we found the place they had recommended and we ate some food which was memorable, but for all the wrong reasons.

The next day we met up with a local woman, Zrinka, who worked in local tourism. Sadly, she had plenty of time on her hands. She took us to her family house where we met her father, Peter. There they recounted stories of how Serbian soldiers had walked up to houses and thrown grenades into the basements, where families were hiding – the madness of war. Her father was held in a makeshift Serbian concentration camp for four months, which was situated a stone's throw from their house. Innocent people, always the victims.

She then took us to a field on the outskirts of town which was used as a mass grave. Thousands of bodies were laid to rest there, following the most horrific of circumstances. It really was desperately sad.

Later that day, we were ready to move on. On the banks of the river Danube we met a maintenance barge that patrolled the river maintaining the navigation buoys.

The borders of Croatia and Serbia met in the middle of the river, so the Croats looked after the red buoys and the Serbs the green. Another of the barge's roles was to keep a check on the state of the riverbanks on their respective sides. This sometimes entailed wielding a chainsaw and pruning back the flourishing fauna. Further down the river, the crew spotted a tree that needed to be cut back so they offered Charley the chance to get his hands dirty.

Both Charley and I hopped off the big barge and stepped carefully around the wooden debris on the riverbank. A member of the crew pointed out which one Charley should cut and then handed him the chainsaw. I stood close to where he was cutting, but not too close. With a crack and a creek the small tree reluctantly leaned over and fell... right on top of my head, with a thud! At first Charley was panicked, thinking that he may have seriously injured me, but when I crawled out from amongst the branches and leaves with a big smile on my face, his fear turned into relief and laughter. Wood hitting wood – no problem there!

Later in the day we left the barge and continued on dry land, working our way to and through the Serbian border. It was another long day (as they pretty much all were) before we arrived in Belgrade – the capital city of Serbia. The city was amazing and the architecture was reminiscent of that which I had seen in Russia or Germany. Our only real purpose in visiting Belgrade was to catch the Balkan Express the following morning. So we checked ourselves into a very grand-looking hotel, which was well past its former glory, yet it was situated right in the city centre. Not long after arriving we wandered around the wide main streets, as always, looking for some food.

Without wanting to sound like a 'letch', we were dumb struck by how stunningly beautiful the average girl was in Belgrade. Sitting outside a corner café wasn't dissimilar to sitting next to the catwalk during London Fashion Week. The local sights held our attention for a good few hours, that was until we noticed enormous black clouds rolling in over the city skyline. Without any real warning, just the odd gust of wind, all hell let loose as an incredibly violent storm raged over our heads. The wind picked up to a blistering pace not far off a tornado, which blew in tremendous gusts through the streets of austere buildings. Suddenly, right next to us, the big umbrellas of an alfresco café were picked up by the wind and tossed down the pavement, smashing windows and sending people flying as they went. The scene had descended into carnage within literally a matter of a few minutes. We offered to help, but with the language barrier, we decided we were far better off back within the sanctuary of the vast castle-like walls of our hotel.

The next day we caught a cab to the main station and climbed aboard the Balkan Express. If you can imagine the polar opposite of the luxurious Orient Express, that was the Balkan Express. This was going to be our mode of transport for the next twenty-four hours!

The cabins were the same size as the Orient Express, though when I previously likened them to wardrobes... I think these cabins actually *were* empty wardrobes. Despite the lack of comfort that we had been spoilt with, there was still a charm that this train held, probably most to do with the knowledge that we were heading to the Far East.

My worst memory of that trip was not the stereotypically rude staff, or the lack of food and water, but the rude awakenings at border crossings. We hit the Bulgarian border in the very early hours of the morning. Police boarded the train and barged their way into each cabin and demanded to see our passports, all the while asking us questions in Bulgarian. It felt like being in an old Second World War film. Not only were you shell-shocked from being woken from a deep sleep (which you always tended to get when sleeping on a train, due to the metronome-like sound and motion), but to be interrogated in a foreign language by a gun-wearing official was somewhat startling. During these border checks, I hid the camera equipment to save any further complications or questioning.

TURKEY

The Balkan Express carried us through the remainder of Serbia, Bulgaria and eventually delivered us safely and on time in Istanbul, Turkey.

Even though trains are a relatively easy and very efficient way of eating up the distance, by now we were utterly sick of them.

Crossing into Turkey was another landmark event for our expedition, as it was here that we officially crossed over from Europe into Asia.

Istanbul was where we were able to have our first real break. By now, we had well and truly lost the concept of a weekend. These few days off happened to fall on my birthday, so that was the perfect excuse to find the best restaurant in town and go large! We made an error though. Before our big night out, we went to visit a traditional Turkish bath.

In short, this is where you strip down to wearing just a towel (of flannel-sized proportions), sit in a steaming hot room with a load of other sweaty men and then get systematically beaten up by one of the Hulk-like masseurs. Once they've beaten you, they then bathe you, by soaping you up in the roughest manner imaginable. Finally, they throw a couple of buckets of freezing cold water over you. Even though this may sound like a strange, somewhat homoerotic process, it was actually very therapeutic and left one feeling like a rag doll, the error being that at this point you are advised to drink bucket-loads of water and then get a good night's sleep – as opposed to drinking large quantities of alcohol and then going clubbing. Still, you're only young once, hey? That night I turned thirty-seven, but when I woke up I felt more like a fifty-year-old.

Having recovered from our hangovers and feeling refreshed from a couple of lazy days, we hooked up with our next means of transport. To cross Turkey we would ride in a Dolmus bus. This is basically an old minibus that drives along with its destination displayed on a sign resting on the windscreen. Along the way, it will pick up people who are heading in that direction and, for a small fee, you can easily get to where you want to go – even though you may risk life and limb doing so.

Our translator and guide for Turkey was a great man called Cenk (pronounced 'Jenk'). The experience we shared with him over the next week would remain as one of our fondest and certainly the funniest aspects of the whole trip.

Cenk was in his mid-thirties and had an uncanny resemblance to Borat (comedian Sacha Baron Cohen's character)! He was very tall, of medium build, had big curly hair and a Tom Selleck-style moustache. With his big grin, kind nature and wicked sense of humour, just sharing his company was comedy.

Cenk had organized a Dolmus for us to drive to Hopa (a port located on the south-eastern shores of the Black Sea that borders with Georgia). This bus came in the form of an old, white, tatty Ford minibus. It really was most unimpressive, but apparently was the perfect example of a real Dolmus.

While I filmed Charley walking around and inspecting the vehicle, Russ started to stick *By Any Means* stickers all over the outside of the van (for TV reasons) and then a big laminated *By Any Means* sign on the dashboard.

It was deemed too dangerous for Charley to drive out of Istanbul, so the owner of the van took the wheel for the first leg out of the city. Once we had reached the outskirts, Charley took over. At this stage, the three of us were still all getting on famously. We had found our places and knew our roles, and so we enjoyed the harmony.

Cenk was a big character, in more than just stature, and before too long he had pulled out his acoustic guitar and started to sing and make up songs, like *The Dolmus Blues*. As he sung, Charley joined in as he drove and I sat in the front passenger's seat filming their singing, conversations and banter. Meanwhile Russ had disappeared into the rear, long back seat and retreated into his own world with the aid of his DVD player and headphones.

At the front we were having a real laugh and we thought at the time it was a shame that Russ didn't join in. However, on such long trips, at some point we all needed to find our own space.

Charley drove for hours through the beautiful rural Turkish countryside. But, we had to remember that we were in a Dolmus and we were supposed to be picking up passengers along the way.

Eventually we came across a figure in the distance waiting at the side of the road. It turned out to be a lovely old man. We pulled up beside him and Cenk opened the window and asked him where he was heading. He was only going a mile or so down the road, to the local village to meet his friends. Cenk (oozing with charm) offered him a lift and the old guy gratefully accepted. That was it – we had our first customer. In really high spirits, Charley and I were whooping and hollering that our Dolmus was now actually working.

We literally drove our first customer for about four minutes to the next village, but it still counted and we had it all on film. We were now in business.

Later that afternoon, we were making our way carefully down a long windy road that led us towards the coast of the Black Sea, when again we saw a lone figure ahead waiting by the road. This time he held his hand and waved us down. We pulled up and Cenk did the talking. This guy was probably in his mid-twenties and was a student who lived not far from where we picked him up. He was looking for a ride into town and as we were first to arrive, he jumped in. Charley welcomed him on board, as he slipped the van into first gear and pulled back onto the road. I filmed, twisted around in the passenger seat, as Cenk began to translate. It is tradition that the Dolmus offers their customers some snacks or refreshments. For this, we had brought some authentic Turkish Delight. As Cenk offered him some of the sweets, Charley started to ask some questions in order to get to know our new customer.

Not surprisingly one of the first questions Charley asked was, "So, what's your name?" Cenk translated and the reply was, "My name is Farty."

I lost it.

The camera started to shake and after the initial guffaw, my shoulders were going ten to the dozen as I silently shed tears of laughter from behind the camera. Charley also cracked up, and then when he saw that I was in pieces, he found that he couldn't hold it together either.

It wasn't our proudest moment, but we were already in a silly mood and that was like the starter gun for an explosion of hilarity.

Not surprisingly, Farty was somewhat unnerved by these two

strange Brits who had shoved a camera in his face and then dissolved into uncontrollable laughter, seemingly at his expense. He soon asked Cenk very politely if he could get out, which of course we let him do immediately. Once we had left him down the road, hot coals were placed on our heads and we both felt really quite bad. That was, until Charley said a piece to camera, "We picked up this young guy called Farty, who shat himself!" That was the final straw – "Farty shat himself" made me collapse into convulsions again. I cried like a baby.

Nearing the end of our crazy Turkish road trip, we were approaching our next hotel when Russ emerged from the back seat. He said, "Look, guys, before we stop we really need to make this Dolmus work, so we have to get some passengers... even if it's only a couple." It turned out that he had managed to remain blissfully occupied in the back, unaware of both our encounters. We told him to relax, because we had nailed it.

GEORGIA

Our journey through Georgia was a whistle-stop tour. We successfully crossed border control in the port of Hopa, where we were met by our Fixer Nick and his colleagues.

Right there we picked up our next mode of transport, a Ural motorbike and sidecar. For the first leg Russ rode in the sidecar as Charley rode the bike. As I filmed them from the back of a car, I chuckled to myself as I thought they looked like Wallace and Gromit. After a number of kilometres I took a turn in the sidecar in order to film closer shots and record comments to camera from Charley.

Georgia is another beautiful country with lush rural countryside, mountains and stunning old cities, like the capital, Tbilisi. Though it is seemingly very poor, we found plenty to see, like the birthplace of Stalin in the city of Gori.

While I was on my stint in the sidecar (playing the dog, Gromit), Charley was riding around a corner and must have been getting tired, as he forgot to exaggerate the turning circle to compensate for the extra weight and lack of turning circle that you get with a sidecar. We took the bend very wide and ended up on completely the other side of the road. Charley quickly and skilfully made the steering adjustments and leaned us back across the white line, just in the nick of time. A split second later an enormous truck came hurtling around the corner and certainly would have crushed us. It was a very close shave and we both laughed nervously, knowing if that had happened a second later, we would have been scraped off the tarmac like strawberry jam. It served as a sobering reminder of just how quickly serious accidents can happen.

Later down the road we were starting to run out of petrol, and at that point we had lost Russ and our support car. Soon we found ourselves kangarooing along due to the lack of fuel. Fortunately, this happened just as we reached the top of a very large hill, so Charley kicked the gearbox into neutral and we freewheeled down the other side. To our amazement just before the hill petered out, we saw that there was a petrol station. So, we kept the speed up and literally freewheeled onto the forecourt and stopped at the pump. Twice we had been lucky that day.

Within a couple of days we had crossed Georgia and found ourselves at the border, crossing into Azerbaijan.

AZERBAIJAN

I had no idea of what to expect from Azerbaijan. To be honest, I had never even heard of it. Yet, if I was to have had a stab at describing the place, I reckon I wouldn't have been too far from the truth.

Our means of transport here was an old Russian 4x4 jeep

called a UAZ. By now we had grown very used to being on the road and quickly got to grips with our new vehicles. We were happy with and adapted to pretty much anything.

I have a particularly short attention span, so this hopping from one vehicle to the next, and in fact one country to the next, suited me down to the ground. Every time I saw it as a new challenge, which is always fun.

Compared to Turkey and Georgia, the landscape here was a lot more barren in appearance. Azerbaijan was obviously poor although, as with most poor countries, it is actually run by a corrupt government who are fabulously wealthy. This country is rich with oil, yet only very few actually see any of the financial return from their treasured natural resource.

Despite this unfair system, the people we met were pleasant enough and welcoming. The food was amazing and we actually had one of our most memorable lunches of the entire expedition in the capital city of Baku. The ingredients of the dishes were similar to Turkish or Lebanese food – a new revelation to me.

We stopped at an oilfield on our way into town and approached two workers who were fixing something mechanical on the edge of a lake of 'black gold' (oil). Clothed in heavy, dark jackets, trousers and flat caps, they looked like they had just stepped out of a photograph taken in the 1920s. Their hands were filthy and their faces belied their younger age. We filmed and spoke with them briefly, but didn't want to get them into trouble, so we moved on.

While in Baku, we had to apply for our Iranian visas and this proved easier said than done.

We waited outside the Iranian embassy for hours and then when we eventually got in, we were told that we needed to pay money into an account through a particular bank that was situated on the other side of the city. No payment, no visa. Also, as it was a Friday, in a short amount of time the visa department would shut and not open again until the following Monday. We had to move fast. Russ stayed outside the embassy, while Charley and I took off in a cab to the bank across the city. It really was touch and go whether we would make it back in time.

The amazing thing was that this was the first real bit of drama on the whole trip so far. The world is now so (relatively) small, and the infrastructures so developed, that as long as you have a mobile phone and a credit card, travelling is really pretty straightforward.

To cut a long story short, we ended up making it back just in the nick of time and thankfully got our necessary visa stamps. The next hurdle was the Iranian border.

IRAN

Of all the countries we would pass through, we expected Iran to be the most difficult to get into. However, before we could worry about getting into Iran, we had to get *out* of Azerbaijan.

The border crossing is literally a bridge over some scrubland. You can easily see each border control from the opposite side, as they are only 100 metres or so apart. However, the ease of your crossing is decided by which country you are in.

From the Azerbaijan side, the Iranian border looked impressive, with a modern building and impressive-looking, military-style uniformed guards. Yet, where we stood at the Azerbaijan gates was an old caravan, with a few scruffy and somewhat rotund, capped guards wading through paperwork.

Before being allowed to leave Azerbaijan, the guards wanted to see our passports. The problem was, we each had more than one passport. The stamp we had to enter Azerbaijan was in a different passport to our Iranian visas. This proved to throw a massive spanner in the works. The guards had obviously never encountered one person holding two passports, so naturally concluded that they must be fakes. Understandable, I guess, but not ideal.

Once again time was not on our side. When we arrived at the border we only had about one hour until the border crossings shut for the day. Seeing that the guards on our side of the fence were utterly confused about what to do with our situation, they took an age to talk it through with one another. Eventually, after our translator pleaded with them to seek advice from a higher-ranked officer, they took our passports away. This was progress... or was it? Where had they gone with our passports? When (if ever) would they bring them back? Time waits for no man and our window for crossing into Iran was quickly ebbing away.

With literally minutes to spare, the guard who took our passports away appeared again from behind the caravan. We waited with baited breath. Handing our passports over he vaguely apologized under his breath for keeping us waiting. We squeezed through the Azerbaijan gate and literally ran across the bridge to Iran.

Not knowing what to expect from this border, we braced ourselves for a long night. But, the guard who stood at the entrance of the border control beckoned us in with a smile. "Where are you from?" he said, seemingly amused by the rag-tag operation on the other side of the bridge. "London, England," we replied. "Well, you are welcome in Iran," he said, as he pointed in the direction of the door to the building. "He was nice," we said to each other, half-expecting that to be the calm before the storm. Yet, we were totally wrong. The Iranian border control was incredibly calm and super-efficient. It took a matter of minutes before we were ushered through, our visas stamped with approval. We were so relieved. Finally, we were in Iran.

Due to what we are led to believe by the Press, I always expected Iran to be the most difficult and potentially dangerous place that we would travel through. The media may well be right regarding the country's political history, though what we were to experience was a quite different story.

Iran is an ancient country, very rich in culture, and the people were as friendly as anywhere else we had been. Yet, it was the landscape that made an immediate impression on me.

We arrived in the north of the country, where the terrain is more similar to that which I would expect to see in China or South East Asia. Once we left the urban area, we drove past lush green paddyfields. I was naively expecting the whole country to be barren, especially considering that we were in the Middle East. We were to find out that Iran is huge and depending which end of the country you are in, the whole landscape dramatically changes.

Driving to Tehran was a real eye-opener. The further south we journeyed, the more fitting to stereotype it became. Tehran itself is a big sprawling city and is far more developed than I had imagined. I actually really liked it, apart from the negative influence of the religions which left a bitter taste in one's mouth.

On a train that we caught from the capital city to the coast, we met a group of girls, who were only too happy to tell us about the way women are policed in Iran. Legally women have to wear headdresses the whole time and the cloth should cover their whole head, including their fringe. If they are showing the fringe (as the younger girls liked to do as a 'fashion statement') to the legal purist, it is regarded as the equivalent of showing one's naked breasts. This would result in punishment.

It's such a shame that so many of these beautiful countries (particularly in the Middle East) are blighted by religious fanaticism and political corruption. It is only right that we should always be mindful to remember the innocent population who always form a majority.

After six hours on a bus and sixteen hours on yet another train we finally arrived in the southern port of Bandar Abbas on the Persian Gulf. This was where we would leave Iran and head over the Gulf to Dubai. During the night before we left, I remember waking in the early hours with the hotel bed shaking and rocking... before you think otherwise, it was a small earthquake! As much as we had our enjoyed our experience of Iran, once again we were ready to move on.

We crossed the Strait of Hormuz (sea that separates the Persian Gulf and the Gulf of Oman) by means of high-speed passenger ferry.

DUBAI

Dubai marked a major stepping-stone for us and also our second scheduled break. We were booked into the Jebel Ali Hotel (beach resort) and this was our first chance in weeks to take three whole days off. That meant no filming, just rest, relaxation and fun. Lucy and Liz from the UK office flew out to join us, in order to hold production meetings with Russ regarding the rest of the trip, as well as taking the next batch of rushes back to the edit. Russ had also flown out his girlfriend, so while Russ was catching up with her or in meetings, Charley and I just hung out by the pool. We could have stayed in our rooms, spent time alone, but as we got on so well, we still chose to hang out together. In the evenings we would all meet up and go out for dinner. On the first night out we ended up in an open-air rooftop nightclub, which was a great chance to let our hair down.

Following our welcome break, Russ stayed on in Dubai to spend some more time with the girls. He would then fly over to India and meet us there. Meanwhile Charley and I headed to the Jebel Ali docks to board an enormous container ship that would carry us all the way over to Mumbai (previously known as Bombay), India.

The ship was gigantic. It was 270 metres long, so if you stood it on its end, it would stand taller than Canary Wharf (skyscraper building in London). We were set to be on this boat for three days and three nights. The extraordinary thing about this vast vessel was that it is manned by only twenty-six people, the roles split between British officers and Filipino crew. They were all incredibly welcoming to Charley and I, I guess because we presented a welcome break from the monotony of sailing for months on end.

If you have seen the Tom Hanks film *Captain Phillips*, this was exactly the same type of ship and scenario, including the high risk of piracy, which required the whole ship to be locked down at night or while passing through certain hostile areas of ocean.

We were shown to our basic but very comfortable cabins and later that evening we set sail. The next three days were spent exploring the ship from top to bottom, playing darts and drinking non-alcoholic beer. We filmed all aspects of the ship's workings and a lot of the time were left to our own devices. Every mealtime was spent in the Officers' Mess where we were invited to sit at the Captain's table.

The ship generates its own electricity, produces its own fresh water and even treats its own sewage. It literally is a self-sufficient floating town.

Three long days later we approached Mumbai, on the Indian coast. The number of ships of all shapes and sizes surrounding the port of Mumbai was breathtaking. Most were simply waiting their turn to be led into the docks to unload and then reload their cargo. When ships are allowed in, a 'Pilot' is brought out to take over the steering of the vessel as it comes into port. Since they know the waters and deep channels so well, this prevented any major mishaps. When the Pilot boarded our ship, Charley and I were there at the door waiting to film him. However, our warm welcome aboard was not reciprocated and he was very aggressive about being filmed. He then said that he would report us to the Port Authorities and have us arrested on arrival. His bark proved worse than his bite and we ended up being restricted from filming the ship docking and that was all. A prime 'Jobsworth' as we call such difficult people in the UK.

INDIA

Reunited with Russ, we stayed at the magnificent Taj Mahal Hotel situated on the water's edge by the 'Gateway of India', a big stone arch monument, built during the British Raj. The Taj is a stunning, five-star hotel and acts as a luxurious oasis, offering its guests breathing space from the crowds, as well as peace from the incessant noise and ever-present chaos of Mumbai.

Tragically, only a month after we were there, the Taj Mahal Hotel was made famous when a group of terrorists raided it and indiscriminately shot and killed 164 innocent people, mostly guests and staff.

We only spent a couple of nights at the Taj and travelled out for day excursions to film a variety of different stories. However, this short stay in Mumbai will remain in my mind forever.

As we were driving along in a taxi on our way to shoot a story about an ambulance, I received a phone call from my mum, back in the UK. She was upset on the other end of the phone and I knew instantly what had happened. Her father, my grandfather, had died.

In my eyes, there are only a few real downsides to my job, but being away from family at crucial times is one of them. My granddad had been fighting cancer for a few years and every time I took another filming trip away I would religiously go and visit him prior to my departure. Doing this I was always aware that it may well be the last time I would see him.

Ken King was a childhood hero of mine. Not only was he a loving, warm and fun grandfather but during the Second World War, while only in his early twenties, he was a Spitfire pilot. He was always very humble about his efforts and rarely spoke in depth about them, which as a kid frustrated me, but later in life I grew to admire. The stories he did share left me aghast when comparing what his generation faced and achieved compared to mine. He was risking his life, dogfighting in the skies over France when, at the equivalent age, I was studying Fine Art and surfing in Australia – could our experiences have been any more different? I am constantly aware that the freedom and privileges that we now enjoy are largely down to the immense effort and unimaginable sacrifices that he and his generation made. Lest we forget.

The news of his death hit me a lot harder than I had imagined it would. As we drove through the streets of Mumbai, I received a call from my Mum who broke the news to me. I sat in the front seat and silently wept. From behind, Charley placed his hand on my shoulder.

Never in one place for long, it was time to move on again. The next overnight train journey heading to Delhi took us nineteen hours. It's here that you have to read in between the lines... *nineteen* hours! There is only a small amount of interest worth filming over this period of time, so the rest is spent chatting, reading and listening to music etc. Hanging out and watching the hours click by was a theme of our trip by now, which we had grown accustomed to. Russ would mostly read, write his diary or watch DVDs. Charley would listen to audio books for hours upon end. Me? I would read or disappear into a world of music and deep thoughts.

We arrived in Delhi to a scene of even more madness than Mumbai. The main train station was teeming with thousands of people. It was hot, humid and somewhat overwhelming. We made a dash for it, pushing our way through the oncoming hordes and eventually reaching the exit of the huge old building. Outside, the chaos didn't seem to end. There were still thousands of people, but now added to the equation were cars, buses, motorbikes and tuk-tuks. We had already filmed in an iconic black and yellow Indian taxi cab in Mumbai, so we decided to jump into two tuk-tuks. One would take two of us and the other would take one passenger and all our kit. Three guys, two tuk-tuks with the goal of seeing who could get to the hotel first. The twenty-minute ride seemed to pass by in minutes and I'm glad to say Charley and I won. Not that I'm competitive, of course.

The Imperial Hotel is one of the finest hotels in Delhi. Our rooms were magnificent and once again the hotel served as another peaceful oasis.

It is a strange existence when one night you are roughing it on a train or boat and the next you are staying in absolute luxury. Most people know just one or the other, so this is why I count myself so privileged to have been able to taste both sides of life. It makes for a richer overall experience and gives you a more comprehensive 'life education'.

Later that afternoon the three of us headed out to visit the Red Fort (a seventeenth-century fort complex constructed by the Mughal emperor – given the name Red due to its bright red brickwork). The fort is an amazing place and a very popular tourist attraction. I filmed a short sequence of us arriving at the Fort, but minutes after entering the great red walls, Russ decided that he had had enough. He told us that he would catch us later back at the hotel, then turned around and got in a taxi. Charley and I were somewhat bemused by this, because that meant that we were being left to shoot the whole sequence by ourselves, and after all, Russ was meant to be the Director.

It is inevitable that on such an intense and long trip there will be a time when tempers will fray and personalities clash. It's not really anything personal, it's just a fact of human nature. On this occasion though, I do think that travelling in a three was not making it particularly easy for any of us. Due to three being an odd number, it is highly likely that there would be times when two get on better with each other, resulting in the third person being left out and feeling isolated. This was definitely the case for us. Before we had left on the trip I fully expected to be the odd one out, seeing that Charley and Russ had known each other for years. I guessed that they would have thought the same. This was something that I was cool with and knew I could handle. However, it was becoming apparent that Charley and I were becoming very good mates, seeing eye to eye and spending far more time together. This seemed to challenge Russ and at times made him withdraw. None of this was calculated, no one was in the right or wrong. It is just something that happens. How this would manifest itself later in the trip, none of us knew.

It's amazing what a good night's sleep can do, and the following day team spirits were high again. By mid-morning we were off, this time heading south to Agra, to visit the famous Taj Mahal (the real thing, not another hotel using its name). We were excited about this leg of the trip as we were back on motorbikes. The Production Team had two brand-new Royal Enfield Bullet motorbikes delivered to the Imperial Hotel. The two bikes were for Charley and Russ. If I'm honest, I was absolutely gutted that I couldn't ride a third bike again, but then again someone had to do the filming. At this point, I had to remind myself that I was employed as the Cameraman and I should rein my neck in and get on with my job.

As the two boys rode their classic-looking Royal Enfield motorbikes, I rode slightly ahead of them, kneeling on the back of a flatbed truck. It had literally been hired while making its deliveries and was still completely covered in dust and dirt. I was given a couple of rugs and a sort of mattress that I rolled up to sit on, or laid out to kneel on. The weather started off wet, which was far from ideal for me, sat on the back of the truck. Yet, soon enough the searing heat overpowered the rain and the Delhi air very soon became like a sauna again. This wasn't really ideal for me either, although I would always rather film in dry conditions as it's so much more manageable.

We drove for hours, the boys zigzagging their way through the crazy city traffic and me hanging the camera off the back of the flatbed truck. After a few hours, when we were in more of a suburban/rural area, I decided that it would be a good time to stop and shoot some 'up and by' shots. This entailed filming from the side of the road, with the subjects coming towards you and then disappearing away – critical for editing sequences of the journey. To get the truck driver's attention, while still kneeling on the back of the truck, I slapped my hand on the side of the truck. This worked and I signalled to him to slow down and stop. Once the truck had stopped I quickly jumped up off my knees and that's when it happened!

The only way I can describe it is as if someone had stabbed a sharp knife into my knee and violently twisted it. I screamed out as I grabbed onto the backside of the truck's cab. I went green and felt physically sick as I tried to straighten my leg. This was a disaster. What had I done? Charley pulled over and quickly ran up to the truck to help me. Balancing on my good leg, I gingerly climbed over the side and was helped to the ground. I stood there and tested to see if it was just a momentary one-off pain. As long as my leg was bent and off the ground it was fine. Yet, the instant I went to straighten it, or put any pressure on it, the twist of the knife reoccurred and I winced in absolute agony. I remember Charley saying to me that there was no swelling, so it couldn't be that serious and sometimes you just have to work through the pain of these injuries. But, I replied saying that I knew my body and have had plenty of minor injuries to know that this was different.

By this point Russ had zoomed off ahead of us, riding in the wake of an ambulance which was clearing the traffic. So, he had no idea of what had happened. We had walkie-talkies and Indian mobile phones, but neither of them enabled us to get hold of him. I wasn't going to die, I was just lame. So, Charley continued on the bike and I was sat in our translator's car, which was following.

Jo (from the UK production office) had joined us in Delhi, to resupply us with tapes and return the rushes. The fact that she happened to be travelling with us for this journey to Agra turned out to be a real result, as she was now handed the camera to film the drama as it unfolded.

Driving along in the car, I felt sick with the injury. Yet, it was not solely due to the acute pain, but also the utter disappointment that this ailment may potentially mark the end of my part in the expedition. I am never weak, I thought. I am usually the strong one on a shoot, and this new experience for me was seriously denting my pride.

We stopped briefly at a garage to get a small oil leak fixed on Charley's bike. I took this opportunity to phone my brother-in-law, Steve Green. As luck would have it, Steve is a top orthopedic surgeon based in Newcastle, UK. I phoned him from my production mobile phone, which never ceases to amaze me. There I was, standing propped up on the roadside in India, chatting to him as he sat in the hospital back in Sunderland. I explained what had happened and my symptoms. He immediately said that it sounded highly like a torn knee cartilage – it was the classic scenario of how they tear. Depending on how serious the tear was would determine the treatment. If small, it could recover with rest. If large, it would require surgery. Not great news at all. Either way, it was going to seriously affect our schedule.

Arriving at our hotel in Agra we met up with Russ, who was obviously very concerned to see what had happened in his absence. We all sat in the hotel foyer and discussed what the plan of action should be. I told them what Steve had said, but the only way of being sure was to see a doctor. So, our local translator booked me an appointment first thing the following morning. It was reiterated in that meeting that if my leg could recover in a few days I would stay on, but if the injury was serious I would have to go home – I was mortified. I felt like I had let the team down and I was desperately willing my knee to not be too serious. It was getting late, so we all retreated to our rooms and I hobbled up to mine.

Lying in bed that night, I was numb. Not physically (as long as I didn't move my right leg I was fine), but mentally and emotionally. It was at this point when I truly realized how much you condition your mind to cope with such a trip. It's like running a marathon; you mentally prepare, train and then run... keeping going even when you are physically, mentally and emotionally exhausted. In marathon running they talk about having to break through 'The Wall'. Maybe this was my wall? The question was, could I break through it? Or had it broken me? I faced a sleepless night before I would find out.

We all went to the doctor's surgery, which was very basic, as one would expect in the middle of India. Having said this, these doctors have an excellent reputation as my brother-in-law Steve had mentioned. We walked straight in. Dr Kapoor was kind, sympathetic and thorough in his examination. He said that he agreed with Steve's diagnosis that it was likely to be a tear or a bruise; however, I would need to have a MRI scan before he could comment on how severe it was.

Following the scan, which was in another clinic a short drive away, we returned with the results. This was the moment of truth...

He looked at the scan results and read out loud that there was a minor tear (Grade 1 or 2) which couldn't be fixed here for at least three weeks. Our faces dropped as the news sank in. That was it for me. My journey had come to an end. Russ asked what I wanted to do. I said, "I have two thoughts. Number one: I want it to heal properly or it'll become an ongoing problem. And number two: It means that I can bury my grandfather." At this point I broke down in tears. The boys embraced me and Russ said, "Well, then you must go home – it's the right thing to do... it's the right thing to do anyway!" Charley then added, "Look, go home, get sorted and then come back out and join us as soon as you're better." I had no choice anyway, I couldn't go on with my knee as it was. Yet, it was almost as if the stars had aligned, because the misfortune of my injury also meant that I would now be able to attend my grandfather's funeral.

Even though I was absolutely gutted to be leaving the trip, albeit for hopefully just a short time, it was a relief to know what the problem was and now I could focus all my energy on getting it fixed, recovering and then getting back out to rejoin the expedition.

Later that day I was put on a business-class flight from Delhi to London, hobbling my way along with my leg in a sturdy splint and leaning on a rickety old Indian crutch. I was met at Heathrow by my dad, stepmum Jan and Lucy from the office (who brought me a brand-new pair of proper crutches). After a quick coffee, they saw me straight onto another flight to Newcastle.

Early the following morning I was wheeled into surgery, with one of Steve's friends, Sean, who would conduct the operation. It's interesting to note that surgeons never operate on their own families – a precaution just in case something went wrong. Following my arthroscopy (keyhole surgery) Steve spoke to Sean and found out that the tear to my knee cartilage was not minor at all. He explained that it was a 'bucket handle' tear, meaning it had torn from one side right over to the other (in the shape of a bucket handle or half moon). This meant that he had no choice but to snip either end and remove 95 per cent of my knee cartilage. This wasn't great and would mean that I would be highly likely to have trouble with it in the future, especially regarding the development of arthritis in the joint. "Still," Steve added in his jovial tone, "when that happens, we'll just give you a new knee!" Again, it wasn't great news, but at least I knew what was what and right now all my focus and attention was on walking again and getting on that flight back out to the boys.

I spent the next couple of weeks convalescing in Newcastle and London. Despite my frustration of being lame, the accident happened almost exactly two months (halfway) through the expedition, so it was actually rather nice to be spoilt by friends and family, as well as getting some proper rest. I also attended my grandfather's funeral which was sad, but important to be there alongside my family.

Two weeks passed before I went back into the Avonmore Road production office to tell the girls that I was ready to go back out. By this time the boys had passed through India and China and were now making their way through South East Asia, heading towards Bangkok, Thailand. I sat talking to Lucy in the upstairs office. She asked if I really was ready to go back out so soon. I was adamant that I was. She seemed to be won over, that was until I got up and walked over to the stairs and hobbled down them. She got out from behind her desk, walked over to me, smiled and said, "Nice try, Mungo, but face the facts, you need at least another week." *Bummer.*

THAILAND

I ended up being away for a total of three weeks (not bad considering all I had been through). I had talked to the boys a few times on the phone during my recovery and I was green with envy when I heard of all that I was missing. I had, however, previously visited most of South East Asia on other shoots, so all was not lost. I was incredibly fortunate to be able to rejoin them in Bangkok, Thailand.

On arrival I got a taxi to the hotel, where I literally bumped into Charley as he was going out. It was so great to see him again and he gave me a big hug and a kiss (as thespians do!). I think he had genuinely missed me too. Unfortunately Russ had come down with an illness and had taken himself to hospital to get checked out. The doctors were undecided on what it was, but Charley was off to visit him, so I joined him. There in the hospital room, the three of us were reunited and it was great to be back together. However, after a chat we all agreed that it would make sense for Russ to have a proper rest and get himself in good health again, so he flew back to the UK for a week or so. The plan was that we would meet him again in Bali.

An old mate of mine, Matt Elmes (self-shooting Director) was hired to carry on the shoot in my absence. Matt was living in China at the time, so it had worked out really well. They also flew out Anne (who shot the prep and first leg of the trip) to lend a hand with Matt. Now I was back, Matt would head back to China, but Anne would stay on for a few weeks to help me out.

Even though I was able to walk and get around, it would still be a while before my knee was fully 100 per cent.

MALAYSIA

Our trip down through Malaysia consisted mostly of traveling south by car. We had set the challenge for Charley to wakeboard from Malaysia to Singapore (not nearly as far as it sounds). It was great fun… until I fell off my perch as the speedboat zoomed off. I landed with a bump and rolled around on the floor by the huge engines until I could recompose myself, desperately hoping no one saw me.

SINGAPORE

Charley and Anne were due another break so we had arranged to stay with some British friends of Charley's who lived in Singapore. We had a great laugh with them, except for when Charley and I egged each other on to have a go on a reverse bungee ride on the waterfront. The ride was fun, but the fact that we had just eaten an enormous meal only ten minutes before made us both go very green and extremely quiet for a good hour afterwards.

INDONESIA (INCL. NIKOI, BORNEO, BALI, GILI ISLANDS, KOMODO, TIMOR)

Indonesia is one of my favourite places on earth. It is made up of thousands of islands, which all vary in size, the most famous being Bali, a section of Borneo, Komodo, Lombok and Timor. But, it is the tiny ones that daisy chain these bigger islands that really impressed me.

Disappointingly we ended up having to fly to Borneo and then Bali, as the original plan went to pot…

We spent a night on a luxurious private island, just 85 kilometres south of Singapore, called Nikoi Island – literally paradise on earth. The plan from there was to take an old, authentic Indonesian wooden boat 526 kilometres across the Java Sea to Borneo. We had spent only two hours on the boat, when a huge wave cracked the bow and sea water started gushing into the hull. It was quickly decided that to try crossing an ocean in this leaking old tub would be irresponsible, if not suicidal. Seeing that Nikoi Island was still in sight, we turned around and headed back to safety. As you can imagine, Charley and I were *gutted* to be forced to spend another night on the most idyllic setting that we had ever seen! The funny thing was our fears were realized. When the boat's small crew launched the lifeboat to get us to shore it instantly sank! We had definitely dodged a bullet.

After a brief three-day stop in Borneo and visiting a few UNICEF projects there, we flew to Bali and met up with Russ again. It was good to see him and have the original team back together again. Including Anne, there were now four of us.

For me, Bali was where the trip became particularly good fun. From the marina we boarded a medium-sized pleasure/game fishing boat. I love boats and this one was definitely not made of wood, but was a state-of-the-art ocean-going vessel owned by an Australian who now resides there. It was magnificent. At this point Anne headed on to Bima, another island further up the daisy chain. She would rendezvous with us a few days later. So, we three boys took the speedboat, island hopping all the way to the Gili Islands (around two hours away). Passing Bali's famous Kuta Beach from the ocean side of the mighty rolling surf breaks was really spectacular.

I remember surfing on Kuta Beach a number of years ago while on another shoot. The surf was so heavy that I broke two boards in one afternoon. As you can imagine I wasn't too popular with the guy who was hiring the boards out – but I sorted him out financially, which eased my guilt.

As we left the security of the Bali coast and headed out to sea, towards the Gili Islands, I moved to the front of the boat to have a change of scenery. I sat on the cushioned seat up front and held on for dear life as we bounced around on the ocean waves. It was there that I saw an enormous grey shark twist its way up to the surface of the ocean, quite close to my right. As its dorsal fin slashed through the inky blue surface of the water it must have heard our speedboat charging towards it, so with one powerful whip of its tail it dived down and safely out of our path. An amazingly lucky sighting, although I was the only one who saw it. I still don't think the boys believed me and thought I was just overexcited.

We arrived at the Gili Islands in the dark and in the nick of time. Earlier our Indonesian driver, Andy, said it wasn't safe to be racing along in the dark, so we had to slow right down and watch for debris in the water. The last forty minutes or so was a drag, but eventually we made it and it was well worth the effort. The Gili Islands are stunning and so worth a visit. That night we had a few beers on the narrow strip of bars along the white sand beaches and bizarrely ended up watching Wimbledon tennis live on a TV in a small outdoor bar. That was a reminder of just how long we had been on the road – now it was summer at home.

The next few days were spent travelling from the Gilis to Bima, which took nine hours – that's a *long* time on a small boat! In Bima we hooked up with a larger traditional wooden yacht (this time a luxury model) on which we went to Komodo to see the famous Komodo dragons. Shortly after that we hooked up with Anne again and boarded a passenger ferry on our way to Timor, from where we would make our final crossing to Australia.

It was on this passenger ferry that Russ and Charley had quite a serious spat. It all kicked off when discussing the final crossing to Australia. To cut a long story short, Russ wanted to fly to Darwin, because he considered it safer than sailing over the Timor Sea at that time of year. Charley, on the other hand, wanted to sail, because that was what had been previously planned. Part of the original vision statement for *By Any Means* was to only ever fly as a very last resort. So, Charley and I felt that it was imperative for us to sail if at all possible in order to stay true to that statement. It was a tricky one, because Russ did have the overall responsibility of looking after us, but then again the whole reputation of the TV series could be in jeopardy if we were always seen to take the safe route. Over the dinner table the tension was high and the two boys weren't happy at all. In the end we all agreed that the best resolution was to split. Russ and Anne would fly over to Darwin from Timor, while Charley and I took the risk and sailed.

Arriving in Kupang, Timor, we were tired yet excited. This was going to be our final push before landing on Australian soil. We knew that once we were in Darwin it was likely to be a relatively easy life all the way to Sydney. But, we had to get there first.

Russ and Anne took off to the airport (tensions still riding high between the boys) while Charley and I joined our Australian skipper, Warwick, and crew on the awesome Phinisi boat.

Warwick had built his Phinisi by hand. Having grown up on the seas, sailing was in his blood. It was a beautiful boat, built out of ironwood, and knowing every inch of the structure Warwick vouched that it was super-resilient and up to the crossing. This was good to know as the Timor Sea at this time of year has a ferocious reputation. Some, including Russ, of course, said we were mad. However, without wanting to sound prejudiced, the fact that Warwick was Australian gave us faith in him. We figured that he would not risk his life or his beloved boat if he didn't think the six-day crossing was possible.

The first two days on *Oelin* (as the boat was named) were

my favourite days of our whole trip up until then. It was just idyllic. As we hugged the north shore of Timor we basked in the perfect conditions. The skies were blue, the air was beautifully warm and the seas were crystal clear and glassy. We were even accompanied by a school of dolphins who bounced and dived in and out of our bow wave. I will never forget seeing the dolphins as the sun had just dipped below the horizon, as they played at the front of our boat. In the dim twilight they were stirring up streaking trails of bioluminescence, which literally made them look like underwater fireworks. We sat and watched, quietly stunned. In all my travels over the years this was one of the most magical things I had ever seen. We couldn't believe our luck and the idea of six days like this was heavenly.

Sadly, our taste of utopia was not to last. While we all slept in our bunks in the belly of the boat, the weather began to turn, picking up the wind and waves. By 3 a.m., I had been physically thrown out of my bunk and onto the hard wooden deck twice. All of us were awake, yet we just lay in our coffin-sized beds, listening to the waves crash against the bow. It didn't sound or feel good. Charley and I eventually got up to see what was going on. We found Warwick up in the wheelhouse. His eyes were like saucers. We were just making the turn around the most northerly point of Timor and the storm was about to give us a serious battering.

We turned the corner and all hell let loose. The seas were huge and the wind was blowing a gale. Unfortunately this didn't subside for the following four days – yes, *FOUR DAYS*! It was horrendous. During the day we could hardly eat, due to feeling so green from the violent rocking. By night, we attempted to sleep, but to no avail. Did we ever think we wouldn't make it? I always had faith in Warwick and ultimately we had safety equipment on board and the Australian Coastguard knew we were in their waters, so ultimately, no. Yet, there were times (particularly in the dark of night) when the huge waves sounded like they were going to destroy poor *Oelin* and take all the souls on board.

I found a swivel chair on the stern of the boat, where I discovered I could sit and swing in the opposite motion to the boat, which somewhat alleviated the seasickness. It was far too dangerous to film (I tried once and almost fell overboard) so I resigned myself to that chair and when I got really bored of the lumpy horizon I dropped a spinning lure over the stern and attempted to catch a fish. I eventually did catch one... which wasn't much bigger than my index finger. The Timor Sea wasn't making us feel welcome at all.

After six days, two of them heaven and four of them hell, we mercifully saw land. The navigation equipment confirmed that it was Australia. We had made it! The release of emotions, relief and sheer exhaustion were free-flowing. We whooped, howled and laughed. The epic crossing had been achieved. Charley and I were particularly proud to say that we had risked and survived by far the toughest leg of *By Any Means*.

Arriving in the port of Darwin, we were greeted by Russ (who had cooled off after his week off in a nice holiday resort), Anne and also Ollie Blackwell (who would be taking Anne's place for the final journey to Sydney). Charley and I were elated and the photo of us both that Ollie took as we pulled into dock says it all. We looked 'alive' and totally invigorated. A tough but great experience to have shared together.

The final four (Charley, Russ, Ollie and I) left Darwin driving in a 'Wicked' campervan. These small campervans had been converted to suit the budget traveller. To focus their marketing on the younger generation they famously graffiti the outside of the vans (ours boasted a spray paint portrait of the band Kiss).

Strange, but it seemed to have worked well, as Wicked vans now pop up all over the world.

The National Highway 1, like an artery vein, carried us from Darwin, cutting right through the outback of the Northern Territories into the heart of Australia. Our sights were set for Alice Springs, which should take us two days to drive to. For miles and miles there was nothing but the scorching, straight road which was surrounded by an ocean of orangey-red dirt and sand. We hardly saw a soul, just the very occasional car coming in the opposite direction.

In Alice Springs we met 'Dingo Dave', an outback expert. Dave's reputation was like that of Crocodile Dundee, yet he looked more like Uncle Albert from the TV series *Only Fools and Horses*. He was your stereotypical 'Ocker' Aussie and we loved his company. Dave and a couple of his mates took us further south to visit the legendary Ayers Rock. We spent the next two nights sleeping under the stars in our 'Swags' (canvas sleeping bags). This was an incredible way to truly taste the immensity and sheer beauty of the Australian outback. Sleeping on the ground made you feel almost part of it. Wild camping is one of my favourite things, so I particularly loved those nights out.

We stopped off in a number of places of interest in South Australia but we still had over 3000 kilometres to go before we reached Sydney. Australia is an *enormous* country.

In the true spirit of *By Any Means* we continued to use a variety of forms of transport including 4x4s, camel, a road grader, steam train, solar-powered car, horses and even snowmobiles in the Snowy Mountains – not your stereotypical form of transport in Australia.

Before we knew it we had reached the penultimate day of our trip and we arrived in Wollongong – a tantalizing 112 kilometres south of Sydney. Here we met up with Charley's wife and daughters, as well as Russ' daughter and girlfriend. As you can imagine it was very emotional for them, especially Charley who was the only one who had spent the entire four months away from home. We spent that night in a beautiful beach-front house. Chatting with Charley later that night, we admitted we had mixed emotions. Part of us was thrilled and relieved to have pretty much completed the epic expedition, yet another part was genuinely sad that it was coming to an end.

The morning of the final day came all too soon. Charley woke up with a spring in his step (and a twinkle in his eye!) having spent the first night with his wife in four months. He couldn't wipe the smile from his face. True to tradition, we had planned to end the trip with a motorcycle convoy to the finish line in Sydney. So, word had been put out about this event through Sydney's media networks. Not dissimilar to way back, four months previously on the M40, we drove down to the rendezvous point unsure of how many people would turn up. Again, we were not disappointed and thrilled to see around two hundred bikers congregated on the coastal headland, waiting to escort us into their wonderful city of Sydney.

Charley and Russ were back on BMW GS motorbikes, while Ollie and sat in the back of a 4x4. I filmed as Ollie took still photos of the train of hundreds of roaring motorbikes that followed us. It took a few hours for us to make that final journey north to the city. As we approached the opposite side of the famous Harbour Bridge, it was very familiar territory for me.

Seventeen years previous, I used to catch the 190 bus from the Northern Beaches into my Art college in Waterloo. Being here again brought back a flood of nostalgic memories. As I continued to film sat in the back of that 4x4, I thought how I would never have dreamed all those years ago that I would be sitting here, having just travelled literally right across the world making a TV series for the BBC. That thought added to my sense of achievement and contentment. It was a good day to be alive.

The crossing of the Sydney Harbour Bridge was symbolic for us. From there we cut through the city streets and soon pulled into the Botanical Gardens and the finish line.

We had made it!

112 different forms of transport
32,948 kilometres
25 countries
102 days

A phenomenal journey and memories I will cherish for the rest of my life.

Postscript:
*Following **By Any Means – Ireland to Sydney**, Charley went on to make a second series, **Sydney to Tokyo**. Russ still produced it, though chose not to actually go on this occasion. I was busy on other projects.*

*A few years on, the three of us regrouped to make **Extreme Frontiers: Canada***

(Channel 5) where we journeyed to all four frontiers of Canada. Well worth a watch!

5

FREDDIE GOES WILD

FEATURING: FREDDIE FLINTOFF

On my way back from a ten-week shoot in the Cook Islands, I decided to take a holiday in Australia. Many years ago, I had spent over three years living on the Northern Beaches of Sydney and I still have many great friends who I take time to catch up with whenever I am visiting 'Down Under'. One of those friends is Todd Kardash. Years previously, while I volunteered as a youth worker in Sydney, Todd had let me crash at his house in Avalon for a few days, just to help me out. I ended up staying there for a full year! Needless to say we got on famously.

Todd works high up in a huge insurance firm, and as with so many jobs of that nature, an important part of his role is to 'entertain' clients. It turned out that coinciding with my holiday was an England cricket tour and a series of Test Matches between the old foes. Cricket has always been a national sporting institution in Australia and there is no greater rivalry than when England play Australia. Through his business, Todd had hired a corporate box at the Sydney Cricket Ground for one of the matches, and to my delight he asked if I would like to join him and his clients. How could I refuse?

I remember having to go and buy a shirt, so I at least looked the part and would fit in a bit more. Prior to leaving for the stadium, we met for lunch in the city and it was here when Todd informed me that I would be the only 'POM' in the box (POM being the slang Aussie term for an Englishman – thought to stand for 'Prisoner Of Mother England')! This meant that I would have to take a lot of flak as the day went on, especially as the booze started to flow. Still, if this meant that I had the chance to catch up with my old mate Toddy and at the same time watch some live international cricket – it sounded good to me.

As the day went on, there was a lot of jibing going amongst the guests in the box, and a great deal of it was aimed at me. At times, I felt a bit like the corporate entertainment! However, things were soon to change. The cricket match was starting to really hot up and it looked as though England may have a good chance of winning.

By now the hot Australian sun had quietly set and the towering floodlights were switched on. This created the most magical and idyllic scene of sporting competition. Gradually the Aussie cricket team began to lose control of their hold on the game, which led my companions in our box to grow quieter and quieter. As they grew quieter, I, the lone POM, grew louder and louder! It was a great feeling, giving back as good as I had got earlier in the day and funny to see that some of the Aussies just couldn't take jibes. The atmosphere in the stadium was tense, and the nervous excitement for both player and spectator was palpable. In the next hour or two, England managed to snatch some quick wickets (getting the Aussies out) and ended up taking a memorable victory. It was the dream scenario for me and I subsequently lost my voice from ranting and raving, revelling in the win. Todd's clients sat still and muted. To this day, I do hope that my revenge didn't cost Todd or his company any loss of business. A loss is hard to swallow, but I had a great day.

So, why do I share this story?

During the match we all shouted at one player in particular, Andrew 'Freddie' Flintoff. As he stood, fielding from the boundary closest to us, the Aussie crowd jeered at him while the Brits (including me) shouted words of encouragement, egging him and the team on.

Freddie was a key player in the England squad, deemed to be able to turn a game around through his fast bowling and powerful, courageous batting. It was said that when Freddie Flintoff came into bat or bowl, the bars and the toilets in the stadium would clear out, as the spectators ran back to their seats in anticipation. This X factor had made him a sporting superstar, and due to being the catalyst for winning the 2005 Ashes series, he became a national treasure.

Little did we know then, while he stood on the cricket pitch in front of thousands and I sat in the box behind him, that in a couple of years we would become close friends. It is funny how life works out.

It was around four years later that I received a call from a Production Company asking me if I would be interested in working on a six-week shoot in Mexico, America and Canada – filming adventure sports with Freddie Flintoff. As the voice on the other end of the phone spoke, I made my calculations with lightning speed; Freddie (ex-England Cricket Captain, Ashes hero and 'Jack the lad' of the sporting world) had recently retired from all forms of cricket, through injury. Like all sportsmen who retire at a relatively young age, he would have to find another career to occupy his time and TV could be it. Other than doing post-match interviews or the odd sport punditry, this would be his first real dabble in television presenting. So, I figured, if he ends up liking working in TV and I get to be the first Cameraman he works closely with and we get on well, then maybe this could become a regular gig? Little did I know. I accepted the job.

I first met Fred at Heathrow Airport on our way to start the *Freddie Flintoff Versus the World* shoot in Mexico. The first thing that struck me when meeting him was his size. Now, I know full well that TV cameras can obscure the size which the audience perceive people (the camera generally makes people look bigger), but I had no idea that Fred was *this* big! He says he is 195cm tall, but seeing that I am 188cm, he certainly seems a lot taller. Not only is he very tall, but he also has a huge frame with broad shoulders and hands like shovels. In short, he is massive.

Seemingly unusual for such a big man, Fred is also very good-looking and the girls love him. Other than being surprised by his size, on first impressions I was incredibly impressed by the way that he welcomed me, a perfect stranger, with the warmest of handshakes and a totally genuine smile. He seemed very chilled (yet, according to this book's foreword, he wasn't) and my immediate sense was that we would get on well. After saying hello, I then turned my attention back to the huge trolley-loads of kit that we had to check in.

Freddie vs the World (ITV) was a series where Fred would travel to Mexico, USA and Canada to compete against other ex-professional sportsmen in adventure sports and other daring challenges. The seven episodes were to be filmed over six weeks in a variety of locations.

The guest list and schedule went like this:

Freddie versus...

Darren Gough (ex-England Cricketer)	Cliff diving, Wrestling & Paintball Paragliding In Mexico City, Acapulco & Guadalajara, Mexico
Kyran Bracken (ex-England Rugby Player)	Rodeo skills (including bull riding) & Shooting In Dallas,Texas, USA
Ian Walker (ex-Premiership Goalkeeper)	Rock climbing, Dune Buggy Racing & Wing Walking In Palm Springs & Los Angeles, USA
Dennis Rodman (ex-NBA Basketball Player)	Jet Fighting (Top Gun!) & Motocross In Laguna Beach, California, USA
Iwan Thomas (ex-GB Athlete – Sprinter)	Rappelling, Kayaking & Stock Car Racing In Sedona, Arizona, USA
Steve Collins (ex-Boxing Champion)	Skydiving, Zip Wire & Drag Racing In Las Vegas, Nevada, USA

Dennis Wise (ex-England Footballer)	Dog Sledding, Bungee Jumping & the Skeleton In Yukon & Whistler, Canada

To make this demanding series, we had a large team travelling with us. The role I played was as the 'Director of Photography' (DOP). It was essential on such a project, seeing that we would be on the road for multiple weeks and working long hours, that each team member were: a) Good at their job, but also b) a good laugh. Back in London the Production Team had worked hard to recruit a crew/team that would make this trip feel not dissimilar to a cricket tour – the theory being that it would ease Fred into his new role as a TV Presenter.

To recount all the finer details of the shoot (especially the epic 'down time' events) would warrant a book of its own. But some of the highlights are well worth a mention...

Filming Fred and Goughie (Darren Gough) jumping from the famous diving cliffs of Acapulco seemed to be where I made my first real impression on Fred.

The cliffs are 35 metres high. Sheer in form they drop away into a rocky channel far below, where churning waves gush in and out. According to the wave, the depth of the water varies from 4-6 metres. So, only when the wave is fully in is there enough water to safely dive in. Yet, given the extreme height of the cliff, it's the length of time that it takes between actually jumping and hitting the water which has to be judged perfectly. Time it wrong and you would hit the sandy bottom with grave consequences. This challenge was not to be taken lightly. There was no way that Fred or Goughie could safely jump right from the top, so I was told that they would be jumping from a ledge about halfway down (still a formidable height!).

In order to capture the tension of the moment on camera, as

well as the jump itself, I figured that the best angle for me would be to be standing right next to them. This meant that I would have to climb down first, along with my camera.

Having done a great deal of rappelling (abseiling) over the years, I have learnt to 'trust my rope' – no matter where you put me now, as long as I have a rope and harness I will do virtually anything.

Fred and Goughie walked up to the top of the cliff just as I was going over the edge. They puffed and cursed as they saw me disappearing down, out of sight, knowing that they would soon have to follow. I think the fact that I was doing all this with a big camera strapped to my back both helped and hindered them; if I could do it, with a camera, then they had no excuse for doing the same without carrying anything. Yet, because I went over with no hesitation and plenty of calm, if they flapped around and showed their fear, they would lose some face. It's been said many times before, but was reiterated multiple times on this shoot, "It's amazing what you will do when there's a TV camera on you!" Cutting a long story short, they both made it down to their designated ledge and jumped successfully and ended up having a number of goes. This was the first stunt of the series – so far, so good. From that point Fred dubbed me as 'Action Man'.

It was good for team morale to have a change of guest each week, as it seemed to freshen up the team dynamic and give us the concept of a new location, new face, new beginning.

The whole team was getting on famously and we were enjoying the down time as much as the filming. This was largely thanks to 'Rooster' (Dave Roberts – Ex-England cricket physio and friend of Fred) who was accompanying us on the entire shoot. He was brought by Fred to keep him in good physical shape, as well as being a familiar face as he dipped his toe in this new world of

TV. While Rooster wasn't treating Fred (or us!) he was keeping a list of 'fines' – as done on cricket tours. If you said or did something daft, it was noted down in Rooster's little black book. On the last night of each week's shoot, there would be a 'Court Hearing' where he and Fred would dish out punishments in the form of drinking shots. We laughed and laughed. Such a simple idea/game created a chance for us to let our hair down, but more importantly bound the team closer together.

Rooster's Court also happened to fall on the first night that the next guest would be joining us, so this was quite some baptism of fire for them. Some dodged the bullet, but one in particular grabbed it by both horns: Ian 'Walks' Walker. Personally, not being a huge football fan, I didn't know who Walks was, though, within minutes of meeting him, I realized that he was a top bloke and was going to be a great laugh. That first night in Palm Springs, California, turned out to be one of the biggest nights of the whole shoot and went on into the early hours. Walks was hilarious and had us in stitches with his face-pulling and wisecracks. The following few days were a struggle though. Climbing huge rocks in Joshua Tree National Park with a raging hangover wasn't easy. Yet, we pushed through with smiles (or were they grimaces?) on our faces.

One of the most daring of all the stunts that we did on that series was Wing Walking. This comprised of Fred and Walks taking it in turns to take off in a propeller-driven biplane, waiting until they had reached a certain altitude before climbing out of the cockpit (with no parachute) scrambling up onto the centre of the top wing and then hooking their backs onto a flimsy metal bracket.

When in the standing position, the pilot would then perform a variety of circus-like manoeuvres, including a corkscrew and a loop the loop! It was a big ask and one that I would definitely have thought twice about doing, yet once again the TV cameras performed their magic and both guys went for it.

To film this was going to be a challenge, so we rigged five GoPro mini cameras to the biplane and I filmed from the open door of a helicopter. The chopper flew parallel and side by side with the biplane wherever possible and the GoPros successfully did the rest.

The stunt was a real spectacle and even though Fred and Walks were terrified (and rightfully so), it turned out to be one of Fred's favourite challenges. That was one of those times when you have to seriously question what human beings do for entertainment.

Over the six-week shoot, Fred and I got on really well. I think he cottoned on quickly that I wasn't going to treat him with white cotton gloves and would treat him like a normal bloke. If he did a piece to camera and it was no good, I would tell him it wasn't good and asked him to do it again, this time trying this or that. Coming from the professional world of sport, Fred related to this. For years he had taken constructive criticism and instruction, in fact he preferred to be told, as he wanted to improve and get better results – as with his bowling or batting. Where others blew smoke up his arse, I refused to.

Like most famous people, when they've got over the honeymoon period with their new-found fame, they desperately want to be treated like a 'normal' person again. Undoubtedly, being well known certainly has its bonuses, but it also definitely has its drawbacks and always being looked at, or treated as 'special', can eventually become superficial, suffocating and sometimes lonely. Eventually they even start doubting whether their friendships are genuine. Are they befriended because of who they are (a celebrity)? Or, because of who they *truly* are, just normal?

Fred and I seemed to particularly bond during the shoot in

Texas. He and Kyran Bracken were going to be riding bulls at the state rodeo. Be under no illusion, this was dangerous, by far the most dangerous challenge they would face the whole series. Most of the other events were controllable to some degree, but to ride on the back of a raging bull was completely uncontrollable and totally unpredictable. In the build-up to the big rodeo night, the boys went through days of training and this was the first time I had seen true fear in Fred's eyes.

The training had been bone-shaking, but the climax of taking part in the famous bull riders' rodeo was all-consuming. To be in his personal space when he was prepping and getting himself focused and psyched up for the ride was extraordinary – he took himself to a place that he said afterwards he had never been before. He was almost in a rage, a frenzy, and he looked at me a few times, as if he relied on my support, and having a mate there gave him strength.

I filmed, while standing on the pen itself, as he took his position, sitting on the bull, waiting for it to bolt. The atmosphere was electric and the noise was deafening. His eyes just looked straight ahead, with tunnel vision and focus. After a matter of seconds (which felt like minutes to me – let alone Fred) the rodeo clowns swung the iron gate open and in a storm of dust and dirt the huge beast swung and jumped sideways out of the pen and into the arena. Fred clung on for dear life!

Admittedly he didn't last long, but he had done it. He flew through the air and hit the dirt with a thud. Managing to dodge some violently flaying hoofs and escape any major injury, he was a survivor. Following the ride, I had never seen him so euphoric – he had done it.

He still says to this day, that after ALL the crazy things he's done, riding that bull was the most scary experience of his life. A great personal achievement.

Each challenge that Fred tackled with his guest competitor, we ended up going through it together. After all, wherever they were, I was stood right with them, filming. This definitely drew us closer together as mates.

Eventually, we ended up in White Horse, Yukon (North West Canada). We figured it must have been called that as it really was a 'one-horse town'. In this small town in the middle of nowhere we were going to do dog sled racing with our new guest, England football legend Dennis Wise. It was strange, but a welcome relief, being in the cold climate of Canada. The snow was a stark contrast to the heat of California.

Having been on the road for around five weeks, we had all just slipped into a mechanical routine when filming. Everybody knew their role and each person got on with it and we were coming out with some great results. The only change at this stage was that at times we all started to need some more time alone. It was no diss to anyone else, but just a natural desire that occurs when you've lived in a group and in each other's pockets for such a long period of time. It was here in White Horse that Fred said to me one evening, "Mungo, why don't you and I go and get some dinner together, because I want to talk to you"

That night we found a small ribs restaurant away from the main drag and sat talking about working together more in the future. Fred said that he had grown to trust me, both in the fact that I knew what I was practically doing, but also from the advice that I was giving him. He said that we should look to do more stuff together in the future and hopefully it could work out well for us both. I was thrilled to hear this, because I knew that I had made a new friend and hopefully I could help him, as well as he could help me. If I could try to advise him on how to play his new TV career, that would be great. But even more than that, if I could pass on some of my personal life experiences down to him, then that would be my privilege, NOT because he was the great 'Freddie Flintoff', but because he was my mate, Fred.

We had no idea where that conversation would lead us, but the words that were said that night, stand firm and true to this day.

FREDDIE FLINTOFF GOES WILD

I was filming fashion stylist Gok Wan in Covent Garden, when I stepped away from my camera to receive a call. This phone call was the Managing Director of a Production Company asking me to work on a new series for the Discovery Channel with Fred. The series was to be called *Freddie Flintoff Goes Wild*. The reason the MD was calling me direct was because Fred had told them that unless Mungo was filming and directing this series then he wouldn't do it. *Good man!* It looked as if the Production Company had no choice but to take a risk on me, so the top man called to vet me himself.

The premise of the *Freddie Flintoff Goes Wild* series was for Fred to travel to various countries, check out the wildlife and spend time with the indigenous people. The countries that were on our list were Tanzania, Africa, Arnhem Land, Australia, Borneo. And finally, the Discovery Islands, Canada.

It turned out that Fred had always harboured a fascination with wildlife and had always dreamed of being able to see the animals in their natural habitat. Bear in mind that even though he had travelled all over the world during his cricketing career, nearly all of those trips had entailed luxury travel, staying in the best hotels and then travelling to and from stadiums. He had never got to truly see the country or had the opportunity to go on any adventures of his own. He was one of the star players and so was wrapped in cotton wool and totally mollycoddled by the England Cricket Board. Heaven forbid that he should take his focus off the game in hand. At the time this was of course totally acceptable, yet since retiring, Fred had yearned to break free and seek out some of the adventures that were kept from him for so long.

Due to spending many months of the year away from home on cricket tours, he (and his wife and children) were very used to him being away. This was the perfect set-up, should he be offered the chance to travel the world and see it from a different perspective. TV was affording him that chance.

The itinerary was a dream, two week trips away followed by two weeks off. I knew from experience that no matter how hard your trip was, if you had two weeks off before the next one, you could achieve anything.

TANZANIA, AFRICA

The first of four episodes was shot in Tanzania. Seeing that this would be my first official 'Director' credit, I was told that for this first shoot they would send Ewen with us (who is a vastly experienced Director and Series Producer) – they were covering their backs. Fred and I were more than happy to have Ewen join us for this first trip. I had met Ewen years before on another multi-camera shoot and we'd got on very well. I knew Fred would enjoy his company and like his laid-back, old school, fun approach to programme-making. Within a matter of days of travelling, we were all getting on brilliantly and Fred had dubbed Scottish-born Ewen as 'McDuff' – priceless.

Our indigenous guide in Tanzania was a Maasai elder called Thomas. He was a big man with a gentle soul, in a way similar to Fred. The two of them hit if off from day one, with mutual respect and a genuine interest in each other's lives. We started off our journey in a Maasai village, seemingly in the middle of nowhere. It had taken us a few days to drive to reach the village in 4x4s, the majority on rough, bouncy dirt roads. On arrival our bodies were shaken to the core and we were already covered from head to toe in red/brown dust.

Despite the rough start we were all in very high spirits.

If you were to ask a kid to draw what they imagined an African village to look like, this was it. Built on a vast, desert-like plain, made up of just sandy dirt and scrub bushes for hundreds of kilometres, it sat in between two ranges of huge hills. We made our tented camp just outside of the brushwood hedge that safely hemmed in the mud hut village. We decided to keep outside of the boundary so that we could film without having to worry about getting our tents in shot.

On the first day, we jumped straight into filming. The first scene was Fred walking into the village and meeting Thomas, which was genuinely their first-time meeting.

I was shooting on a small camera (Canon XF305) and had two radio mic's, of which the receivers were clipped to a 'T' bar on top of the camera. The two were pinned to Fred and Thomas. This set-up was relatively simple, but also ergonomically unbalanced the camera, so was super-hard work on my forearms. Radio mic's can be a nuisance with their multiple frequencies etc. and this first day was no exception. Usually the Sound Operator (who is an expert in this equipment) would have this audio well in hand, yet, as I had seemed to cut myself a niche in 'one-man banding' (operating both camera and sound), I was left to muddle through. Eventually the audio issues were sorted.

Thomas took Fred on a tour of the village and explained a bit more about their lives. As the conversation developed, Fred also asked about the local wildlife etc. We were told that lions were a threat, hence the thorny brushwood barrier surrounding them. The Maasai kept goats, chickens and the occasional cow, but goat was their main source of meat. With this Thomas then invited Fred to join with the men of the tribe to slaughter and feast on a goat. What Fred didn't realize was that in order to be accepted as a man and Maasai warrior, Fred would have to do the dirty work.

The goat was understandably reluctant, as it was pulled into a small, round, mud-walled hut with a thatched roof. Fred, Ewen and I were already in the hut along with Thomas and about six more Maasai elders. It was tight but I managed to find enough room to work in, and the camera rolled. While a couple of the men lit a fire with twigs on the opposite side of the hut where Fred and Thomas sat, the goat was brought over and Fred was shown how to grab its feet and get it laid out on the floor. Once it was down, he was told to keep a knee on it to stop it from wriggling away. Thomas then explained that the Maasai way of dispatching the goat was to suffocate it, opposed to cutting its throat. They do this because it is a tradition for the Maasai to drink the animal's blood. Sounds gruesome, but they do this so that literally every part of the animal is used, thus making the butchering of the animal justified and worthwhile.

Fred's face was a picture. He looked up from the goat under his knee and looked at Thomas explaining that he had never killed anything before. Thomas couldn't believe it. How was it possible for a man to get to the age of thirty-three without killing anything? He translated this into Swahili and the rest of the men in the hut collapsed with laughter. Fred smiled and smirked, but also winced, as his time to 'come of age' had come. Better late than never, in the Maasai's eyes.

By now the small fire had produced enough smoke to create a white haze that filled the hut. As the harsh African sun hit the stick roof, perfectly straight rays of light shot down through gaps into the hut. With the light making shapes and the smell of the wood fire, the setting for the drama was set. Despite the overwhelming heat and the sweat dripping from the end of my nose, I kept filming. Thomas led Fred through the process. He had to place his knee onto the goat's neck and hold its hind legs with his left hand. His right hand was placed over the goat's nose and mouth at the same time, thus causing it to suffocate.

Fred was clearly distressed by this, but said that it was made easier knowing that every part of the goat would be eaten or used. It only took a few minutes for the goat to pass away. The body jolted once or twice which made Fred groan, but ultimately it was quite a peaceful way of passing. Over the years I've seen many animals slaughtered for feasts or ceremonies, but compared with others this seemed by far the most humane way of doing it.

Next came the actual butchering, but aware that he may cock it up, Fred gracefully passed on this and just watched. However, Thomas wouldn't let him get away without drinking some of the warm blood, though he did manage to avoid eating the kidneys and liver.

It wasn't long before the goat meat was filleted and left to cook on sticks leaning over the fire. As I filmed, Fred dropped some of the perfectly cooked meat into my mouth... it was beautiful and easily as good as any roast lamb I've tasted. After all, you don't get meat much fresher than that.

Day one finished with Fred being taught to fight 'Maasai-style' with a spear and a round wooden club. Thomas said that if, while we were walking tomorrow, we came across a lion, Fred should know what to do. We played along with this and thought it sweet that Thomas was playing along with the filming so naturally. It had been an eventful day and we returned to our camp, where our local driver, Cliff, was cooking us supper. That night in our tents, we found out that Thomas wasn't joking or playing up for the camera, as from our sleeping bags we all heard the distinctive call of lions in the local area!

The following day, Thomas, Fred and I set off on a walk to another village. The Maasai people are famed for their ability to cover a huge amount of kilometres on foot in just one day. Thomas told us that the walk would take us four hours, so we prepared accordingly. We packed some snacks to see us through until we reached the next village for lunch, and only took enough water to last us four hours (a few water bottles each). I checked that I had enough memory cards and batteries for the camera and then we took off. Ewen was left to break camp and would rendezvous with us at the next location.

The scenes that we passed through that day, both landscape and Maasai communities, hadn't changed since biblical times. It was quintessential Africa. The only downside was that the four-hour walk ended up taking over *eight* hours! This wasn't due to us walking slowly. We kept up a good steady pace and I filmed on the move most of the time to keep us on the move. Thomas had just miscalculated how far it was. Part of the walk included climbing quite high up a craggy hillside to cross a range of scrub-covered hills. During the steep hike we ended up walking an extremely long way around the shortest possible route. Due to the heat and our lack of food and water, we were famished and incredibly thirsty. The Maasai are perfectly acclimatized, so Thomas hardly broke into sweat, but we were dripping wet. We went through waves of feeling the strain, taking it in turns to go very quiet and grumpy, which then would turn into hilarity and silliness. The only real saving grace that kept us going was seeing a large herd of zebra running right over the path in front of us and then the golden ticket for Fred, a giraffe! For some reason, he loves giraffes. Out of all the other magnificent big game he could choose to adore, he chose the gangly, rather odd-looking one. When we had our sightings of these typically African animals, adrenaline raced through our veins. Excitement for Fred and concentration for me, making sure that I captured the moment on film.

After a gruelling eight-hour hike, as we descended the backside of the range, we thankfully saw the next village in the far distance. We eventually walked in, absolutely knackered. Ewen was there to greet us with water and snacks as we collapsed on the ground and were soon surrounded by dozens of overexcited kids. At least their enthusiasm and joviality lifted our spirits again.

We spent the next few days hiking a number of kilometres further north-west towards the Serengeti National Park. The ultimate plan was to see the natural phenomenon of the wildebeest migration, which was dependent on the rain. Every year around one and a half million Wildebeest follow the seasonal rains that water the parched African soil. The normal cycle of the rains will cause these beasts to cover a roundtrip of well over 3,000 kilometres. It is one of the natural world's most spectacular events.

For us, realistically, our chances of seeing this were slim. We only had a window of around ten days while we were on the ground. Not only that, but the rains had not come to our region yet. We pressed on regardless, hoping that our luck may change. We laughed in camp, while we talked about how TV people always expect the earth to move for their projects. For us to throw ourselves into Africa and just expect the rains and vast numbers of wildebeest to follow suit was pretty ridiculous. However, all was not entirely lost.

Days later, while crossing a vast expanse of high land we saw in the distance that the sky was growing very dark. We couldn't believe our luck. Later that evening the huge billowing clouds had formed mighty stacks into the heavens and then the black, pregnant sky broke into a massive electrical storm. The thunder and lightning was electrifying (literally) and to us this signalled one thing... "Wildebeest". The problem was that the African landscape is so enormous that it's hard to comprehend any accurate scale of distances. Yes, the storms were raging, yet there was no rain. Certainly not where we were, anyway (I'm sure somewhere the tribes and animals were copping it). We woke in the morning to an overcast sky, but no sign of rain. Still undefeated, we pulled on our boots and our packs, left camp and carried on walking.

A day later we reached the end of our road. We had seen plenty more zebra, giraffes (much to Fred's delight), and even some baboons. However, we still hadn't seen the illusive 1.5 million wildebeest! In our idealistic TV world, we had originally planned on filming Fred walking close to the beasts, watching the masses pass by. Now at the gates of the Serengeti National Park, the Rangers told us there were some in the local area, but we were not allowed to leave the safety of our vehicle while inside the park. We had no choice but to pay our fee and begrudgingly drive into the park, just like any other tourist. With the wind somewhat taken from our sails, we did find a fair number of wildebeest, but nothing like the numbers we were hoping for. As a bonus prize for all our efforts, we also saw an impressive herd of elephants and the crowning glory, the king himself, a resplendent male lion.

National Parks exist for just this reason, to allow magnificent wildlife to roam, undisturbed and free in their natural habitat. In these safe havens, the desperately fast growth and development of man's world will not be allowed to encroach on, or destroy, those wildlife cycles that have been going on since time began. Long may it last. Also, no matter who TV people think they are... they can't always have their way!

ARNHEM LAND, AUSTRALIA

Two weeks later, Fred and I met at Heathrow again. This time we were flying to Australia.

I must have done OK according to Ewen's feedback to the Production Company, as this time it was just me and Fred travelling. Having said that, maybe this decision was made to save the cost of an extra long-haul flight? Following our two-week rest from the African shoot, we were fresh-faced and raring to go.

One of the benefits of it just being the two of us on the flight was that Fred always flies Business Class, so he strongly suggested that it would be wrong to sit me in the back while he was up the front being pampered. Miraculously, they agreed, so put us both in Business Class. When we were on *Freddie vs the World,* I remember getting on a rare flight where Fred did have to fly 'cattle class'. As we entered the plane, he turned around with a wry smile and said to me, "Oh! I didn't realize you could turn right on a plane." Don't worry, I gave him a deserved amount of grief for that comment.

The flight to Darwin was long, but relaxed. On arrival we spent a day and night in the city, before catching a small bush plane out to Arnhem Land.

The Production Company back in the UK had agreed with me that it was useful for us to have another pair of hands on location, even if it was only to be a point of contact for safety in case of emergency etc. They asked if I knew of anyone in Australia. I knew Jo, who I had met on *By Any Means* a few years earlier. Jo was a Brit who, it turned out, was originally from Preston (sharing Fred's birthplace). She had moved to Australia and set up her own business, producing TV amongst other things. Jo agreed to fly over from Sydney and help us out, acting as a Producer on location and arranging some of the logistics before we arrived. She is good fun and I knew her and Fred would get on OK. The funny thing about having Jo with us was the fact that she's tiny. Fred and I are pretty tall, whereas she is tiny. Looking back at the photos we looked like giants stood next to her. Needless to say she got endlessly ribbed for being so short.

With a couple of bounces and a big puff of red dust, our small plane landed on a dirt airstrip that had been cut out of the thick Australian bush. We had landed in a place that looked not that dissimilar to Jurassic Park.

Arnhem Land is located in the far north-eastern corner of the Northern Territory, about 500 kilometres east of Darwin. In area it covers over 97,000 square kilometres (60,000 miles), yet only has a population of 16,000 people. Declared an Aboriginal Reserve in 1931, it remains one of the largest Aboriginal Reserves in Australia and is best known for its remote isolation, art and the strong traditions of its indigenous people. It is a well-protected area, and any non-Aboriginal visitors need a permit visit it.

Jo and the Production Team back in the UK had found Max, an older white Australian who had spent years visiting Arnhem Land for fishing and hunting trips. Over the years he had built a good friendship with an Aboriginal elder and landowner, Charlie. Charlie was now in the later years of his life, and incredibly we were told that only sixty years ago, Charlie and his father were living in a cave! *Only in Arnhem Land.* Max wanted to help Charlie make the most of his precious land, and so joined him in setting up a hunting lodge, built in the bush. Hunters from all over the world now come to experience this unique, stunning and untouched wilderness.

Max and Charlie have hosted a number of film crews over the years and bizarrely the last crew before our arrival was Bear (Grylls) and the boys – small world, hey?

Disembarking the plane, we were met by Max and Greg. Our first impressions were that Max was a stereotypical older Aussie. He wore shorts with long socks and boots, sported a big white bushy beard, had a portly figure and a very upbeat, jovial and welcoming personality. Greg, on the other hand, was the incarnation of Crocodile Dundee. Probably in his mid-forties, he was a quiet, lean, hardy professional outdoorsman. We loaded our bags into the back of an old, and somewhat decrepit, roofless jeep, and took off down the tyre-grooved track towards the lodge. In Arnhem Land, nature is all-encompassing, and the small hamlet of single-storey, corrugated iron buildings that made up the lodge sat in a clearing surrounded by wild bush.

Settling in and already starting some playful banter between the Aussies and POMs, we knew this next adventure was going to be good.

Getting straight into it, we were driven back out to the dirt airstrip, where Fred was taught by Greg to shoot a rifle, using some old Melbourne Bitter beer cans for target practice. Fred had originally stated how he wasn't a fan of guns, but as with so many people, when you actually have a go at shooting, you catch the bug. Fred is one of those annoying characters who seems to be good at everything. He only missed a few shots and Greg was impressed.

After a good Aussie steak supper, washed down with a number of tinnies (beers), we hit the hay in order to get some rest before our shoot really started.

The plan over the next week was to meet up with our Aboriginal guides and then 'go walkabout', hunting, fishing and foraging for 'bush tucker' (wild food) while camping out in the bush, just how the Aboriginal people had been doing for many thousands of years.

Greg was going to accompany us on the trip, but would stay behind camera. He would act as our backup and generally look out for us. He explained that even through the locals were welcoming and up for the trip, they lived in their own world, in their own timeframe, and so were notoriously unreliable. There was a good chance that they may just not turn up at all, but we had no choice but to hope for the best.

When we arrived at the rendezvous point on the grassy bank of a large river, we were relieved to find our hosts waiting for us. Connie – who was probably in her early forties – was the talkative one. She would be our key character for the shoot. Her husband, Joseph – probably a similar age – was a super-efficient hunter, though a man of very few words. It is a fact that Aboriginal people are well known for being shy and softly spoken – it's just part of their nature. Finally, there was Moses, their five-year-old grandson, who would also be joining us.

I filmed as Fred met them, introducing himself and inquiring about them. The response from them was stilted and very self-conscious – this was not going to be easy. It was interesting working with people who were so unfamiliar with cameras and TV. It was certainly going to be a challenge to direct them, but as you will know by now, I love a challenge.

Fred did what he could and we stepped aside to chat away from their hearing. The only way we would get them to open up was to set them at ease. So we focused on befriending them, not asking them to open up too much before we had gained their trust, and, using the universal language of humour, we found out very quickly that they had a twinkle in their eye and responded well to some banter and gags.

Fred loved having Moses along, as it reminded him of his youngest son, Rocky, back home. I also loved having Moses along because he created the perfect bridge and distraction from the adults getting too heavy. Within just over an hour, we were making good progress, and suddenly had all our focus turned onto our first potential target.

As we walked and talked, Joseph suddenly raised his arm to signal us to be quiet. He had spotted a wallaby (small kangaroo) in the trees about 20 metres straight ahead of us. Joseph's instinctive hunting senses were remarkable. I used the camera lens to zoom in and see the prey, but I couldn't find it. Fred, Connie, Moses and I hung back as Joseph walked a few paces in front of us and started to stalk the wallaby. Not more than ten paces later, he stopped, raised his rifle to his shoulder, took aim and fired. Bang! He turned around and moved his head to beckon us to follow him. Surely he can't have hit it that quickly, we thought. But we were wrong, he had nailed the shot and there, lying on the ground, was our first meal. He lifted the body by its hind legs and gave it a whack on the back of the head with a log, just to make certain it was dead. Fred reeled at the crack, as wood hit skull.

Things were looking up. What we thought was going to be like wading through treacle was actually going very well. Now they had a focus. Fred was designated by Connie to carry the dead wallaby and was shown how best to do it – resting the main body on your back and holding the hind legs over your shoulders. As Fred picked up the still body and twisted it over his back, the hind legs snapped with a 'crack'. This wasn't the most pleasant experience for the big lad, but then again neither was the warm blood that ran down his back. It actually looked more like *he* was the one that had been shot!

Fred continued to carry the dead wallaby, as Connie led us on, looking for a good place to skin, butcher and cook the meat. Along the way, they also showed Fred how to cut paper bark from a tree, which they used to wrap the meat in as it was cooked, and it also doubled up as a picnic rug/tablecloth.

Eventually we reached a group of huge rocks that would offer us shade from the punishing sun and also shelter, should the rains make an appearance. This was a good place to camp, so we dropped our bags and our prize catch in order to get a fire going and start cooking. Filming all this as it happened was pretty straightforward, although the heat was unbearable and I had to consciously keep stopping to take on water.

The cooking sequence took hours. After all, Joseph had to skin and butcher the animal while Connie humorously barked instructions at Fred, who she had hard at work making the fire.

I mentioned earlier that Fred was one of those annoying characters who can do anything... well, actually he cannot do *every*thing. Fire-making was *not* one of his strong points, in fact he didn't have a clue, although, in his defence, there would be cause for concern if a Preston boy was naturally adept at making fires. This was a world away from home.

Hours later, we sat and ate the meal. The freshness of the meat was evident, and although on the tough side, was tasty. Connie explained that her people eat pretty much all of the animal, as she offered Fred some offal. As she cut open some of the guts, the insides spewed out green mush which was crawling with white worms! Fred squirmed at this, which made her laugh out loud.

She gave him a piece to try which he pretended to eat, smirked at the camera and then threw it over his shoulder when she wasn't looking. But Connie was too smart for that and pulled him up as being a coward for throwing it away, as she offered him another piece of gut. This time he had no choice but to eat it. His face was priceless as he quickly chomped on the intestines. She asked him what he thought. He replied, coining a famous Crocodile Dundee phrase, "Well, you can eat it, but it tastes like shit!" With lightning speed, Connie retorted, "That's because it is shit!" Brilliant. With that, we all laughed out loud and realized that this wasn't going to be as hard as we thought it might be. Connie was a great character, Joseph was a great hunter and Moses was a little legend.

That night, the three of them headed back to spend the night at the lodge, as Connie was not happy about Moses being out for too long (after all, she was looking after him for his mum, so it wasn't worth taking any risks. Also I was aware that when filming with children you have a 'duty of care', which means you should give them proper rest etc.). This left Fred and I out in the bush alone. Greg said he would come back and sleep not too far away from us, but we weren't sure if he was joking or not. He left us the rifle, just in case we had any visitors, which again made us think that he would opt for a bed and a few tinnies. Either way, we were happy.

In the big rock formations that stood behind where we had cooked, we found a deep and tall cave. This was the perfect spot to camp. I filmed as Fred put up his mozzie tent (a dome tent with no rain sheet, just a mesh covering to keep the mozzies and other creepy crawlies out) and then as he set about making a camp fire. He tried about four times, but couldn't get the fire to start, so I put the camera down and did it for him. As it was growing dark and I still had to put my tent up etc. I started the fire and then finished filming the night sequence as the sun set and our world fell completely dark. It was only about 6:30 p.m. by the time we had our tents up and a fire roaring in the mouth of the cave. We had borrowed two camping chairs from the back of Greg's old jeep (we had learned in Tanzania that there was nothing more uncomfortable when camping than not having decent back support when sitting around for hours on end), so we placed them by the fire and sat talking.

As we sat, we realized that we still had a good two and a half hours to kill before we should turn in for the night. We would be up early with the sun and we wanted to sleep right through, so we didn't want to climb into our tents too early. That meant we had no choice but to sit up and chat. As it would be for many blokes, this seemed a bit daunting – being forced to chat one on one with a mate for a full two and a half hours. What would we talk about? We started off with the usual subjects, work, home life and social life etc.

To be honest, at this stage in our friendship, I would totally forget that Fred is famous. After all, there we were, sat in middle of Arnhem Land in a cave. However, when I did think about it, I then realized that some people would (and do) pay great sums of money for the opportunity to meet Fred, let alone have so much time to grill him one on one. So, I took the opportunity to interrogate him about what it was like to play cricket for England at Lord's Cricket Ground, which was a boyhood dream of mine. Hearing his stories was fascinating and a real insight into a world that was a million miles away from our cave.

Every now and then we would have to break the chat and go looking for more firewood. At times we took this in turns, but one time we went together. Not too far away from our cave was a medium-sized eucalyptus tree; it was dead but still standing. We were both foraging around the base of this tree in the dark with our head torches providing just a spot of light. I then stopped and gave the dead tree a shake. It moved quite easily, so I suggested that we should try rocking it over, because that amount of firewood could save us scrabbling around all night for odds and ends. Fred agreed, so we went at it. We're both pretty big guys and we're also competitive, so even though the tree didn't seem to want to fall over, we kept at it with ever-increasing force. At one point we were shaking it back and forth so violently that we heard a massive 'crack'! We looked at each other and I shouted, "Come on!" A split second later there was a second crack, and a huge branch fell from the top of the tree and hit me square on the head! I doubled over in pain and held my head. Fred stopped shaking the tree and came over to see if I was OK. I burst out laughing, partly out of shock and partly because of the bizarre situation we were in. We decided that given our remote proximity, in the middle of nowhere, it was probably stupid to be risking seriously hurting ourselves. So, we returned to camp without the tree. When back seated by the fire I held my head again and then realized that there was blood on my hand. Fred then checked the cut and we decided that it wasn't life-threatening, so I cleaned it with a wet wipe and we picked the conversation back up.

Due to being like my father and also being brought up with three talkative sisters, I think I am probably an exception to the rule of being a normal bloke when it comes to talking openly. I love nothing more than a good chat, but I'd much rather talk about things that *really* matter, opposed to just idle chatter. Fred is from a totally different upbringing – where traditionally northern men don't readily talk that deeply and certainly wouldn't offer up their weaknesses etc. It's seen by them to be much safer, carrying on with the banter. (Please forgive the sweeping generalization.)

Seeing that we had covered the general chat, I thought I'd delve a bit deeper and asked, "So, what moves the great Freddie Flintoff?" Fred went silent as he thought for a moment. He then replied, "I don't think I can answer that question, because I've never thought about it before." I said that it didn't matter, I was just interested to get to know the '*real* him'. I then changed the subject and brought the topic back to our Australian shoot. It was about ten minutes later, by which time I had forgotten about my question, that Fred piped up and said, "I've thought of an answer to your question." "What question?" I asked.

"About what moves me..." he said. "Go on, then," I said, while throwing another stick on the fire and sitting back in my chair. "What moves me are random acts of kindness." Fred said this with a sense of happiness, in being able to share his heart. "That's great, Fred." I was impressed by the thought process and soul-searching that this had taken. Also, this was the point when I knew that he fully trusted me 100 per cent, to accept him for who he really is. We then went on to talk about far deeper matters into the night. Fred seemed to enjoy it.

Eventually, my watch hit more of a reasonable hour to go to bed, so we loaded up the fire (to burn as long as it could through the night) and retreated into the cave and zipped ourselves in our mozzie tents.

In the early hours of the morning, I had been lying awake desperately fighting the call of my full bladder. Eventually I had to give in and get up for a pee. I considered just kneeling in my tent and unzipping it a touch, though I was still so groggy and tired that I didn't trust my aim. So, I reached in the dark for my boots, gave them a few knocks (to wake up any lodgers that may have crawled in for the night) and pulled them on, forgoing the tying of laces. Unzipping the tent fully I quickly spun out and re-secured the zip after me. I then walked about three paces and stood on the sandy cave floor. I sighed with relief as I splashed my boots, but suddenly I felt a rush of wind sweep my head. There was a squeak and then another rush of wind pass my face. In an instant, there were multiple flybys as hundreds of bats flew down to scare off the big shape that was peeing all over their home. I held my breath, concentrated on the job in hand and finished up, before quickly zipping myself back into the sanctuary of my mesh dome. Caves are overrated, I thought, as I settled back to sleep.

The next few days were spent walking for huge distances

across some of the most breathtaking, untouched scenery I have ever seen. We saw no one. No cars (there were no roads), and not even one plane flew overhead. It was like being in the very far corner of the world. There can't be many places on our planet left like this now, and I said a silent thank you for having the privilege of witnessing it.

We may not have seen any other people, but there was an abundance of wildlife. As we walked, Joseph and Connie would point animals out. Even Moses joined in and beat them to it at times. At one point we were crossing a very wet, muddy marshland that led to an overflowing river. There we saw fresh, enormous foot and tail tracks of a crocodile. Joseph estimated that it would have been around 4 metres long. We cautiously followed the tracks in the direction of the river and then saw the distinctive log-like head floating in the creek about 10 metres out. We must have spooked him. This sighting created new jeopardy for Fred and I. Now we knew that this paradise also commanded great respect.

With far more care, we carried on foraging and hunting for food, which was plentiful. Joseph continued to amaze us with his supersonic hearing and his eagle eyes. He heard a colony of bats high up in the trees, so he stopped us, raised his gun and shot a couple of times into the leafy canopy. It rained down dead fruit bats. There must have been at least five that fell from the two shots.

Later that day, we reached a lush green plain that stretched out as far as the eye could see. Dotted around in this panoramic paradise were white specks. "Magpie geese," Joseph said, in his thick accent. He told Fred and I to drop our bags and stalk quietly forward with him. All three of us silently stepped our way towards a head-height rock formation by the lazy river. I filmed, as Fred followed Joseph, who settled while hiding behind the cover of the rocks. In one smooth motion, Joseph rose up on the rocks and swung his shotgun to aim at a flock of geese. Bang, bang! He let off two rounds, and to our astonishment, he had hit four birds. The other geese bolted as we all ran over to claim the catch. Magpie geese were the local delicacy and Joseph's favourite dish, so Connie and Moses were both delighted when we returned to camp with supper that night.

There are strict hunting rules enforced in Arnhem Land. Only Aborigines are allowed to kill native animals. This enables the indigenous species to keep strong in numbers and protects their interests. Yet, wild boar was open for the taking, and this time it was Fred's turn to take the rifle. We were walking through a thick forest of gum trees, when yet again Joseph raised his hand and stopped us. I stepped a foot forward to get a better angle for my frame, but he said, "Mungo, stop!" After a few seconds of all standing dead still, he beckoned us forward, but with a finger to his lips signalled to keep quiet.

We crossed under the immense trunk of a fallen tree and regrouped on the other side. Without a word said, he tapped Fred on the shoulder and pointed out into the bush. Fred followed Joseph's finger and then nodded. All this while I was looking at the camera's monitor to check my framing held on the boys, while also desperately trying to see what it was they had seen. I couldn't see a thing. Sticking on the action, I focused on Fred as he turned his cap back to front and then raised the rifle to his shoulder. Joseph stood right next to him, all eyes were rigidly set on the target. With a deep breath Fred took aim, paused and then, bang! The rifle recoiled and smacked him just above the eye. Joseph lurched forward as did Fred, so I followed behind. Running about 25 metres we found a huge black pig lying on its side. The shot was good and it had hit him cleanly in the back of his neck. Just to be sure that he was dead, Joseph got Fred to put one more bullet in its head. Once the adrenaline had worn off, I asked Fred on camera to talk me through it. As he was speaking a stream of blood trickled down from his cut eyebrow. Blood for blood.

The boar was massive and far too big to move in one piece, so Joseph expertly butchered it right there on the spot. It was a messy business, but eventually the huge hind quarters were ready to go, so Fred hauled one up onto his right shoulder and then grabbed the other with his left hand. Again he was soaked in blood, but this would provide food for a good few days.

It wasn't all blood and guts. Connie also taught Fred how to forage from the plants and local fauna. There were plenty of vegetarian options when you knew where to look. In fact, we included them in our bush tucker meals as a sort of dessert.

Over the next few days, we found a good variety of camping spots for Fred. In order to create a bubble within which he really got to taste being in the wilderness, he camped out every night. I would have to return to the lodge with all the camera equipment and sort out the following day's plan etc. I actually would've liked to have stayed out more, but the camera batteries had to be charged, the rushes given to Jo (who was logging the details of them onto a computer as we went along), and also it was important for me to get as much rest and undisturbed sleep as possible. I had a lot on my plate, shooting, recording sound and directing the whole show. Someone had to be on their 'A' game.

It was a whole new experience when, at the end of a tough day, everyone would turn to me and ask what the plan and call time was for tomorrow. I would generally be mentally and physically exhausted by this stage of the day, but still had to drum up some enthusiasm to rally the troops. Although it was added responsibility compared to just doing the camerawork, it was also nice to be able to respond to what I felt we all needed.

We were doing well, and as we had a lot of great content and footage, I was able to make the call time later or wrap a little earlier than usual. Fred loves his sleep. In fact I'm pretty sure he would sleep all day long given half a chance, so despite the sun rising at dawn over his camps, he would always stay in his bed until I dragged him out.

Fred has never been shy to admit that he is scared of the dark. Yes, you read that correctly. This thirty-five-year-old giant is literally afraid of the dark. Apparently it stems back to a man showing him and his mates a horror movie when they were still at a very young age. That experience scars Fred to this day. It's sobering to think that the irresponsible act of an adult can have such a long-lasting impact on a kid's life – in some aspects it's a sad world we live in. Due to this fear, it was a big undertaking for Fred to sleep out in the bush by himself. However, he learned a few facts of wild camping that can be of great comfort. First, your tent becomes your fortress and your safe haven. No matter where your tent is pitched, when you are in the small enclosed space, you really do feel a sense of security. That is your personal space. Secondly, a fire (if you can start one) is a great companion. Not only will it give you warmth and scare off wild animals, but it's actually like having another living being with you. This may sound ridiculous, but it's very true.

On the penultimate morning, near to where Fred was camping, was one of the most beautiful landscapes I have ever seen. The wide river wound its way through the thick bush and ended at a magnificent waterfall, surrounded by an incredibly dramatic rock formation. On the edge of the large waterfall was a series of descending rock pools that all ran water into each other, cascading down and ending up in the main river. We decided that it would be great to film Fred taking a bath in one of those rock pools. As you can imagine, after a number of tough days working in the hot sun and all those nights sleeping rough, it's fair to say he was minging! Joseph scooted us over the river to the base of the rocks and held the boat as we took shots around the pools above.

This scene was stunning, the rising sun glowing over the red rock. Fred stripped down to his Calvin Kleins and sat in one of the bigger pools. It was effectively a natural hot tub, with the water churning down from the higher pool. I stood on the edge and filmed him having a wash. It wasn't quite Brooke Shields in the movie *The Blue Lagoon*, but it was quite amusing to watch. Having shot the sequence, I stripped down to my undies and climbed in too. The water was disappointingly warm, which was hardly surprising given that it is baked all day long under the inferno in the sky. Still, it was nice to be refreshed, even if only minimally cooled down.

We sat in up to our chest in the water, laughing and joking, but then to my horror I felt something snap very sharply on my big toe! As if I was having an epileptic fit, I screamed like a girl and shot out of the pool. Fred jolted from my actions and then burst out laughing. He was roaring with laughter as I professed that something really had bitten my toe. Not to risk himself going through the same, he edged out of the pool and sat wet on the hot rocks, still guffawing at my expense. As my blood pressure settled, I still banged on that something had attacked me. Then, from a few pools down little Moses appeared holding in his hand a tiny baby crocodile. "That was it!" I said, as Fred wheezed again with laughter. It may have only been three inches long, but its pin-sharp gnashers packed a serious punch. I'm sure Fred will dine out on that one for quite some time.

Prior to leaving the UK for this trip, we had discussed (in our TV way) how incredible it would be if Fred could catch a crocodile.

We had no real idea of how possible it would be, but we knew it would make great TV.

It was the last day of our shoot out in the wilds of Arnhem Land and the goal was to do just that – catch a real live croc. By law, Joseph would have to actually kill the reptile, but Fred could certainly help him catch one. It was definitely a long shot and we honestly didn't know just how realistic our chances were or what the outcome would be. One thing was certain on these shoots – *nothing* was set up.

We started off the day on the boat. The waterways around this particular area were swollen from the daily afternoon torrential storms. Some rivers slithered their way around ancient rock formations and others spliced through huge plains of grassland and swamps. Most of the rivers had tributaries, the smaller of which were favoured by the crocs as a menacing hiding place from which to pounce. The boat that Joseph had borrowed from Max was a 'Tinnie' as the Aussies call them (not a beer, as referenced earlier, but a small steel-hulled boat about 8 metres in length and 2 metres in width). Balanced on the back end was an outboard motor that spun its propeller to push the craft in a forward motion. Joseph took the tiller (arm of the motor), revved up the engine and steered us away from the riverbank and onto the dark, seemingly bottomless water channel.

Moses sat by Joseph's feet at the back, as Connie sat with Fred further up towards the front of the boat's square nose. I kneeled and leaned overboard, moving all over the flat deck, hoovering up as many shots as I could to make a good sequence to tell the story. The blazing sun was relentless, as we had no shade while on the water, but the scenery was absolutely breathtaking. There was nothing man-made visible for as far as the eye could see in all directions. As we hummed along the waterway, leaving a white frothy trail, we all had our eyes peeled for our 'catch of the day'.

It wasn't long before we realized that we were definitely not alone on this river. Far from it. Without any exaggeration, literally every 20 metres or so, we would see the surface of the water move in an unmistakable 'V' shape as a submerged monster would dip its head and with a swish of its prehistoric tail would glide, then dive into the murky depths. Connie would point out lily leaves that would turn over in previously undisturbed glassy water. This, she said, was the sign of crocs. With my Director's hat (figuratively) on, I couldn't help but think that this sequence could be TV gold, if we witnessed Fred catching a crocodile. There were hundreds of them, everywhere. To cut a long, boring, painfully hot story short...

Ten hours later, we had still yet to catch one. We had a number of close calls and had even managed to corner and attempt to spear a few, yet all to no avail. There was obviously a reason why these frightening creatures had managed to exist since the ancient times of the dinosaurs. They were super-smart and intrinsically evolved to survive. They certainly seemed to be under no threat from us.

At one point, around midday, we had butted the front of the boat up onto a muddy bank and hopped out in pursuit of a smaller, freshwater croc. As the long-limbed reptile scarpered off, Fred and Joseph were in hot pursuit. In the process they skirted around a big tree that was sat on the water's edge of a large pond, set back from the main river. I followed them, totally oblivious to my surroundings while filming. Suddenly, I saw them jump out of their skins! They blurted out some graphic expletives and ran back in my direction. It was like a scene from Laurel and Hardy. Without realizing, we had run straight into the path of a huge female 'Salty' (saltwater crocodile, which can grow to over 5 metres long and run in short bursts up to 30 k.p.h.). She was sat, wallowing in the pond, completely motionless, guarding her nest of eggs. We estimated that she must have been at least 4 metres long – she was enormous. Fortunately, she can't have felt that threatened by the three amigos prancing around her nursery. If she had been, I doubt very much that I would be sat here writing this. Needless to say the small freshwater croc made its lucky escape.

The hope of our prize catch seemed to be slipping out of our reach. The sun, having done its damage, was bidding a hasty retreat to the horizon, while we were still sat on our floating steel platform, frazzled and dehydrated. Morale was at its lowest ebb, but no one could say that we hadn't tried.

We decided to give a small cluster of rocks on the opposite side of the river one final look. Somewhat half-heartedly we skirted around the bulbous sandstone masses and our wake lapped against the rough, sun-bleached surface of the rocks. We looked for any sign of life within the lush green reeds, any movement or rustle of sound. As we turned a corner, there lying on a lower rock ledge was a crocodile. Instantly adrenaline pulsed through our veins and we all found our second wind. Quickly, but quietly, Joseph reached down for his spear, Fred hopped up close behind him, while I pressed RECORD and focused up on the pending action. In one fluid motion Joseph threw his spear at the creature, but with a loud scrape on the rock it missed its target by an inch. With the surprise attack, the croc shot off into the reeds that carpeted a narrow creek between the two largest rocks. Joseph and Fred leaped out of the boat and onto the rocks, desperate to not lose sight of their prey. The chase was on.

I moved as quickly as I could with the camera and also jumped out of the boat behind them, but in order to get a better vantage point (as opposed to just a cramped over the shoulder shot) I leapt across to the other rock formation. Now we were on opposite sides, separated by the narrow creek of reeds, running and hopping parallel to each other, in a pincer-like formation. This was a risk, because if the action happened on the other side of the rocks, out of my view, the sequence would be compromised. But, due to the lack of 'action' all day, I thought for the sake of an exciting chase, the risk was worth taking. Fortunately, my instincts proved right.

As the croc ran for its life, Joseph retrieved the spear, while Fred gingerly hopped back and forth on the rocks, looking for any sign of the animal. Joseph joined him and within a minute or so later Joseph (with his X-ray vision) saw the croc. He didn't hesitate and with a 'whoosh' he lobbed the spear at the dark shape, barely visible in the shallow water. Miraculously, with a dull thud, the spear found its target! It stood up in the air like a cocktail stick stuck in a piece of pineapple and Joseph grabbed the end of the long bamboo spear to prevent their catch escaping. It was a flurry of action, as Joseph tussled with the spear and Fred leaped across the creek to help. There was an air of excitement, disbelief and nervousness as they were desperate to finally secure this one. Not surprisingly the croc was going berserk, water was splashing everywhere and Joseph was clearly struggling to hold the strong beast. With a strained voice, he told Fred to grab its neck, just below the head. Fred threw himself down on his belly, reached over and with his huge right hand took a strong hold on the croc. Joseph and he in unison then lifted the croc onto a higher rock behind them. I quickly jumped over to them, still filming as the croc touched down. Fred put all his weight on the back of the leathery body (a technique he learnt from the Maasai with the goat). This time it wasn't going anywhere.

This was the first chance we had to have a good look at the impressive creature. It was a freshwater crocodile, around 1½ metres long from nose to tail.

We were ecstatic! All our patience, determination and hard work had finally paid off. Fred still knelt on the wriggling reptile while saying a 'piece to camera'. He was thrilled and couldn't believe that he was holding a real, wild crocodile in his hands. I filmed him, while gurning behind the camera, knowing that we had nailed our dream sequence. What an achievement, amazing.

Joseph then took my Leatherman knife and dispatched the crocodile by unceremoniously cutting its throat from side to side. After a few seconds the creature's body stopped wriggling and it lay motionless and lifeless. Fred then stood up and we all shook hands, high-fived and whooped with delight. We had done it. Yet, to our astonishment, despite being almost fully decapitated, the dead croc came back to life and ran off, falling into the water in the creek below. With a yelp of surprise and horror Fred and I stood stunned, as Joseph jumped straight into the water after it. Thanks again to Joseph's finely tuned hunting instincts, the fact that the animal's nerves still pumped adrenaline and had caused it to run off, he was able to retrieve the body from the creek. When he climbed back out of the water, he took the knife and cut its head completely off, proudly stating, "It's dead now!"

As before, this was just a kill for the sake of a TV show, but Connie and Joseph still hunt like this in their everyday lives. They live off the wild land as much as possible, keeping their Aboriginal survival skills and traditions alive. Moses' presence during this hunt was purposeful, as they hope that he will carry these ancient practices onto future generations. That night, back at camp, the croc was cooked in a fire and eaten with real gratitude. A fitting scene to end the great adventure in Arnhem Land – a memorable experience in a wild paradise on earth.

BORNEO

Following another welcome two-week break, it was now leading up to Christmas as Fred, McDuff and I regrouped at Heathrow Airport and boarded a plane for Borneo.

My previous experience of the jungle, in the Amazon, had left me with memories of it being an incredibly hard and uncomfortable place to be. You are wet with sweat from the minute you walk in to when you walk out. That includes night-time as well as the day. The insects that thrive in the rainforest are generally aggressive and incessant, while the wildlife, despite being spectacular in most cases, is to be held in respect, if not feared. The whole environment is damp, dark and often claustrophobic due to the overpowering plant life and overwhelming dense tree canopy.

To be honest, it was only the fact that our trip was focused on seeing wild orangutans and pygmy elephants in their natural habitat that made me look forward to this next adventure.

Three flights and over two days later, Fred, Ewen and I arrived exhausted in Sandakan, Borneo and were greeted by our team. Jason (a Brit who lives out there) was leading the logistics of our trip and he had a small team of locals including Eric, a jungle survival expert, and a couple of drivers. That night, we all went out for a seafood meal in what turned out to be one of the best seafood restaurants we have ever eaten in. It was nothing flash to look at, in fact it was pretty rough and mostly built of wood, balancing on stilts that disappeared into the sea, but the seafood was incredible. We knew full well that this would be our last decent supper before a tough week out in the wilds, so we appreciated every morsel.

The next day we drove for around three hours across the country to reach our next stop, the Kinabatangan River. I started filming Fred's journey in the car, to show the effort that it takes to reach such remote locations. There we met Alim, our local guide who would be accompanying Fred for the duration of his jungle experience. Yet, we had *still* yet to arrive. When at the river, we then boarded a couple of long thin river boats and journeyed on for another hour or so, before eventually reaching our final destination, the Pangi Forest Reserve.

It was hot, steamy and damp jungle. The real thing.

While Jason and Eric showed us the immediate surrounding area, the team of locals set about pitching a line of small dome tents on top of the steep riverbank. This small huddle of blue tents would serve as 'base camp' for the next week or so, and was going to be Ewen's and my home. Fred watched with envy as we chose our tents and placed our kit bags inside, as he knew he would not be granted such relative luxury.

Soon we were shooting our first real jungle sequence, following Alim as he led Fred into the dense jungle to look for a suitable location for their wild camp. The conditions underfoot were testing, as thick mud caused our feed to get stuck or slide from under us. The temperature soared as we left the slight breeze by the river and delved further into the tropical rainforest. The humidity wrapped around us like a big sweaty blanket. It was heinous, but we had better get used to it.

Mercifully it didn't take long for Alim to find a good place to build camp. After a fairly short climb up a steep, muddy hill, we found the site where a huge tree had grown on top of a leaning, huge rock. The ancient tree had closed its grip around the rock and its huge roots hung over and dropped down to the ground – perfect to hang a hammock on. The face of the wall leaned over, which created natural shelter from any rain. Seeing the amount of mud that swamped the jungle floor, rain would be certain. After all we were in a 'rainforest'.

The two guys started to build camp. Alim, who is probably aged in his late forties or early fifties, is a physically tiny man, yet he has a heart the size of a lion. Stood next to Fred he was dwarfed and looked like a schoolchild in comparison. However, knowledge is strength and he certainly knew the jungle. He had grown up in the rainforests and much preferred to be living within the trees than in a modern-day town or city. From day one, he took Fred under his tiny wing and looked after him with complete selflessness.

The first thing Alim did was to rig Fred's hammock using twine that he picked from the trees. Fred helped where he was able. Alim then set about trying to find some dry wood to light a fire (easier said than done in the wet forest). While he went gathering, Fred cleared an area of ground from rocks and stones where Alim would sleep. It was Alim's choice to sleep on the floor, with a small thin mat and a sleeping bag – this was what he was used to. Eventually camp was set. The boys were happy with what they had created and they were getting on famously, with Fred being very impressed by Alim's gentle nature.

As it was the first night out and due to the excessive travelling that had taken most of the day, we decided that the two of them should join us in base camp for supper. So, we all trudged our way down the treacherously muddy slope, back to the relative comfort of our river camp. When we appeared from the darkness of the trees, we saw that there was far more daylight left than we had realized – hence the domineering cover of the vast tree canopy deeper in the jungle. Base camp looked so inviting with the generator-powered lights popping out like stars in the twilight setting. Not only was there more light, but also an extremely slight, but most welcome breath of wind that drifted off the river. This made the constant sauna effect just that tiny bit more bearable. We sat on a tarpaulin, played some music from one of our phones, and tucked into some basic, but more than adequate food. Spirits were high. We knew this week would be tough, but so far so good. When it got later in the evening, Alim and Fred reluctantly headed off back into the jungle to their camp. Fred filmed the journey back and the first night on his own little diary camera, which had an infra-red setting. This suited me fine, as it saved me having to make the same return journey in the dark.

The overall goal of this trip was twofold: To see wild orangutans and pygmy elephants in their natural habitats. Whatever other wildlife Fred could see, while learning how to survive in the jungle, would be a bonus. Most orangutans, when encountered by tourists, are spotted in purpose-run sanctuaries, but we wanted to see them in the wild. This was partly for authenticity, but also to make the point that the primary rainforest in which they thrive is under huge threat of decimation from huge palm oil plantations. The same goes for the ever-decreasing numbers of pygmy elephants who are rapidly being pushed out of their natural home and close to extinction.

Spotting orangutans in the wild was said to be challenging and finding the small tribes of pygmy elephants in the dense jungle was said to be very risky. In fact, only a week before we arrived in Borneo, an Australian veterinary student had been tragically tusked and killed by these elephants. Our challenge was set.

Having established setting up camp within the deep jungle and having a scout around the immediate area, a small group of five, Fred, Alim, Ewen, Jason and I set off on foot to seek out some orangutans. The area of jungle we travelled through was dense, hilly, wet, muddy, and the further inland we headed the more stiflingly hot it became. We started off walking for a few hours, up steeps hills, over a multitude of dead, rotting trees. Our eyes continuously swept the path of our careful footsteps, looking up into the domineering tree canopy that hung suspended hundreds of metres above our heads. We looked for any sign of movement, noise, or a flash of an orangey colour... but nothing. Along the way we were constantly distracted by the incessant dripping of sweat running into our eyes and the fear of stepping on a snake. However, worst of all was the regular discovery of leeches, who would jump on you as you swept past leaves and plants. Once on board, the leeches would follow the heat source generated from your body to find a good source of blood to feed on. They would then inject a form of anesthetic into your skin, allowing them to burrow their teeth into your flesh, unbeknown to you. Whenever we stopped to take on water we would check each other over. The most common place we found them was around the waistline of our trousers and around the top of our boots. The biggest telltale sign that you were carrying some of these bloodsuckers was the fresh blood stains that slowly appeared on your sweat-drenched clothes. One time I found six on Fred in one go. They aren't dangerous, apart from the risk of infection from their jaws that sometimes remained in your flesh as you tore them off, but it was more of a mental battle. Just knowing something was sucking on your blood was surprisingly disturbing. The joys of the jungle!

Still we marched on, going through phases of talking, filming, laughing, singing and then stopping, looking up in silence, watching and listening. This went on for hours. In fact, that day we walked for about six hours – which in the jungle is no small feat. We weren't only exhausted but also exasperated by the fact that all that effort had resulted in no sightings at all. What a waste of time and effort. We had purposely walked in a huge circle and when only 100 metres from camp again my walkie-talkie crackled into life. Eric, who was back at HQ by the river, had his eyes on two orangutans in the trees right above our camp. Typical. We had walked all day long and the great apes had practically come to us. We couldn't believe it. With no hesitation, we all ran as quickly yet as quietly possible into camp and sure enough, found our prize. Two beautiful orangutans sat high in the canopy.

Despite the fact that we could have saved ourselves walking large distances during the day and simply stayed at camp to see this, we stood and looked in awe as the human-like apes sat high above us. They seemed almost as interested in us as we were in them. I trained the camera onto them, making sure I bagged all the shots I needed to make up the sequence, before then turning the camera onto Fred, whose excitement was palpable. It was like the first time in Tanzania when he saw his favourite wild giraffes for the first time. He smiled from ear to ear and couldn't stop saying how brilliant it was. The difference between an orangutan and, say, a giraffe, was that due to their human-like appearance you felt like you could properly communicate with them. As I crouched low behind Fred to frame up a 'relationship' shot (showing Fred and the orangutan in the same picture – to prove it was all real and not a clever editing trick), he stood there and kept calling to the ape. "'Ello!" he would say in his broad Lancashire accent. "'Ello, mate, look at you!" It was a great moment, as the orangutans looked intently at us, and even though they couldn't speak back, we felt as though we had connected in some very real way. What turned out to be a seemingly wasted day ended up being a triumph. We had nailed our first orangutan scene on the second day, which had always been a huge gamble when looking for wild animals with such a limited amount of time.

The next few days were spent filming various other sequences. We explored more of the local area near camp, where we stumbled across an enormous cave which we climbed deep down into. In the dark, cold and stony cathedral-like chambers we happened to disturb thousands of bats. They flew around us swooping and ducking, never hitting us, but creating a massive swirl of air and movement, so if we closed our eyes we could feel them flying around us. The noise of their screeching was piercing and their huge numbers looked more like a swarm of flies opposed to large bats. It was eerie, yet fascinating.

Later, one evening at dusk, we went for a ride on the boats further upriver. Armed with a powerful spotlight, we shone the luminous beam along the bank of the swollen river. Every now and then we would pick up two small shining lights, which indicated that something, or should I say someone, was watching us. We would cut the boat's engine and quietly drift towards the sparkling set of eyes, hoping to get a glimpse of what animal it was. The most incredible experience of this night-time safari was seeing the kingfisher birds. I am certainly no twitcher (normally the only 'birds' I'm interested in are blonde with two long legs!), but on this occasion I was spellbound by the feathered creatures. When hit by a bright light, the kingfishers' plumes became illuminated in the most incredible electric colours. We saw a number of these little birds as they utilized the still conditions to fish from the river as the sun went down. The piercing blues, bright yellows and stark green colours completely wowed us. Yet, most surprisingly for me, was how close we were able to get to the birds. As the boat engine stopped and we silently drifted towards their perch on a branch overhanging the river, they would stay completely frozen, as if believing if they didn't move that we wouldn't notice them. On more than one occasion we got so close that I stood in the boat and filmed them from a distance less than a metre.

It was magnificent and I'm sure only possible due to their lack of contact with humans, hence their lack of fear of us. The jungle may well be a tough place for us humans to live in, but the dense protective canopy also shelters some of the most incredible wildlife on earth.

After a number of days, filming different points of interest, exploring the jungle and observing Fred deal with it all (including making him build another camp, to see how much he had learned from Alim), we finally faced our biggest challenge – to seek out the pygmy elephants.

It turned out that one of our local boat drivers had a great story to tell.

Osmund lived with his family on the steep banks of the local river, just a few kilometres from our jungle camp. His house, made from local wood, was skilfully balanced on stilts to protect the homestead from any risk of flooding. Although predominantly being a boatman (using his long, narrow wooden craft to ferry local people and goods up and down the long river, to and from towns and villages), he also had great ambition. He dreamed of being able to create a wealthier life for his wife and five children by setting up an 'authentic home stay' in their home. In recent years it has become popular for the more 'right on' travellers to forego the holiday resorts or hotels and rather pay to stay with a local family. By doing this, they would experience a more realistic view of what life was like in that country. The new business venture was proving slow to start when we arrived, so he was very keen to offer his boat services as well as his wife's excellent home-cooked food for our shoot.

Throughout his life, Osmund had always been aware of the local herd of pygmy elephants and would regularly see them on the riverbanks while scooting past on his boat. It had even been known for the occasional elephant to wander onto his land and approach the family house, only through curiosity of his much smaller two-legged neighbours. Yet one afternoon he was to have an encounter that would change his life.

Sat on his tall wooden veranda, Osmund was enjoying a beer after a long day working on the river. However, his late afternoon relaxation was broken by a sudden flurry of the distant, disturbing squeals of what sounded like a baby elephant. The higher-pitched screams were then echoed by loud, distressed-sounding calls of an adult elephant. He tried to ignore it, but curiosity and concern got the better of him. Something seemed wrong. Leaving his seat and heading down the steps to the lawn below, he looked upriver and saw a heartbreaking scene. A herd of elephants had gone down to drink from the river and a small infant had ventured far too deep into the water and was desperately fighting to stay above the water. The infant's mother was rocking back and forth on the shore in a very agitated state. You could see from the high mud line on her front legs that she was unable to reach her baby due to the deep mud that prevented her from getting out into the water.

Osmund acted on his instinct. He ran down to his boat, which was tied up just below the house. He pulled the ripcord on the outboard motor and revved the throttle which sped the boat into action. En route to the elephants he didn't have a clue how he could help, but he had to try, and anything would be better than nothing. Within a minute or so he was right in the thick of the drama. The baby was floundering and splashing around in the deep water. Its head kept disappearing below the water. The mother was desperately trying to reach out with her trunk, but to no avail. Both creatures were going crazy. Without any consideration of the danger, Osmund expertly swung the boat around in a violent turn. With his right hand still on the tiller, he reached out and grabbed the baby's head in a sort of headlock. Despite its relative size and strength, the small beast was exhausted and close to giving up, so fortunately it didn't put up a fight. It seemed to humbly accept the helping hand that Osmund was potentially risking his life to give. The mother's screaming grew louder and increasingly more desperate. Osmund clung to the infant's head and steered the boat towards the shore. It seemed to be working. It wasn't far to the riverbank, but the difference meant life or death to the little elephant. As he and the baby reached the shoreline, he pushed the baby and helped it onto a drier, more stable bit of mud which the mother immediately ran to. Fearing the retaliation of the massive mother's fury, Osmund started to bark like a dog... he still doesn't know why he did this, but it worked and pacified the mother. Perhaps it indicated that Osmund was a fellow animal? The mother and baby were reunited and, thanks to Osmund's heroic intervention, the little one regained the chance to live a long life.

It doesn't end there.

You must have heard the saying 'Elephants never forget'. Well, Osmund's story proves this proverb to be true. Ever since that day, Osmund has been bizarrely accepted by the herd and amazingly, when he barks like a dog, the mother replies to his calls and comes to greet him.

What a wonderful, heartwarming story. But, being the cynical British TV types that we were... we thought it was all just a little bit too good to be true. We expected that Osmund had somewhat embellished the story as great patter to boost his new tourist trade.

When Osmund offered to take us to visit this same herd of pygmy elephants, we decided that if it *was* true it would make an incredible story, and even if it wasn't true, it would lead us to the elusive elephants. We had nothing to lose.

Early the following morning we took off in the boat to where Osmund had heard from other locals the elephants were. The river journey took around forty-five minutes to the border of a huge palm oil plantation. There, we were told, we would be met by a four-wheel drive vehicle which would drive us to where the last sighting was. In our minds we pictured a lovely Land Cruiser in which we could sit back in a luxurious seat and catch up on some much-needed sleep – a welcome break from camping in the jungle. On arrival, to our dismay, there was no Land Cruiser, but just a small, beaten-up yellow tractor with a dirt-tipping bucket on the back – yep, this was our luxurious 4x4. Not only were we bitterly disappointed by the vehicle, but then to top it all... it started to rain. This was not the epic closing story of our jungle adventure that we were expecting. Fred, Ewen and I climbed into the bucket which was filling up with puddles of muddy water and were driven for a good hour or so through a palm oil plantation.

What we saw was desperately sad. The beautifully wild, primary rainforest had been torn down and clinically farmed into long, neatly lined up rows of palm trees. In theory this doesn't sound too bad, until you witness firsthand the vast scale upon which this is happening. Another tragic example of mankind bullying nature into submission to feed his greed, gain and self-interest. Meanwhile the precious indigenous wildlife get forced back into an ever-decreasing paradise, being reduced to the size of a postage stamp, which is unsustainable. Something will have to give and unless circumstances rapidly change, it will be the animals that lose the battle to survive.

Included in this wildlife, of course, are the pygmy elephants. For centuries these creatures have roamed around their paradisiacal natural habitat, yet due to the recent increase of oil plantations, they are now an endangered species. It was on the far outskirts of the plantation that we found them.

The three of us were told to wait in the bucket, parked at the side of the dirt road. As we sat obediently, Osmund disappeared into the thick bushes to see if he could locate the herd. He followed the signs of crushed bushes, broken branches and great swathes of mud tracks, all indicating that huge beasts had pushed their immense bodies through that way.

He was gone for about an hour, during which time Fred, Ewen and I remained in the muddy, wet tractor bucket. After venting about how disappointing this was, we managed to lie down (like a tin of sardines) and get some sleep. Oh, the glamour of TV!

Eventually Osmund came bursting out of the bushes and corralled us to follow him. We must be quick but also quiet. As you can imagine it wasn't hard to muster us from our cold metal bed – I grabbed my day sack and the camera and filmed Fred as he followed Osmund into the bush.

Due to the tropical rainfall, the jungle was saturated with water. Every bush you brushed past would soak you to the skin and underfoot was literally a grassy, muddy swamp. Here the foliage was quite low slung, so the fact that all three of us Brits are over close to 2 metres tall meant we had to bully our way through the undergrowth. Despite the rain, the temperature was still incredibly high. Typical jungle conditions. Mixing the heat and the moisture spelt disaster from my camera lens, which started to severely steam up. This was a nightmare.

When filming with wildlife you only have one take. You can't explain to them that due to technical issues you missed the shot, so could they please return to the first position and go for a second take. I knew the action would unfold whether my camera was able to shoot or not – and the further we went into the steamy swamp, the worse my lens fogged up.

I was huffing and puffing as I trudged behind Fred, spitting and swearing at the camera, as I desperately wiped the glass with my less-than-clean lens cloth. Still on the move, pushing through the bushes, Ewen asked me what the problem was… I could hardly answer him out of frustration and a looming sense of failure. Being pretty unflappable, Ewen pacified me by saying that the misty lens would only add to capturing the atmosphere and tension of where we were and what we were doing. I wanted to agree, but by now I couldn't see anything through the camera but shapes.

Despite my frustration, urged on by Ewen I continued to film. Thankfully, Fred was caught up in the excitement of the moment and barely knew that I was having a meltdown, so he kept on talking to the camera. We had pushed deep into the jungle when Osmund stopped, hunched down by the base of a tree trunk and signalled for us to do the same. It was like being in a Vietnam War movie, when the soldier on point holds his fist up and everyone in the patrol stops. We all stopped in our tracks and tried to calm our heavy breathing. I alternated from frantically wiping the lens, filming for as long as I could and then wiping the lens again... I was not a happy bunny.

Just as I started to film again, Osmund began barking like a dog (just as he had in his story). At this I filmed continuously as Fred told the TV audience about what was going on. This would be the moment of truth, verifying or vilifying Osmund's tale.

He kept barking and we kept listening. Around the sixth time we almost jumped out of our skins as to our amazement there came an enormous trumpet call from an elephant! He barked again and the elephant replied again. To our astonishment, it was clearly replying to Osmund's bark. Fred was as flabbergasted as the rest of us and brilliantly laughed in shock as he acknowledged the events to the camera. Osmund looked behind to us all, with a huge smile on his face. He had spectacularly silenced his critics. This was amazing! There was clearly a large herd of elephants just a matter of metres away from us, hidden by the trees and bushes.

Seconds later Osmund jumped to his feet and thrust his back against the tree trunk. He shouted to us all to do the same.

Recall the tragic story from earlier about the Australian veterinary student who was tusked to death by these pygmy elephants, just a matter of weeks before? This was not a safe position to be in.

As he did this, a huge elephant burst out of the bushes, from seemingly nowhere. Yet, by Osmund's reaction we could see that this was not his friend. This huge grey beast had one tusk and a crazy look in his eye. In an instant the atmosphere had turned from elation to trepidation. I carried on filming through the steamy lens as Osmund jumped forward and fronted up to the elephant, flapping his arms and making more barking noises. To our relief the crazy elephant turned on a dime and dived back into the dense undergrowth, but then Osmund lunged forward and slapped its behind as it retreated. We couldn't quite believe what was unfolding before our eyes. Osmund then said that we should back out, as this was now very dangerous. He feared the crazy elephant would come back for retaliation. As we turned on our heels and made a hasty retreat, Fred said to me that we might have been alright if he hadn't slapped the beast on the arse! Either way, we weren't going to hang around to find out.

We arrived back at the dirt road, with adrenaline still pumping through our veins. We were shocked, amazed and startled by the encounter that we had just experienced. I had pretty much forgotten about the lens issue, but still ran some of the footage back to check we had caught it all on camera. The images were misty, but the sound and action played out well enough. Good job done, and to Ewen's credit he was totally right to just carrying on filming.

By now the sun had come out and the wet jungle had become a stiflingly hot steamy sauna. We took our time to calm down, get some water down our necks and dry ourselves out. We had an action scene on film, but now we had to attempt to get some pretty positive scenes of the elephants, to reinstate their rightful majestic stature, as opposed to being terrifying monsters.

After a short while we were led by Osmund back into the bush, but this time in a different direction. He was sure they were moving to our left and within minutes we had caught up with them again. This time we weren't so close (thankfully) but were separated by a small stream. The truth was, if they had any interest in 'going for us' they easily could have, but this stream at least gave us some sort of a barrier.

We crouched down again, not wanting to pose a threat and this time, through the thinner bushes, we could get clear glimpses of a number of enormous adult elephants and a few smaller baby ones. It was an incredible privilege to witness the wild creatures so close in their natural habitat. The thing that struck us the most was the noises the herd made. They growled and gurgled deeply like a lion or tiger, and then occasionally they would trumpet. We were able to stay in this position for some time, while I filmed Fred as he talked about this special moment he was experiencing. Osmund was clearly more relaxed at this distance and once again he barked. Yet again, there was a specific reply from one of the elephants – amazing.

As I mentioned before, wildlife will wait for no man. And so, after a few minutes of checking each other out, the mighty herd moved on.

We headed back out to the road, where we appeared further up from where the tractor was parked. We stood around there, hoping that the herd may come and cross the road not far from our position. Within twenty minutes or so our patience was rewarded and we were treated to see the entire herd out in the open. The scene was magnificent and one we shall never forget. We shot some great footage, particularly one scene of Fred watching a young elephant running around and throwing grass and mud with its trunk, onto its back. It was literally as if he was performing to Fred, who was actually quite moved by this encounter. Yet another life-changing experience for the big man.

A few days later we were relieved to head out of the jungle and back to civilization. As I'm sure you can imagine, that first shower was epic! We were totally exhausted, but thrilled to have another great show 'in the can'. Seeing that it was only a few weeks to Christmas, we decided to have our Christmas party back in Sandakan – all I will add is that we very nearly missed our flights the following day.

CANADA

It was early the next year, when as fat as the Christmas turkeys that were in our bellies, we boarded a plane for Vancouver, Canada.

This aim of this, our final trip in the *Freddie Flintoff Goes Wild* series, was to explore the Discovery Islands, situated just north-east of Vancouver Island.

Fred and I had been to Vancouver before while filming the *Freddie vs the World* series, and we loved it. Vancouver Airport was particularly familiar, as last time we had been on board a horrific flight, which was aborted three-quarters of the way from Vancouver to Whitehorse in the Yukon, due to terrifying weather conditions. We were forced to return to Vancouver Airport in the early hours of the morning, where we all camped out, literally on the floor of the airport, until the following morning flight at 7 a.m. The flight had been one of nightmares and the airport floor was far from comfortable, however we put it down to experience and went on to thoroughly enjoy the rest of our experience in Canada.

The novelty that made us particularly look forward to this trip was the fact that it was going to be cold. Every other location, Africa, Australia and Borneo, had been *so* hot. To actually wear lots of clothes and wrap up warm in your sleeping bag at night would be a very welcome change. In fact, compared to the intensity of the heat on all the other shoots, we secretly viewed this journey as a bit of a holiday.

Due to working on another project, this time Ewen was unable to travel with us, so taking his place was Charlotte, the Series Producer. We had only spent a small amount of time with Charlotte while visiting the production office, yet we were confident that she was going to be fun and very capable of supporting us on location. We were not disappointed. Also joining us on the ground was going to be Rob, a local Canadian who had worked for years as a Fixer for TV and film shoots. Rob is very warm, kind and is the stereotypical Canadian outdoorsman – we were in very good hands.

Having flown into Vancouver we spent a quick night in the city, before heading to the ferry port to cross over to Vancouver Island. If you've never been – put Vancouver high on your 'bucket list' of places to see. Canada (in my opinion, particularly the west) is stunning. It boasts deep blue, inky waterways lined by snowcapped coastal mountains; it's teeming with wildlife and is home to a very warm nation of people.

Landing on the big island, we drove up to Campbell River where we boarded another ferry to the smaller island of Quadra. As the car and passenger ferry pulled up, we met our indigenous host for the next few days – Vernon. Having lived on Quadra Island for the majority of his life, Vernon was from a long line of native Canadian Indians – referred to as 'First Nations'. Fred and I immediately warmed to Vernon as he had a real twinkle in his eye. He was a real character and must have been close to the age of sixty. He was dressed in a denim jacket, jeans and he sported a black beard and longish black hair. He had tattoos on his arms and was missing a number of fingers! He looked the part and was certainly the real deal. We soon found out that he had lived a very colourful life. There wasn't much that he hadn't done – he had been a fisherman, lumberjack, artist, truck driver and had even done time in prison. By his own admission, he had worked and played hard, yet now in his later years had calmed down and was focusing on far more important matters. His passion is to pass on the First Nation's heritage and culture to the younger generation, which is sadly being lost as the new age of development and technology takes over. This sounds like the usual mantra coming from native elders, yet we could very quickly see just how much this meant to Vernon and his family.

He picked us up in an old 4x4 flatbed truck. I mic'ed him up and asked him to ignore me and the camera, unless I spoke to him. He chuckled and spoke in his slow, broad Canadian accent. Physically he appeared to be doddery and slow – a little older than his years. It was obvious that his body had taken the toll of many years of brutally hard work and partying, yet we were to find out that he was still more than capable of looking after himself in the Canadian wilderness.

My aim on these shoots was to never over-direct, but rather just follow what happened and see what would unfold. If there was need, I would step in and ask Fred or his host to answer a question to camera, do a certain thing or simply pause while I got a shot from another angle for the edit. This method of shooting allowed the three of us to just go on adventure, not on a film shoot. We got on really well and the camera would enable the viewer to make up number four in our group.

Arriving at Vernon's home, built right on the coast, I jumped out ahead of Fred. I then asked Vernon to drive back down the road, so I could film an arrival shot. Again, shooting in Canada proved to be a dream, because English is their first language. The vehicle carrying Vernon and Fred rumbled off down the street and turned around. As it drove back up I filmed an 'establishing' shot to place where they were. The truck pulled up and without any cue from me, Vernon just led the way straight into his garage and there, to our surprise, was a deer strung up by its hind legs by a rope to the ceiling. Vernon then handed Fred a large hunting knife and told him to start skinning it.

This was playing out perfectly as Vernon was adamant that Fred should get his hands dirty and truly get involved over the next week. This made my job so much easier, as I just had to follow the action.

Later that day we also met Michael, Vernon's son. In his late twenties, Michael worked as a traditional wood carver. Yet, don't picture a young guy whittling away at a small stick, Michael would take huge cedar tree trunks and carve huge totem poles and traditional figureheads from the timber. They were extraordinary pieces of art and very intricate in their detail.

Being Vernon's son, you can imagine the pressure that Michael felt to be the perfect heir, embracing the tribal culture, thus keeping their heritage alive. He shared with us how he had also succumbed to the temptations of the more modern side of society and had dabbled in certain vices. However, he was now on the other side of those experiences, and was committed to championing Vernon's mission. Other than carving, Michael's real passion was hunting.

Before we knew it we were all on a private, medium-sized pleasure cruiser boat charging up the Discovery Passage.

The Discovery Islands are a collection of hundreds of islands that vary in size, found in the Discovery Passage which is situated between Vancouver Island and the British Columbia mainland. These islands would once have been a solid land mass, but over thousands of years the North Pacific Ocean had worked its way in to form an archipelago.

Fred, Vernon, Michael and I were on the smaller boat and Rob and Charlotte were on a larger boat that we had hired for the week. The idea was that wherever possible Fred, Vernon, Michael and I would be alone, to create a bubble within which they would forget that the bigger picture was to shoot a TV programme. This would hopefully enable Fred to have more of an authentic experience in the wild. Wherever the three boys would camp, Charlotte, Rob and I would make our camp a good distance away, to maintain that bubble. On these types of shoots, we the crews have a lot of work to do. This is physically demanding, yet also mentally tiring. Seeing that it isn't us who are 'experiencing' living in the wild on camera (although of course we are in essence). It is important that we sleep as well as we can and eat as properly as possible to maintain our energy levels.

Before we reached the location where we would spend the first few nights, we passed a pod of playful porpoises, and then we turned a corner only to see a large colony of Steller sea lions. Fred was blown away by the amount of wildlife we had seen in such quick succession. He was particularly taken by the sea lions. There was a huge number of them and the fact that some of them were so big really caught his attention. Adult males can grow up to over 3 metres long and can weigh up to one ton. As a Cameraman, I never got bored of Fred's genuine childlike enthusiasm and love for wildlife. We stopped the boat in the water, filmed, sat and watched them for a while. Vernon told Fred all about the sea lions and then they laughed as Fred compared the noises coming from the big males to him lying in bed after a few pints and a curry! The boys were getting on famously.

Our first camping location was a peach. Set on a small peninsula jutting out from a small island, the ground was mossy and soft (perfect to sleep on) and there was plenty of accessible firewood. Wild food in the Discovery Island is not a problem to find. There is plentiful fishing to be had (the area is famous for its abundance of wild salmon), the hunting is great and foraging on the beaches will present you with a treasure trove of fresh oysters and clams. Compared to the other locations we had visited on this series, camping and eating here was hardly a chore. The view from the camping site was like the winning entry from a nature photography competition – glassy waters, reflecting pine and cedar tree-covered islands, with snow-peaked mountains as a backdrop. This is easily the most idyllic camping spot of all my years in the job.

I filmed as the boys pitched their tents, and meanwhile Rob and Charlotte were making our camp 100 metres away around the bay.

Making camp took most of the afternoon, as the boys took the opportunity to gather enough firewood to last them a few nights. In order to save time on that first night, Vernon had brought a huge fresh salmon with them and so, that evening, the boys taught Fred how to fillet the fish and make a butterfly stick contraption, to cook it over the fire. With a roaring fire and the cedarwood smoke creating a beautiful aroma around camp, the scene was that of a boy scout's daydream. I filmed long after the sun set, as Fred, Vernon and Michael sat, ate huge chunks of fish and shared stories of their lives.

Eventually, after shooting Fred getting into his nice cold tent, I called it a day. I bid the three boys goodnight and then walked over to my camp. Rob had done a sterling job and we too had a roaring fire, the tents were pitched and ready to crawl in to, but best of all was a huge saucepan of hot pasta and a cup of red wine. What a great day.

It turned out that, due to other commitments, Michael would have to leave us a few days into the shoot, so the following morning we set off on our small island to go deer hunting. To keep the numbers and noise down, Vernon stayed at camp where he would do some 'fishing' (sleeping!). So, Michael, Fred and I headed off up the hill and into the unknown. The gradient of the hill was very steep and the further we headed up a bluff, the less tree cover there was. It seemed that most of the trees had fallen down on their own accord, maybe to do with the soft soil of the damp darkness of the past winter. Michael taught us that this more open terrain was bad for hunting as the prey would see, hear or smell us far sooner than we would ever see them. Despite this fact, we walked on for a good four or five hours and covered a lot of difficult ground. I filmed sequences of Fred and Michael crossing logs, taking water breaks and willing on some action… yet with no joy. One of the problems was that Fred and I were being so noisy. Due to our synthetic waterproof trousers every step we took there was a 'swooshing' noise. Michael was quick to inform us that true hunters would wear a quiet material for stalking. Yet, it wasn't only our trousers that was the problem.

While filming, with me operating both the camera and sound, meant that I had to wear headphones to make sure that we were recording good quality sound. If you have experienced the embarrassment of sitting on a train with headphones on and you try to speak to someone, you shout. This is not intentional, it's just the way you naturally compensate the volume of your voice so that you can hear what you are saying.

You guessed it, I was barking out large orders, "RIGHT BOYS, LET'S STOP HERE AND HAVE A CHAT", "FRED, CAN YOU STOP AND LET ME PASS?", "DON'T KNOW ABOUT YOU BUT I'M BLOODY STARVING!" etc. Fred found this ever so amusing, whereas Michael just rolled his eyes and shook his bowed head.

It was clear by now that we were never going to see a deer, let alone shoot one, so we decided to head back to camp. Seeing that we had climbed up and down some seriously high ridges, we decided to try and skirt around them on the way home. By this time I'd stopped filming our failed attempt to hunt and so we just walked normally and crashed through the dead sticks etc. The funniest part of the day for me was when Fred just started to lose the plot. He started to recount out loud the story of the Gruffalo. But not just a few lines. From years of reading it to his three kids, he knew the whole book, word for word. This had me in tears of laughter and again Michael shook his head.

Hours later it was dusk as we re-entered camp. Vernon had woken up by then and had made sure the fire was going strong. We collapsed into camp, exhausted. Yet, in the wilderness there is no time to sit down and rest. We had to find supper. Of course, my food was being lovingly prepared by Rob back in our camp, but that was out of bounds to the boys. So, half-heartedly we dropped our packs, got back on our feet and walked down to the beach to forage. Fortunately, all the talk of ample supplies of shellfish proved to be true and in under an hour the three guys had collected a small sack full of fresh oysters and clams.

As they dug for the shellfish, the huge sky blew up into a breathtaking sunset and looked as though it had caught on fire. I placed the silhouettes of the three figures on the beach in bottom of frame and nailed a stunning scene to close the day.

On Michael's last day we decided to give the hunting scene one last try. So, we hopped into the boat and got dropped off on the opposite side of the small bay. Michael was confident that there was better terrain for hunting on that side.

There is really very little to say that is interesting or entertaining about that day. We spent all day long walking many kilometres, sitting motionless on bluffs in stakeouts, tracking signs of deer and even chasing after a possible sighting far away on an opposite hill. Once again all to no avail. In fact the only thing we saw of interest was some wolf scat (poo!). It was really no one's fault, but Fred blamed me, I blamed Fred and Michael blamed the weather (but really he blamed us both). We just had to face the facts, Fred and I aren't born hunters and we were actually quite alright with that. Our loss was the deer's gain of another day in paradise.

Losing Michael was a shame, but it did mean that we would get to spend more quality time with lovely old Vernon. The next few days were a raucous riot of fishing excursions, failed attempts at wild animal baiting (to film not kill) and moving to a couple of more beautiful camps further up the passage. All these activities were filled with much laughter and joviality. We really were having a great time.

On our penultimate evening we had journeyed by boat to an ancient, traditional First Nation site. Vernon told us that it was here that he would come as a boy with many of his older family, who had since passed away. They would congregate and camp around 'The Tree Of Life'. The setting was stunning with a white sandy beach, and we hoped that Vernon had got the right location, as he admitted that it was a long time since he had been there. On the beach of virgin sand we were greeted by a track of enormous wolf prints – each print literally the size of my hand. We asked if it was wise to camp here, so Vern went to inspect the tracks. "It's fine," he said. "That lone wolf was here a few days ago, but he would be long gone by now." Fred and I looked at each other and knew we were really up for staying in this cool location, whether it was the right place or not. Before dragging our camping equipment up the beach, we decided that we *should* check that this was where The Tree Of Life stood. Scrambling up a few small mounds of sand and foliage we walked into a clearing in a wooded area just back from the beach. There before us stood a ginormous cedar tree, which in fact on closer inspection was about five big cedar trees entwined altogether – twisting and turning their way up into the sky. The sight was really quite impressive and that's when we knew why the First Nation people would've considered this as a magical, sacred place.

We worked hard to make camp before the sun set too low and I filmed snippets of this, while also helping the other two with their kit. While Fred was down at the shoreline collecting some more of our gear, Vernon took me aside and asked me if he could surprise Fred, and would I help?

It was tradition that a First Nation elder could adopt a child into their family by taking them to The Tree Of Life. Ceremoniously placing some strips of bark like a crown around their heads and saying a few words, this would make the adoption, in their eyes, official. The only other factor was that all this had to be witnessed by one other person to make it stand up in their traditional beliefs.

Always having to think about the TV side of things, I encouraged Vernon that this was a great idea, but urged him that we'd have to do it before the sun got even lower, as I was running out of light to film in.

So, when Fred returned, Vernon asked him to come over to the base of the tree and take a seat. He then placed a 'crown of bark' on his own head, then one on mine (as the witness) and finally another on Fred's head. He then said words to the effect, "Here under The Tree Of Life, with Mungo as my witness, I offer Freddie the chance to be adopted into my family of many generations." Fred and I were completely taken aback by this, and despite having to film it all we were both clearly moved. Fred humbly accepted Vern's offer, with almost a lump in his throat. As an elder of his tribe, Vernon then gave Fred the Indian name 'Deisum' which he said means 'Big Stone'. It was totally off the cuff, yet also an incredibly moving moment between the three of us. I am sure some cynics will say, what are three grown men doing acting out ceremonies at the bottom of a 'sacred' tree? If so, they are missing the point and I pity them for it. There was a level of total acceptance and respect that Vernon passed onto Fred, to whom it meant the world.

That was it. The friendship was sealed and from a film's point of view, it was pure gold.

Later that night, we lit a huge fire on the beach and attempted to make wolf calls, howling loudly then waiting to listen for a reply... no reply was heard, apart from one from Rob, who was listening from their boat which was anchored out in the bay. We all laughed.

The final nemesis of our trip to the Discovery Islands was to see the famous black and white Orcas (otherwise known as 'killer whales') that reside in those waters. Yet, considering the size of the waters, the distance the whales can travel in a day and the lack of time we had to achieve this, it was the equivalent of looking for a needle in a haystack. Fred and I joked nervously that it was the wildebeest scenario all over again. No matter what, we would stick to our guns and never set up anything, but only let it happen for real.

We broke camp first thing in the morning, and up until this point we had enjoyed a lucky window of beautiful clear weather and flat seas. Fortunately, the sea was still relatively flat, but a thick sea fog had rolled in and visibility was terrible – not the conditions you want when whale-spotting. We had no other choice but to take to the waters and see what would happen. We *had* to spot and film them during this one day or we had missed our chance.

During the first few hours it was not looking good at all. Visibility was very poor and there was no sign of movement anywhere to be seen. We started off really enthusiastic, and slowly as the hours ebbed away we became less hopeful and less interested. However, due to the fact that we all got on so well, spirits were still high and Fred and I were shouting out "Come on whales" (in heavy Welsh accents, as you hear at the rugby internationals). Then Fred started singing 'Bread of Heaven', the Welsh national rugby song. Along with Vern we laughed our way through hours of sitting around staring into the milky fog. Every now and then we would have a sighting and a flutter of activity. But, alas no, it was another drifting log or black sea bird in the distance.

The clock was ticking and we had now commandeered Charlotte, Rob and their boat into the search party. Yet, inevitably we came to the dreaded point when we had to turn and head for base, with our adventure over and with no sighting of whales. We reluctantly turned the boat around and headed down alongside one of the islands.

In less than thirty minutes, our VHF radio crackled to life and it was Rob's boat calling us. By chance they had headed down the opposite side of the island and it was there that they found a pod of four enormous Orcas. We couldn't believe our luck, just when we had given up all hope!

Fortunately we had the faster boat, so we doughnutted around and pushed the throttle onto full power. The race was on. Adrenaline had kicked in again and we were all hollering and whooping in anticipation.

Before we knew it we were in the area we had been tipped off about, and as we approached we slowed the boat down to a steady cruising speed. To our right in the distance, just as we had hoped for, we saw an almighty spurt of water, shooting into the air from one of the Orca's spouts. It must have shot 5 metres up into the air. I filmed as Fred and Vernon were cheering, high-fiving and slapping each other on the back. "There she blows, Freddie," Vernon said, as we moved closer.

To top it all, the sun also burned through the mist, just as we slowed up and respectfully tracked alongside the Orcas. We stayed with them for a good twenty minutes. Fred was totally enchanted by the sight. It was also my first time being so close to these magnificent creatures. There was a tangible sense of calmness and almost wisdom in the way that they gracefully moved their huge hulking bodies, seemingly effortlessly, through the clear, cold water. There were spells when they would dive and we would think that was it, show's over, only to hear another huge blowout from the spout 50 metres out in front. At one point two of them changed at a 90° angle and started heading straight for our boat. There was nothing we could do in time, so I filmed their approach and we all held on, in case they 'T-boned' us, knocking our little boat over. But instead, it was more like they were playing with us, as the two enormous whales dived straight under our boat. Seeing that the water was crystal clear I got an incredible shot of them doing so. We were like kids in a sweet shop and the whales were putting on a great show.

After a while, we decided that we should leave them in peace and head back to Quadra Island. So, I asked Fred to say one last piece to camera, wrapping up the trip. As I filmed and he spoke the final words of the series, behind him all four Orcas moved into a formation like the Red Arrows air display team and rushed past us. It couldn't have been scripted or choreographed better. This really was the icing on the cake of a cracking week. That was a 'Wrap'!

Freddie Flintoff Goes Wild had been a phenomenal series to work on. Great countries visited, where we had spent time with amazing people. Beautiful wildlife was appreciated and new skills had been learned. Best of all for me was the true friendship that Fred and I had developed. We had shared some experiences together that no one else could understand or appreciate. We had made a new friend for life.

Following that series, Fred and I went on to work on many more projects together, noteworthy ones being: *From Lords to the Ring* – where Fred was trained over four months to become a professional heavyweight boxer, culminating in a professional fight in front of 9,000 people at Manchester's MEN Arena. That project was my first Producer/Director credit and (fortunately) it was a roaring success and a three-part series that I'm very proud of.

The secret to the success of the boxing series was that it was firmly built on the trust that Fred and I have in each other, following all our adventures; I can ask him very personal questions and he just spills out his heart, and as any Director will know, that's a winning combination. In the security of this trust and friendship, during this series Fred seemed to shed a skin. He admitted for the first time publicly to have struggled with bullying as a kid and being plagued by eating disorders throughout his early professional cricketing career. Being this open and honest proved to be a real release for him, on the back of which he explained of the unspoken pressures of always having to be who *others* wanted him to be. In the final interview of that series, post his fight (which he narrowly won on points), he stated that "the professional sportsman was left in that ring" – it was time to live his life, for himself and his family.

Most recently, Fred was asked by Sky to go to the Amazonian rainforest to champion their charitable cause of saving one billion trees. He refused to go without me. So, a small team of us (including Ewen as Director) journeyed out to Brazil for a month-long expedition, where Fred and Rob Penn cycled down the Trans-Amazonian Highway – a dirt logging road that cuts straight through the heart of the Amazon jungle. It was a tough four weeks, but the results were great and Sky were over the moon with the two-part series.

I hope there will be many more stories to come from Fred and I in the years to come, but far more important than the TV adventures is our friendship.

6

AND FINALLY...

I believe I have one of the best jobs in the world.

Since the mid-nineties I have been fortunate enough to travel to over eighty countries, film some of the biggest names on television and work for most of the world's major broadcasters. It has been an incredible ride.

I started my career as a young, enthusiastic twenty-four-year-old man – full of hopes, dreams, confidence and a very real sense of invincibility. The world was my oyster and I was going to discover the pearl of all it had to offer me.

For the first ten years I worked almost non-stop. I soaked up knowledge and information like a sponge. I learned the skills of a Cameraman, slowly built a steady client base of Directors and TV contacts, which resulted in laying a solid foundation upon which to build my career.

Now in my early forties I am older and hopefully wiser. I am still, however, trying to run around like a twenty-year-old. I hope that I am more patient, far more skilled as well as having a huge library of experiences under my belt. Through this book, I have shared some of the stories and some of what I've learned along the way. I hope you have enjoyed it.

My life has certainly not been 'normal'. The road that I have taken has led me to places of enormous privilege, yet there are also missing pieces in my domestic life. I am still single and I have no kids, both of which I would have expected and loved to have had by now. As with most achievements, there is always a degree of sacrifice to be made.

Without doubt, a large part of my success as a Cameraman, specializing in travel and adventure filming, is due to the fact that I *am* single. As touched on before, there are very few guys of my age, with my level of experience, who can just get up and leave at the drop of a hat. Most have wives and families to put first, whereas I can just go... and I do.

Eventually, this maverick lifestyle catches up with you and the desire to fit in to 'normality' and the pressure that society places on us, wishing us all to conform to its rules, kicks in.

A year ago I decided that it was time for me to be 'sensible', plan for the future and start to begin a gradual exit from camerawork. I was thinking this way, partly because I am getting older and partly because I needed to respond to my body – which has taken a lot of punishment over the years.

I have had operations on *both* knees and my right camera-bearing shoulder, all caused by wear and tear from the job. I am acutely aware that the older I become the harder I have to work at keeping in good shape. Put simply, I need to stay on top of my game. I guess you could call it a 'mid-life crisis'.

A while ago an opportunity arose for me to take on a role in developing TV ideas and concepts within a new Production Company. Maybe this could be my new spin-off career, diverting my path into production?

To cut a long story short, I lasted four weeks!

Being sat behind a desk for days on end was simply not me. It was here that I realized just how good I had it, in my camera career. When I made the sidestep into this new role, I was pretty much on top of my game in the adventure camera genre. Starting a production job proved to be excruciatingly difficult. Especially having to learn the ropes again. It is hard to teach an old dog new tricks, particularly one who has had such a colourful career in the field.

While working in the office I had taken calls from my mates, still cameramen, who were all over the place, working on all sorts of jobs. Deep inside, I just knew that I had to be back out with the troops on the ground and not chained to a desk. I had given it a shot, well sort of. I was excruciatingly embarrassed to tell my bosses that this just wasn't for me (certainly not yet) and, to my great relief, they were incredibly gracious and understanding.

Two weeks later I was in the Italian Dolomite mountains, on a shoot with Bear (Grylls) filming the *Escape From Hell* series. On location my old mate Duncan (1st AD) asked me, "What's happened to you, Mungo? You've changed." I asked him what he meant by that. To which he replied, "You just seem chilled out and peaceful." I joked with him, "What do you mean? I'm always chilled and peaceful!" We laughed how I could be a miserable git at times... *especially* when hungry. I then went on to tell him about my recent 'open prison sentence' in an office, at which he said it all made sense to him... but then the penny dropped for me too. I just don't belong in that office environment. As my father brilliantly put it, "You in an office is like trying to fit a round peg into a square hole" – it just doesn't work.

I was back and I was more up for it than ever. It honestly felt as though I had been given a second chance at life. Since then, whenever I have found myself about to moan or complain while on a camera job, I stop myself and remember that desk. Then I keep my mouth shut and quietly count my blessings. I think my four-week sabbatical was one of the best things that could have happened to me at this stage of my career.

I may state that I reckon I have one of the best jobs in the world, but believe me, there is SO much more to life than work. It is reading between the lines and looking at the other aspects of our existence where I find true value and understand what our lives are really all about.

Personally, I am not driven by money or material possessions at all. I was brought up in a lower middle-class family, but we never really had a lot of money or privileges. However, mostly because of my job, I now have a small degree of material wealth which I hold onto very lightly. I have a flat in London (which is the only investment I ever made and is turning out to be the best I could have ever made) and I own a Land Rover Defender. That's about it on the bigger scale of possessions. Yet, when valuing my 'life' as a whole, including my wonderful, loving family, great friends and a job that I enjoy, I have riches beyond compare.

Some of my friends have made a lot of money. They have flash cars, big houses and all the benefits that go with great wealth. Hats off to them – they are all self-made and have earned their success. However, with great wealth also comes great responsibility. A few of them are currently facing difficult issues in handling aspects of their wealth responsibly. Contrary to belief, life is certainly not made easy by having lots of money.

Those who are from normal, working-class backgrounds struggle to find a balance between the upbringing they received and the opportunities that they can now offer their kids. They want to give them the best, but don't wish for their kids to devalue the more down-to-earth aspects of life that had shaped their parents into the great people they are today. Some might say that this would be a nice problem to have, but make no mistake, it carries with it huge consequences. My view is, no matter what school they go to, whether it's Eton, Cheltenham Ladies' College or the local comprehensive, what will truly shape these kids is their relationship with their parents. If you love them unconditionally, teach them at home what it is right and wrong, demonstrate how important it is to earn your rewards and then share what you have with those who aren't so fortunate, then they will develop into good, well-rounded people and that will put them in good stead for their future lives.

I firmly believe that leaving your kids with a legacy of unconditional love is of far more value than an estate of millions of pounds (which is likely to just complicate their lives).

Love makes the world go around.

I'm no prude and I'm certainly no religious zealot or a Bible basher, but I do have faith. I *have* to have faith that there is the hope of the existence of some*thing* or some*one* bigger and better than us, someone who is in control of this world and our lives within in it.

It is very clear to me too that there is good and evil in this world.

From my experience, it is possible to clearly sense danger when someone bad walks into a room – you don't *know* it, you can just *feel* it... a sixth sense, if you like. I have been in situations over the years when I have felt fear, not always in the obvious way (when teetering on the edge of a high cliff), but rather in the most unlikely circumstances. For example, I have been filming among a group of people when something changes. The atmosphere and the attitude turns and that's when your instincts tell you to get out of there! Similarly, at other times, I have sensed a deep unrest about a situation and so have backed out from taking part (sometimes resulting in losing face in the process), but every time my instinct has proved right and so, I have learned to observe and listen.

Certain events in our world can only be described as 'evil'.

I have witnessed the aftermath of atrocities in Rwanda and Cambodia, where pure evil has visited.

When you see a dead body, you know it is dead, far more than the simple fact that it's no longer breathing. You can tangibly sense that the person's 'soul' has left the body. I realize now that our bodies are effectively 'skin wetsuits' and what truly makes 'us' are our souls. Without the soul living in the body, it is reduced to being just a lump of flesh/meat.

When people meet me, what they *see* is a tall, big lump of hairy meat. But, *who* they are truly meeting is my soul, who is the *real* 'Mungo'. One day my flesh will give up and fail, my soul will leave my body behind. Only then will the truth about what happens to our 'souls' be discovered. I find this exciting.

I remember when leaving Rwanda, I was totally disillusioned regarding the country's hope for long-lasting peace. Multiple tribal conflicts have taken place over many generations and I couldn't see what would stop this reoccurring, devastating cycle. 'Man' always seems to eventually screw things up, ultimately, due to greed, pride and self-centredness. My well thought-out conclusion was that this cycle could only be stopped if the heart of man changed. To my knowledge the only one who can truly change the heart of man is God.

In the past I have not been as brave as the likes of Bear, who unashamedly publicly declares his Christian faith. But, I do believe in God. I seem to be on a constant rollercoaster ride with my beliefs – up and down like a yo-yo. However, I can't deny my hope and faith in a higher power that holds all things together.

There is hope. As well as evil forces present in our world, there is also an overriding goodness. I believe the majority of people are good, to the core, and they understand what it takes to live side by side in peace and harmony. These good people treasure this world and take seriously the responsibility we have for looking after it and all who live in it.

It's really so simple: if we all treated each other as we want to be treated, then this world would be a far happier place – there lies our challenge!

This begs the question of what will we do with our lives? Will we be one of the good people, responsibly making the most of all we've been given? We may not be able to change the world, but we can make a world of difference within it.

One of my favourite quotes ever was by a Western journalist who once asked Mother Theresa, "Mother, don't you realize that your life's work is just a drop in the ocean?" To which she replied, "Ah, yes. But the ocean is made up of many drops!" Her life was her offering. She did the best with what she had and, no matter how big or small, she made an impact.

I realize that my camera is far more powerful than a gun. If I had a gun, I could shoot one bad person at a time and make a small impact in a localized situation. However, if I shoot something with my camera, I can potentially show the footage to literally millions of people. And I believe that people standing together in unity can have a powerful effect and make long-lasting change for good.

I wonder, what is your skill? How can you impact the world around you with your humble 'drop'?

This world is a wonderful place.

Choosing to look beyond the negatives and focusing on the positive, we simply must appreciate the richness of all that this world holds, a lot of which, given the means to, we can experience in our lifetime. There is a multitude of people groups who live in a kaleidoscope of colours, a cacophony of sounds and a barrage of smells. They speak a thousand languages, yet share the same biology and can all communicate through the simplicity of silence. There are landscapes that will blow our minds, from the highest soaring peaks to the secretive murky depths and a range of temperatures that will both scorch and freeze. Living right alongside us are whole other worlds of animal and insect species, many of which are still yet to be discovered. This place is special, as are you, being part of it.

No one institution seems to be able agree on just how many countries there officially are, as some aren't recognized as independent 'countries'. However, the common number seems to be around one hundred and ninety. You may consider my travelling tally of over 80 countries to be impressive, but in the bigger picture there is still a whole world out there to be discovered and I've hardly scratched the surface. I look forward to learning more and wherever possible experiencing these places firsthand. Given the chance I would love to visit them all, but that is not practical and highly unlikely (unless someone commissions a TV series about it – any offers?).

I celebrate and champion those in my industry who, from past to present, have used their cameras to explore, share and educate us all about this, our amazing universal home. And as for my part in the big picture, I am humbled and honoured to offer my 'drop'. With the new revolution of the digital computer age and all the viewing platforms and communication networks, our generation has an exciting opportunity to make a positive impact on our world, leading the way for generations to follow after us.

In theory, I am only just reaching the halfway mark in my working career. If the next twenty plus years are anything like the past twenty I will be exhausted, but blessed beyond my wildest dreams. I am excited by the future and all that it holds.

I have a good friend 'Clifford', who always calls me "Mungo, the luckiest man in the world". I freely admit that I am lucky. But then again, to a degree, all of us can make our own luck. I know that writing this book will not make me a lot of money, but that is not my motivation. If you genuinely seek to add to the world, play your part, then you will be genuinely rewarded.

I may never become a millionaire, but when it comes to life experiences, I am a billionaire!

"That's a Wrap!"

For more information on Mungo visit:

www.mungothecameraman.com

To follow Mungo:

MUNGO The Cameraman – Facebook Group
@mungomungeam - Twitter